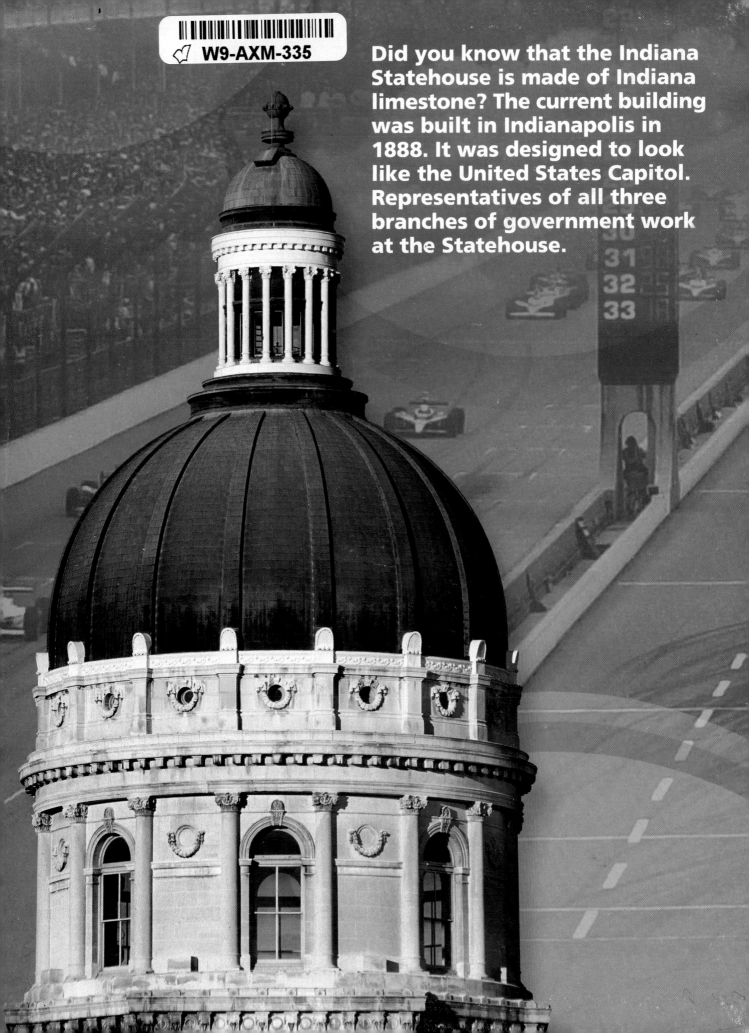

Did you know that the Indiana Statehouse is made of Indiana limestone? The current building was built in Indianapolis in 1888. It was designed to look like the United States Capitol. Representatives of all three branches of government work at the Statehouse.

INDIANA
SOCIAL Studies

Indiana History

HOUGHTON MIFFLIN HARCOURT
School Publishers

INDIANA

Indiana History

Series Authors

Dr. Michael J. Berson
Professor
Social Science Education
University of South Florida
Tampa, Florida

Dr. Tyrone C. Howard
Associate Professor
UCLA Graduate School of Education
& Information Studies
University of California at Los Angeles
Los Angeles, California

Dr. Cinthia Salinas
Assistant Professor
Department of Curriculum and
Instruction
College of Education
The University of Texas at Austin
Austin, Texas

Series Consultants

Dr. Marsha Alibrandi
Assistant Professor
Social Studies Teacher Education
Department of Curriculum and
Instruction
Graduate School of Education and
Allied Professions
Fairfield University
Fairfield, Connecticut

Dr. Patricia G. Avery
Professor
College of Education and Human
Development
University of Minnesota
Minneapolis/St. Paul, Minnesota

Dr. Linda Bennett
Associate Professor
College of Education
University of Missouri–Columbia
Columbia, Missouri

Dr. Walter C. Fleming
Department Head and Professor
Native American Studies
Montana State University
Bozeman, Montana

Dr. S. G. Grant
Dean
School of Education
Binghamton University
Binghamton, New York

C. C. Herbison
Lecturer
African and African-American Studies
University of Kansas
Lawrenceville, Kansas

Dr. Eric Johnson
Assistant Professor
Director, Urban Education Program
School of Education
Drake University
Des Moines, Iowa

Dr. Bruce E. Larson
Professor
Social Studies Education
Secondary Education
Woodring College of Education
Western Washington University
Bellingham, Washington

Dr. Merry M. Merryfield
Professor
Social Studies and Global Education
College of Education
The Ohio State University
Columbus, Ohio

Dr. Peter Rees
Associate Professor
Department of Geography
University of Delaware
Wilmington, Delaware

Dr. Phillip J. VanFossen
James F. Ackerman Professor of
Social Studies Education
Director, James F. Ackerman Center
for Democratic Citizenship
Associate Director, Purdue Center for
Economic Education
Purdue University
West Lafayette, Indiana

Dr. Myra Zarnowski
Professor
Elementary and Early Childhood
Education
Queens College
The City University of New York
Flushing, New York

Indiana Consultants

Dr. Jay D. Gatrell
Associate Professor of Geography
Department of Geography
Indiana State University
Terre Haute, Indiana

Dr. M. Gail Hickey
Professor
School of Education
Indiana University-Purdue University
Fort Wayne, Indiana

Dr. Chrystal S. Johnson
Assistant Professor
Social Studies Education
Department of Curriculum and Instruction
Purdue University
West Lafayette, Indiana

Dr. Jason S. Lantzer
Lecturer in History
Indiana University-Purdue University
Indianapolis, Indiana

Dr. Richard B. Pierce
Associate Professor of History
Chair, Department of Africana Studies
University of Notre Dame
Notre Dame, Indiana

Dr. Phillip J. VanFossen
James F. Ackerman Professor of Social
  Studies Education
Director, James F. Ackerman Center for
  Democratic Citizenship
Associate Director, Purdue Center for
  Economic Education
Purdue University
West Lafayette, Indiana

Classroom Reviewers and Contributors

Pamela A. Gresk
Teacher
Sunnyside Elementary School
Indianapolis, Indiana

Alan Hagedorn
President, Indiana Council for Social
  Studies
Teacher
Center Grove High School
Greenwood, Indiana

M. Jeannine Mattingly
Teacher
Skiles Test Elementary School
Indianapolis, Indiana

Pamela R. Zehren
Teacher
Lydia Middleton School
Madison, Indiana

ISBN-13: 978-0-15-377044-9
ISBN-10: 0-15-377044-9

2 3 4 5 6 7 8 9 10 0914 17 16 15 14 13 12 11 10 09

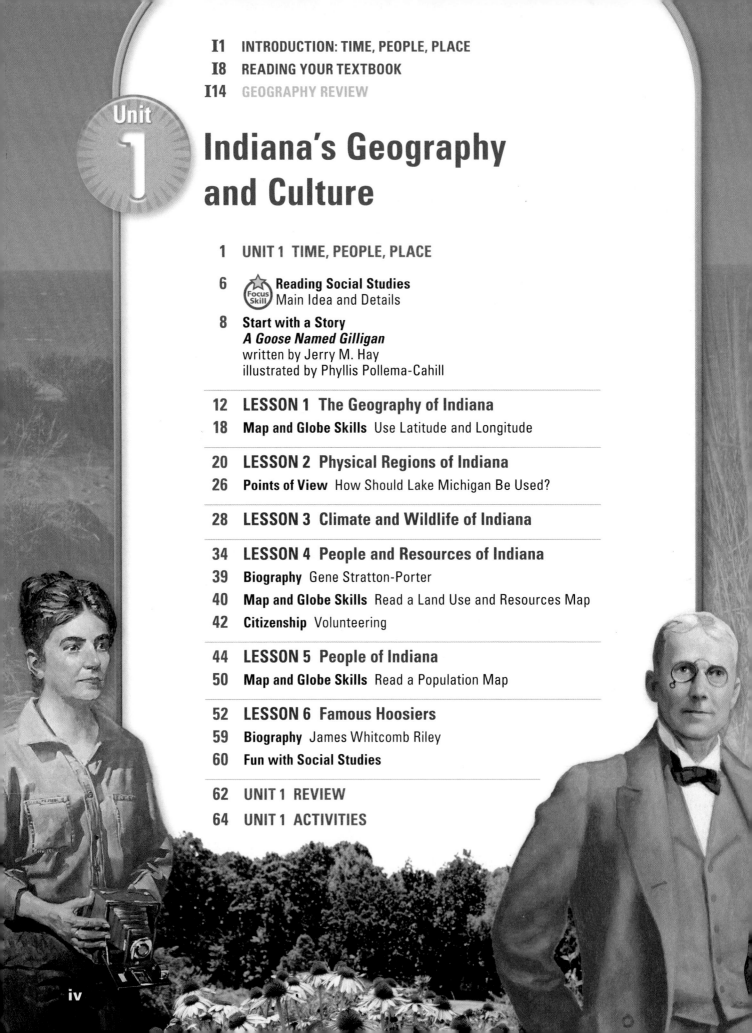

Unit 1

Indiana's Geography and Culture

Unit 2

Indiana Long Ago

v

Unit 3

Indiana's Later History

Unit 4

Indiana Today

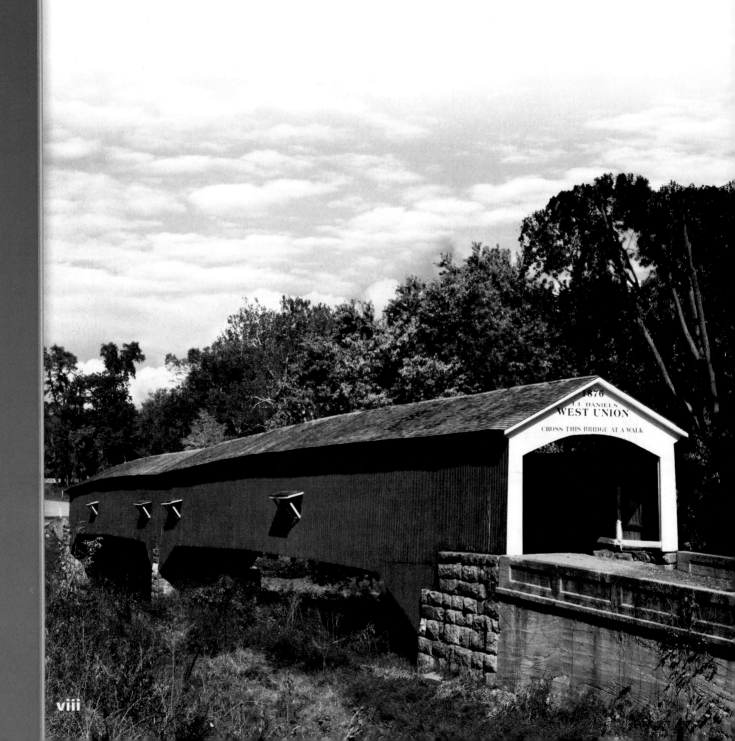

FOR YOUR REFERENCE

Features

Time Lines

Illustrations

The Story Well Told

"Doubtless future generations may see Indiana a flourishing place."

Lydia Bacon, pioneer, 1811

Have you ever wondered what makes up the state of Indiana? You know it is made up of many places, but do you know what those places are like? This year, you will find out.

You will study the geography of Indiana. Geography is the study of Earth's surface and the ways people use it. You will also learn about history, economics, government, and culture. You will learn how areas change over **time**. You will find out how **people** change the places they live and are changed by these places. Throughout your study, you will also discover the importance of **place**.

Time People Place

Indiana History

As you read this book, you will learn to think as a geographer, or a person who studies geography. Learning about geography involves not only the present but also the past. Studying history helps you see how the present is connected to the past. It also helps you see how some places change over time and how other places stay the same.

As you learn to recognize these connections, you will begin to think the way a historian thinks. A historian is a person who studies the past.

Historians **research**, or carefully study, the time in which events in different places happened. They look for clues in the objects and papers that people left behind.

They read journal entries, letters, newspaper stories, and other writings by people. They also look at photographs, films, and artwork.

By carefully studying such **evidence**, or proof, historians are better able to understand what the world was like at the time. It helps them **interpret**, or explain, the past.

Historians look at how events in a place are connected to one another. One way they do this is by using time lines. A time line shows the **chronology**, or time order, in which events happened. A time line can also show how one event may have led to another.

Geographers look closely at people who live in places around the world. After all, places would not be what they are today without people. People locate places, build them, change them, and make them grow.

Because of this, it is important to study not only people of the present but also people of the past. Geographers need to know about the people who founded a place. They also need to know about any newcomers who caused the place to grow or change. In addition, they need to know about the people who make a place what it is today.

When studying people in a place, it is important to think about points of view. A person's **point of view** is how that person sees things. A point of view is shaped by

a person's background and experience. It can depend on whether a person is old or young, male or female, or rich or poor. People with different points of view may see the same event or the same place in very different ways.

People from the past can often serve as models for how to act when troubling events take place. People today can identify key **character traits**—such as trustworthiness, respect, responsibility, fairness, caring, and patriotism—that people from the past showed. They can look at how these character traits help make people into good leaders today, just as they did in the past.

It makes sense that geographers spend much of their time studying places. Places are fascinating. Every place on Earth has features that set it apart from all other places. Often those features affected where events happened in the past, and they may affect where they will happen in the future.

To better understand the features of a place, geographers often study maps. Maps show a place's location. But they can show much more. They can tell a lot about the people who lived there long ago. For example, they can show the routes people followed, where they settled, and how they used the land.

Maps can also tell about people who live in different places today. They can show which people live where, how many people live in each place, and how people in a place earn their living.

Maps, like other evidence, help geographers write a clearer story of the past, present, and future. They are just one valuable tool geographers use to show how time, people, and place are connected.

THE PEOPLE OF INDIANA WELCOME YOU

Reading Your Textbook

GETTING STARTED

Unit Title ●

● Your textbook is divided into four units. Each unit has a title that tells what the unit is about.

● Each unit begins with Indiana's Academic Standards for Social Studies covered in the unit.

● The Big Idea tells you the key idea you should understand by the end of the unit.

● These questions help you focus on the Big Idea.

LOOKING AT TIME, PEOPLE, AND PLACE

● TIME pages tell you when some important events in the unit took place.

● PEOPLE pages introduce you to some of the men and women you will read about in the unit.

● PLACE pages show you where some of the events in the unit took place.

READING SOCIAL STUDIES

The Reading Social Studies Focus Skill will help you better understand the events you read about and make connections among them.

This statement explains why this Focus Skill is important.

The Focus Skill is modeled for you, and you will be asked to practice it.

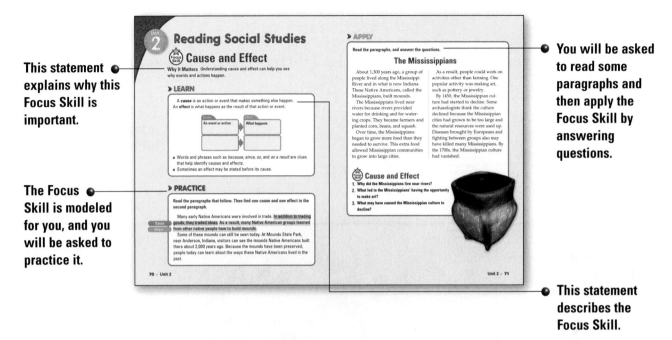

You will be asked to read some paragraphs and then apply the Focus Skill by answering questions.

This statement describes the Focus Skill.

STARTING WITH LITERATURE

Each unit begins with a song, poem, journal, story, or another special reading selection.

Questions let you practice the Reading Focus Skill and relate the literature to your life.

READING A LESSON

This question helps you focus on the lesson's main idea.

These are the new vocabulary terms you will learn in the lesson.

Some of the people and places you will read about are listed.

Remember to apply the Focus Skill as you read the lesson.

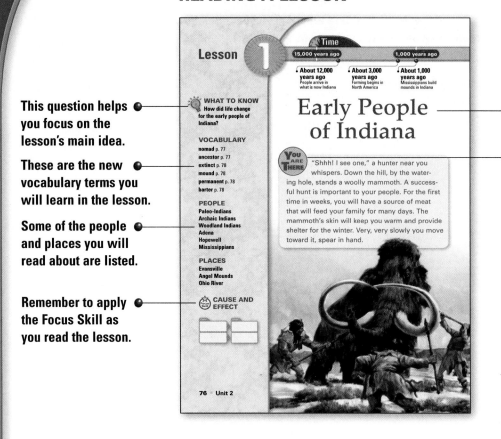

Lesson **1**

Time
15,000 years ago — 1,000 years ago

About 12,000 years ago People arrive in what is now Indiana

About 3,000 years ago Farming begins in North America

About 1,000 years ago Mississippians build mounds in Indiana

WHAT TO KNOW
How did life change for the early people of Indiana?

VOCABULARY
nomad p. 77
ancestor p. 77
extinct p. 78
mound p. 78
permanent p. 78
barter p. 78

PEOPLE
Paleo-Indians
Archaic Indians
Woodland Indians
Adena
Hopewell
Mississippians

PLACES
Evansville
Angel Mounds
Ohio River

CAUSE AND EFFECT

Early People of Indiana

YOU ARE THERE
"Shhh! I see one," a hunter near you whispers. Down the hill, by the watering hole, stands a woolly mammoth. A successful hunt is important to your people. For the first time in weeks, you will have a source of meat that will feed your family for many days. The mammoth's skin will keep you warm and provide shelter for the winter. Very, very slowly you move toward it, spear in hand.

76 ▪ Unit 2

Lesson title

You Are There puts you in the time when events in the lesson took place.

Some lessons have special features in which you can read about Children in History or Primary Sources.

Children IN HISTORY

Miami Children

Miami children grew up doing many of the same things children do today. They played and did chores. From an early age, they were taught to follow the laws and customs of their tribes. Fathers taught sons, and mothers taught daughters.

Boys played sports that involved running, swimming, and jumping. They learned how to use bows and arrows. These activities helped them grow strong and develop their skills as hunters and warriors. Girls played house by following what their mothers did. They had dolls made from cornhusks.

Make It Relevant Think about some of the games you like to play. What skills do you learn by playing these games?

Lessons are divided into different sections.

Key people and places are boldfaced.

The Miami

During the late 1600s, the **Miami** people moved into what is now northern and western Indiana. They settled along the **Maumee River**, where Fort Wayne is now located.

Village Life

The Miami built a settlement called **Kekionga** (kee•kee•OHN•guh). Over time, the Miami became the largest group of Native Americans in what is now Indiana.

The people in each village elected two chiefs. One chief led them in times of peace and the other in times of war. A council of older men and women helped chiefs make decisions. The

Miami lived in dome-shaped houses called wigwams. An opening in the roof let out smoke from the fire.

Miami men hunted buffalo, deer, rabbits, and beavers. They also fished and carried on trade. The women cared for the children, prepared meals, and made clothing. They grew beans, squash, pumpkins, melons, and corn.

As farmers, the Miami did not have to spend as much time looking for food. Some people could specialize in other jobs, such as making pots or weaving. To **specialize** is to work at one kind of job and learn to do it well.

READING CHECK MAIN IDEA AND DETAILS
What were some sources of food for the Miami?

84 ▪ Unit 2

Vocabulary terms are highlighted in yellow.

Each short section ends with a **READING CHECK** question. It helps you check whether you understand what you have read. Be sure that you can answer this question correctly before you continue reading the lesson.

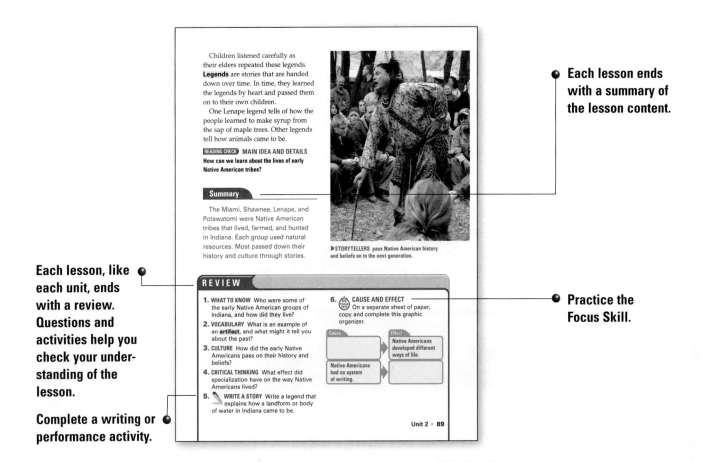

Children listened carefully as their elders repeated these legends. **Legends** are stories that are handed down over time. In time, they learned the legends by heart and passed them on to their own children.

One Lenape legend tells of how the people learned to make syrup from the sap of maple trees. Other legends tell how animals came to be.

READING CHECK MAIN IDEA AND DETAILS
How can we learn about the lives of early Native American tribes?

Summary

The Miami, Shawnee, Lenape, and Potawatomi were Native American tribes that lived, farmed, and hunted in Indiana. Each group used natural resources. Most passed down their history and culture through stories.

➤ STORYTELLERS pass Native American history and beliefs on to the next generation.

Each lesson ends with a summary of the lesson content.

REVIEW

1. **WHAT TO KNOW** Who were some of the early Native American groups of Indiana, and how did they live?

2. **VOCABULARY** What is an example of an **artifact**, and what might it tell you about the past?

3. **CULTURE** How did the early Native Americans pass on their history and beliefs?

4. **CRITICAL THINKING** What effect did specialization have on the way Native Americans lived?

5. **WRITE A STORY** Write a legend that explains how a landform or body of water in Indiana came to be.

6. **CAUSE AND EFFECT** On a separate sheet of paper, copy and complete this graphic organizer.

Cause		Effect
		Native Americans developed different ways of life.
Native Americans had no system of writing.		

Unit 2 ■ 89

Each lesson, like each unit, ends with a review. Questions and activities help you check your understanding of the lesson.

Complete a writing or performance activity.

Practice the Focus Skill.

LEARNING SOCIAL STUDIES SKILLS

Your textbook has lessons that help you build your Citizenship Skills, Map and Globe Skills, Chart and Graph Skills, and Critical Thinking Skills.

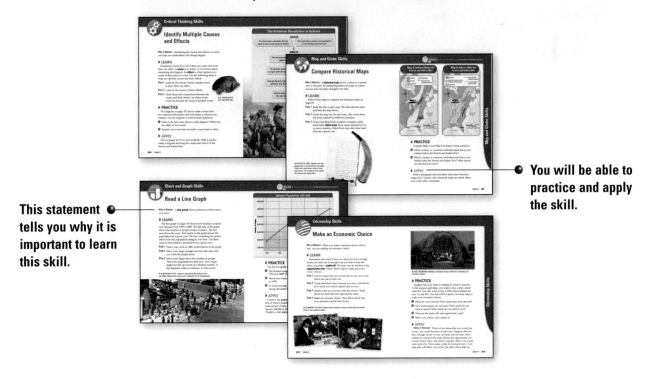

This statement tells you why it is important to learn this skill.

You will be able to practice and apply the skill.

SPECIAL FEATURES

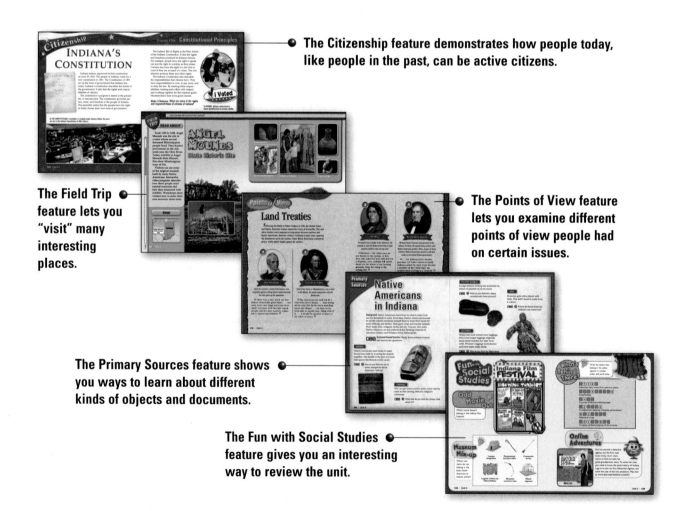

Biographies give in-depth background about some of the people who lived at the time.

Each biography focuses on a trait that the person showed.

A time line shows when the person was born and died and some key events in his or her life.

The Citizenship feature demonstrates how people today, like people in the past, can be active citizens.

The Field Trip feature lets you "visit" many interesting places.

The Points of View feature lets you examine different points of view people had on certain issues.

The Primary Sources feature shows you ways to learn about different kinds of objects and documents.

The Fun with Social Studies feature gives you an interesting way to review the unit.

FOR YOUR REFERENCE

At the back of your textbook, you will find different reference tools. You can use these tools to look up words. You can also find information about people, places, and other topics.

Almanac
Facts about Indiana and its leaders

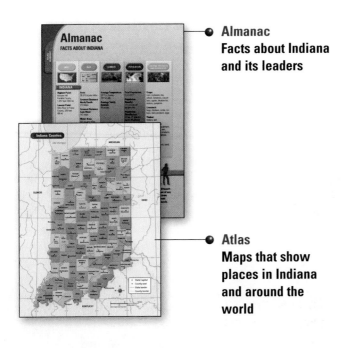

Atlas
Maps that show places in Indiana and around the world

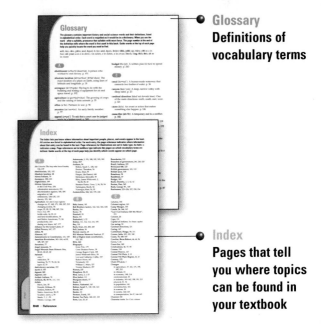

Research Handbook
Guidelines for researching and giving reports

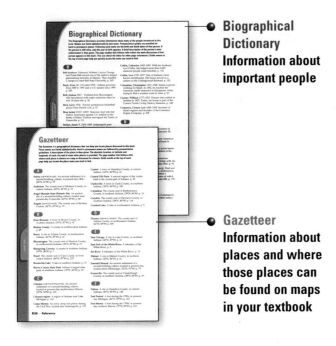

Biographical Dictionary
Information about important people

Gazetteer
Information about places and where those places can be found on maps in your textbook

Glossary
Definitions of vocabulary terms

Index
Pages that tell you where topics can be found in your textbook

The Five Themes of Geography

Learning about places is an important part of history and geography. Geography is the study of Earth's surface and the way people use it. When geographers study Earth and its geography, they often think about five main themes, or topics. Keeping these themes in mind as you read will help you think like a geographer.

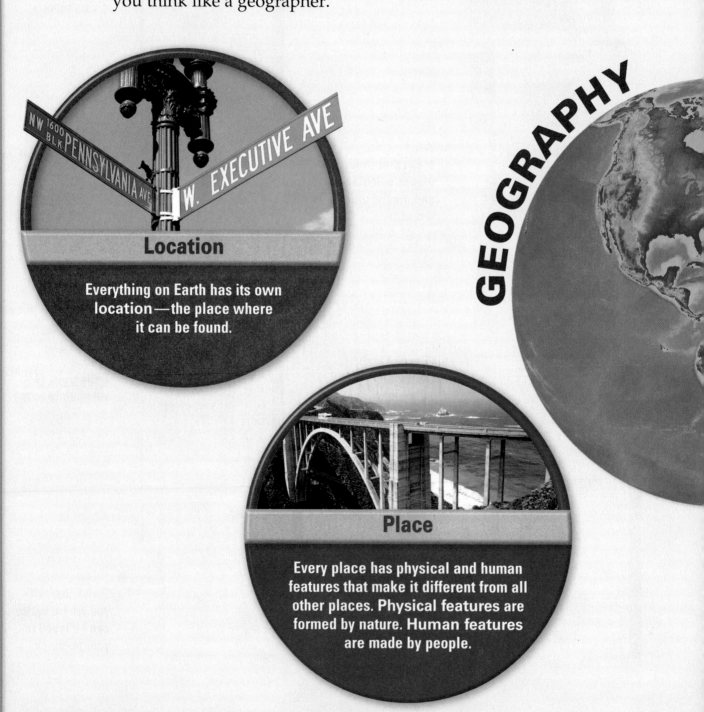

GEOGRAPHY

Location

Everything on Earth has its own location—the place where it can be found.

Place

Every place has physical and human features that make it different from all other places. Physical features are formed by nature. Human features are made by people.

Human-Environment Interactions

People and their surroundings interact, or affect each other. People's activities may change the environment. The environment may affect people. Sometimes people must change how they live to fit into their surroundings.

Movement

People, goods, and ideas move every day. They move in your state, our country, and around the world.

THEMES

Regions

Areas of Earth with main features that make them different from other areas are called regions. A region can be described by its physical features or its human features.

Looking at Earth

A distant view from space shows Earth's round shape. You probably have a globe in your classroom. Like Earth, a globe has the shape of a sphere, or ball. It is a model of Earth. It shows Earth's major bodies of water and its continents. **Continents** are the largest land masses. Earth's seven continents, from the largest to the smallest, are Asia, Africa, North America, South America, Antarctica, Europe, and Australia.

Because of its shape, you can see only one-half of Earth at a time when you look at a globe. Halfway between the North Pole and the South Pole on a globe is a line called the **equator**.

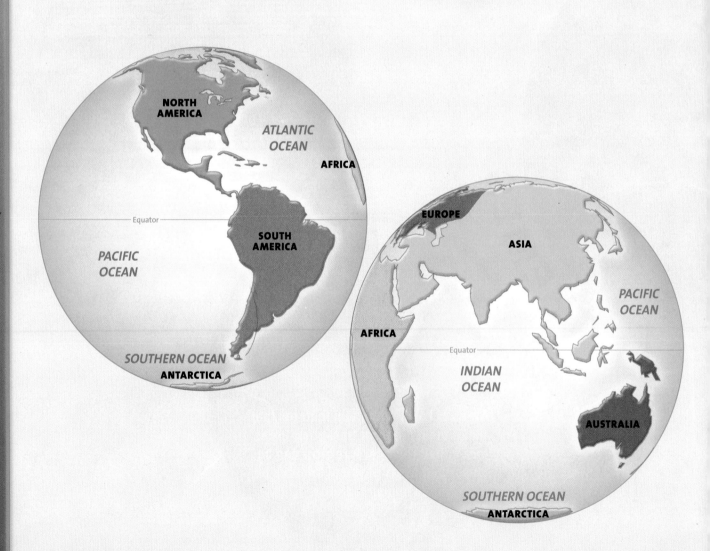

The equator divides Earth into two equal halves, or **hemispheres**. The Northern Hemisphere is north of the equator, and the Southern Hemisphere is south of it. Another line on the globe is called the **prime meridian**. It is often used to divide Earth into the Western Hemisphere and the Eastern Hemisphere.

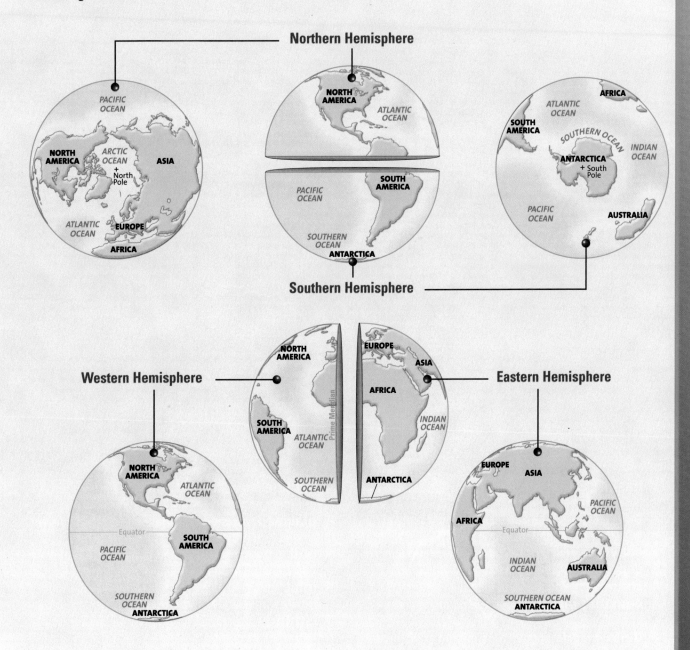

Geography Terms

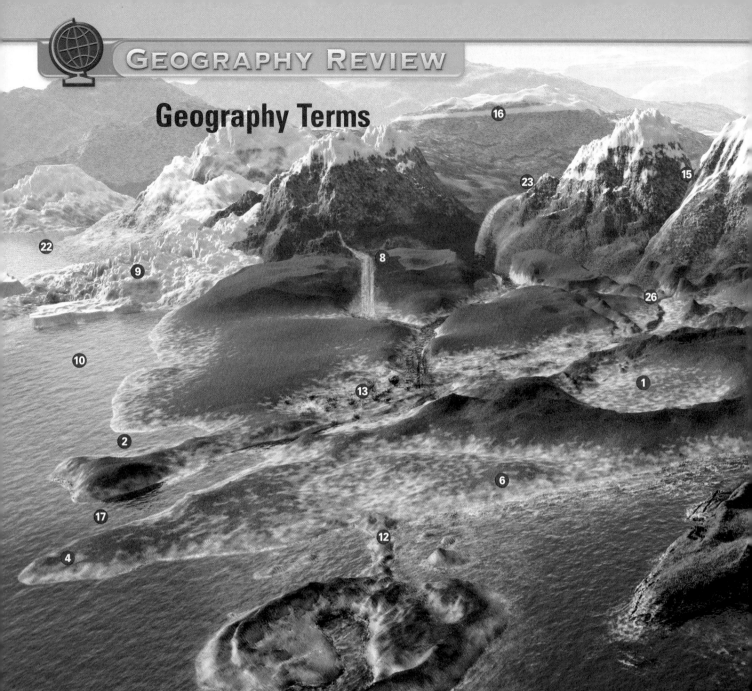

1. **basin** bowl-shaped area of land surrounded by higher land
2. **bay** an inlet of the sea or some other body of water, usually smaller than a gulf
3. **canyon** deep, narrow valley with steep sides
4. **cape** point of land that extends into water
5. **channel** deepest part of a body of water
6. **coastal plain** area of flat land along a sea or ocean
7. **delta** triangle-shaped area of land at the mouth

8. **fall line** area along which rivers form waterfalls or rapids as the rivers drop to lower land
9. **glacier** large ice mass that moves slowly down a mountain or across land
10. **gulf** part of a sea or ocean extending into the land, usually larger than a bay
11. **inlet** any area of water extending into the land from a larger body of water
12. **isthmus** narrow strip of land connecting two larger areas of land

14 mesa flat-topped mountain with steep sides

15 mountain pass gap between mountains

16 mountain range chain of mountains

17 mouth of river place where a river empties into another body of water

18 peninsula land that is almost completely surrounded by water

19 plain area of flat or gently rolling land

20 plateau area of high, mostly flat land

21 savanna area of grassland and scattered trees

22 sea level the level of the surface of an ocean or a sea

23 source of river place where a river begins

24 strait narrow channel of water connecting two larger bodies of water

25 swamp area of low, wet land with trees

26 tributary stream or river that flows into a larger stream or river

27 volcano opening in Earth, often raised, through which lava, rock, ashes, and gases are forced out

Reading Maps

Maps give important information about the world around you. A map is a drawing that shows all or part of Earth on a flat surface. To help you read maps, mapmakers add certain features to their maps. These features often include a title, a map key, a compass rose, a locator, and a map scale.

Mapmakers sometimes need to show certain places on a map in greater detail. Sometimes they must also show places that are located beyond the area shown on a map.

A **map title** tells the subject of the map. It may also identify the kind of map.
- A **political map** shows cities, states, and countries.
- A **physical map** shows kinds of land and bodies of water.
- A **historical map** shows parts of the world as they were in the past.

A **map key**, or **legend**, explains the symbols used on a map. Symbols may be colors, patterns, lines, or other special marks.

An **inset map** is a smaller map within a larger one.

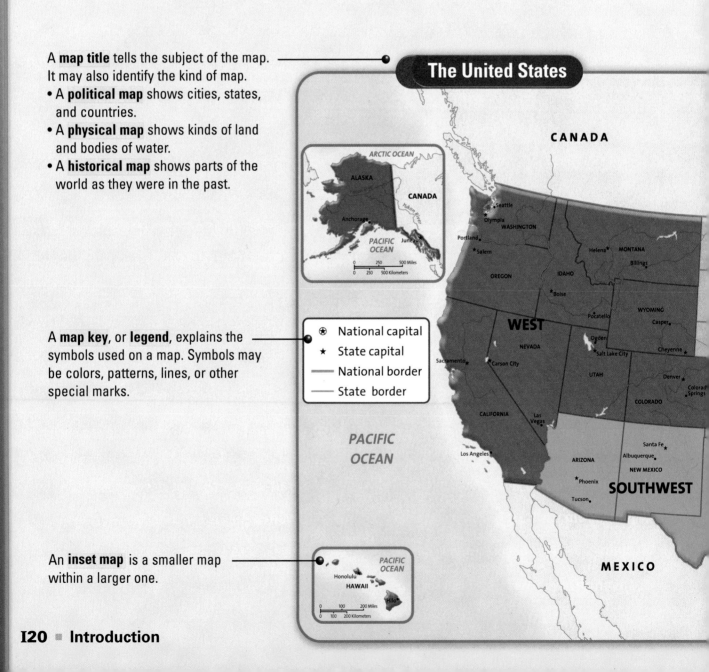

Find Alaska and Hawaii on the map of the United States on pages R8–R9. The map there shows the location of those two states in relation to the location of the rest of the country.

Now find Alaska and Hawaii on the map below. To show this much detail for these states and the rest of the country, the map would have to be much larger. Instead, Alaska and Hawaii are each shown in a separate inset map, or a small map within a larger map.

A **locator** is a small map or globe that shows where the place on the main map is located within a larger area.

A **map scale**, or **distance scale**, compares a distance on the map to a distance in the real world. It helps you find the real distance between places on a map.

A **compass rose**, or direction marker, shows directions.
- The **cardinal directions** are north, south, east, and west.
- The **intermediate directions**, or directions between the cardinal directions, are northeast, northwest, southeast, and southwest.

Finding Locations

To help people find places on maps, mapmakers sometimes add lines that cross each other. These lines form a pattern of squares called a **grid system**.

Look at the map of Indiana below. Around the grid are letters and numbers. The columns, which run up and down, have numbers. The rows, which run from left to right, have letters.

Each square on the map can be identified by its letter and number. For example, the top row of squares on the map includes square A-1, square A-2, square A-3, and so on.

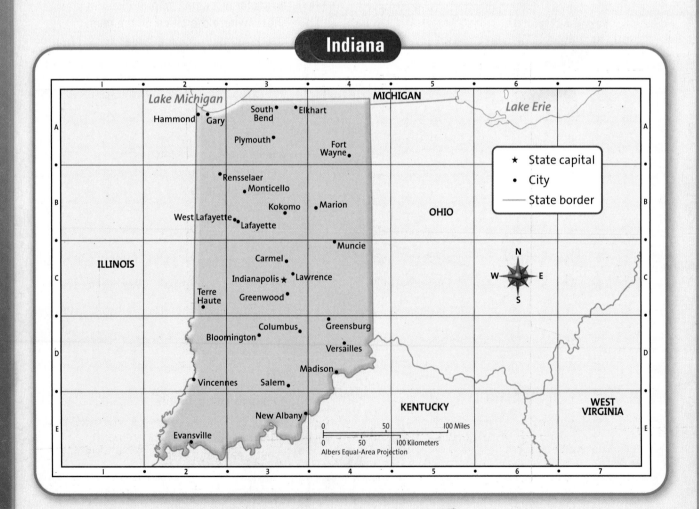

Indiana

Indiana's Geography and Culture

Unit 1

Start with the Standards

INDIANA'S ACADEMIC STANDARDS FOR SOCIAL STUDIES

History 4.1.11, 4.1.13, 4.1.18

Geography 4.3.1, 4.3.2, 4.3.3, 4.3.4, 4.3.5, 4.3.6, 4.3.7, 4.3.8, 4.3.9, 4.3.10, 4.3.11, 4.3.12

The Big Idea

Geography and People

Indiana has diversity in its land and its people.

What to Know

- Where in the United States is Indiana located?

- What is unique about each of Indiana's physical regions?

- What are Indiana's climate and wildlife like?

- What is the relationship between Indiana's people and its natural resources?

- What are the people of Indiana like today?

- How have Hoosiers contributed to culture?

Indiana State and National Parks

❯ **Indiana Dunes National Lakeshore**

Indiana has more than 20 state parks. It also has 3 national parks. These parks allow visitors to enjoy the outdoors. They are also places to learn about Indiana's environment. Many parks in Indiana are known for their land and water. These features include canyons, waterfalls, caves, and sand dunes.

Clifty Falls State Park is best known for its canyon and waterfalls. Water from Clifty Creek drops 70 feet into the canyon, forming the park's largest waterfall. The park has many smaller waterfalls. It also has walls of limestone rock. Many of these rock walls have fossils from animals that lived long ago.

❯ **The many trails in the forests of Potato Creek State Park are perfect for hiking.**

❯ **The waterfalls in Clifty Falls State Park were formed long ago by glaciers.**

Among the hills of southern Indiana is the Hoosier National Forest. The forest is named for Hoosiers, or people living in Indiana. It has rock walls, caves, and underground rivers. The park is Indiana's largest natural area.

One of the national parks in Indiana is the Indiana Dunes National Lakeshore. This park stretches 15 miles along the shore of Lake Michigan. The park is known for its dunes, or hills made of sand. Many visitors hike on Mount Baldy, a dune that rises more than 120 feet above Lake Michigan. The park also has swamps, prairies, rivers, and forests.

Indiana Parks

 ❯ Visitors to Turkey Run State Park can canoe on Sugar Creek.

INDIANA TEST PREP

1 **For which physical feature is Clifty Falls State Park best known?**
A its plains
B its waterfalls
C its marshes
D its hills

2 **Which park has underground rivers?**
A Clifty Falls State Park
B Indiana Dunes National Lakeshore
C Hoosier National Forest
D Potato Creek State Park

3 **Which physical feature is found in Indiana Dunes National Lakeshore?**
A hills made of sand
B ocean
C desert
D cliff

4 **Writing** Why are state parks important?

Plains and hills are two of Indiana's main landforms.

Indiana has a temperate climate.

Indiana's Geography and Culture

Indiana is rich in natural resources.

People from many different backgrounds live in Indiana.

T.C. Steele

1847–1926
- Impressionist painter known for Indiana landscapes
- Considered the most important of the Hoosier Group of Painters

James Whitcomb Riley

1849–1916
- Wrote about 1,000 poems
- Known as "The Hoosier Poet"

People

1800	1840	1880

1847 • T.C. Steele

1849 • James Whitcomb Riley

1863 • Gene Stratton-Porter

1869 • Janet Scudder

1886

Dorothy Buell

1886–1977
- Founded the Save the Dunes Council in 1952
- Her work influenced Congress to form the Indiana Dunes National Lakeshore

Oscar Robertson

1938–
- Won a gold medal as the co-captain of the U.S. basketball team at the 1960 Olympics
- After retiring, helped build affordable housing in Indianapolis

Gene Stratton-Porter

1863–1924
- Wrote more than 20 novels, some of which took place in Indiana
- Worked as a wildlife photographer, taking photographs mainly in the Limberlost Swamp

Janet Scudder

1869–1940
- Made sculptures and carved furniture
- Frequently marched in parades and demonstrations supporting women's rights

1920   **1960**   **Present**

1926

1916

1924

1940

• Dorothy Buell   1977

1938 • Oscar Robertson

1950 • Jane Pauley

1956 • Larry Bird

Jane Pauley

1950–
- Born in Indianapolis
- Has worked as a television host and journalist since 1976

Larry Bird

1956–
- Inducted into the Basketball Hall of Fame in 1998
- Serves as president of basketball operations for the Indiana Pacers

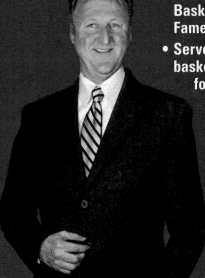

Unit 1 ■ 3

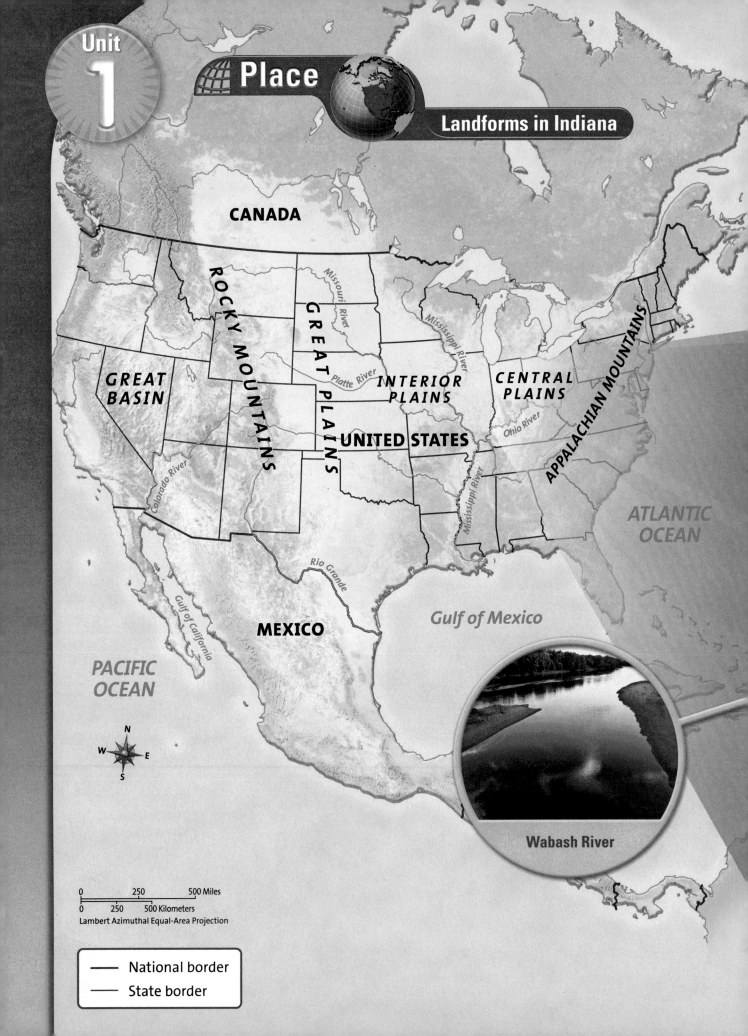

CANADA

ROCKY MOUNTAINS

GREAT PLAINS

Missouri River

Mississippi River

Platte River

INTERIOR PLAINS

CENTRAL PLAINS

APPALACHIAN MOUNTAINS

GREAT BASIN

Colorado River

UNITED STATES

Ohio River

Mississippi River

ATLANTIC OCEAN

Rio Grande

Gulf of California

MEXICO

Gulf of Mexico

PACIFIC OCEAN

N
W   E
S

Wabash River

0   250   500 Miles
0   250   500 Kilometers
Lambert Azimuthal Equal-Area Projection

—— National border
—— State border

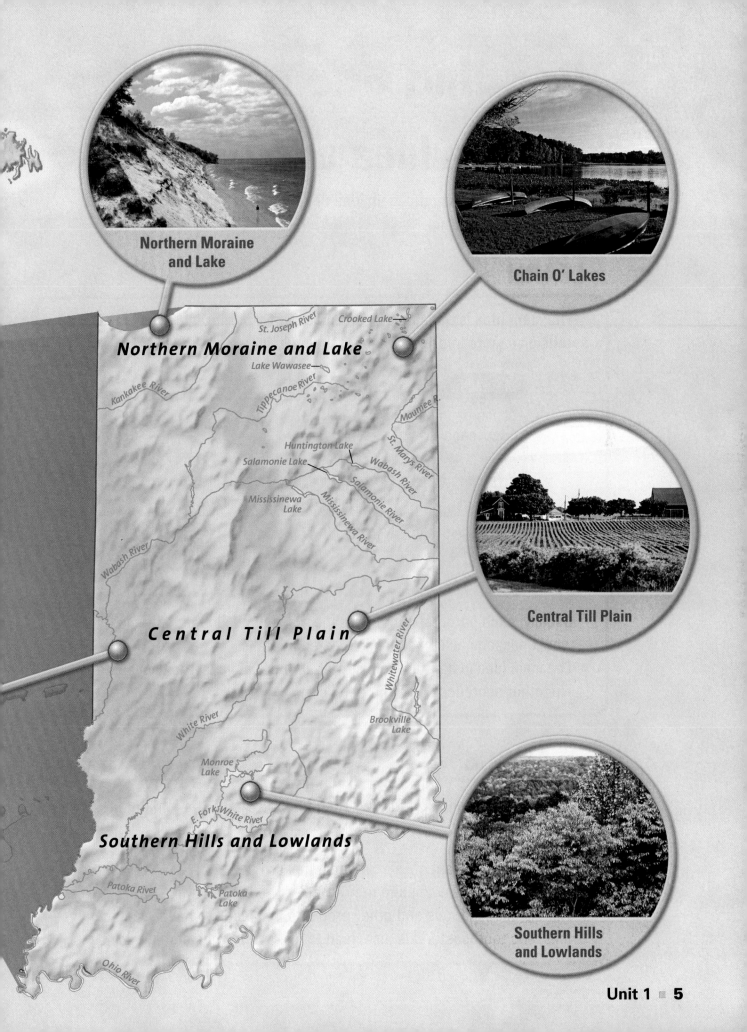

Northern Moraine and Lake

Chain O' Lakes

St. Joseph River

Crooked Lake

Northern Moraine and Lake

Lake Wawasee

Kankakee River

Tippecanoe River

Maumee R.

Huntington Lake

Salamonie Lake

St. Marys River

Wabash River

Mississinewa Lake

Salamonie River

Mississinewa River

Wabash River

Central Till Plain

Central Till Plain

Whitewater River

White River

Brookville Lake

Monroe Lake

Southern Hills and Lowlands

E. Fork White River

Southern Hills and Lowlands

Patoka River

Patoka Lake

Ohio River

Reading Social Studies

⭐ Focus Skill Main Idea and Details

Why It Matters Finding the main idea and details can help you understand what you read.

▶ LEARN

The **main idea** is the most important idea of a paragraph or passage. The **details** give more information about the main idea.

> **Main Idea**
> The most important idea of a paragraph or passage

⬆

> **Details**
>
> | Facts about the main idea | Facts about the main idea | Facts about the main idea |

- Usually, each paragraph in a passage has a main idea and details. The whole passage also has a main idea and details.
- The main idea in a paragraph is often, but not always, the first sentence. The other sentences give the details.

▶ PRACTICE

Read the paragraphs that follow. Then find the main idea and details in the second paragraph.

Main Idea
Details

Mint is an important crop in Indiana. It is grown mostly in the northern part of the state. The soil and the climate there are good for growing mint.

Mint is used in foods and other products. It is used to flavor gum, candy, drinks, and toothpaste. It is also used to make perfumes and medicines.

Read the paragraphs, and answer the questions.

Southern Indiana's Caves

Southern Indiana has more than 2,600 known caves. Only four of them are show caves. A show cave is one that people pay a fee to enter and view. Indiana's show caves are Wyandotte (WY•uhn•daht) Cave, Marengo (muh•REN•goh) Cave, Bluespring Caverns, and Squire Boone Caverns.

Most of southern Indiana's caves formed in the same way. Water caused limestone—a kind of rock—to dissolve. Where the limestone dissolved, it left hollowed areas, or caves, in the rock. This process took place slowly over time.

Southern Indiana's caves offer a variety of features. These include rock formations that look like icicles. Some are stalactites, or rocks that form on a cave ceiling and hang down from it. Others are stalagmites, or rocks that form on a cave floor and build up from it. Animals living in the caves include crickets, bats, and blind cave fish.

Main Idea and Details

1. **What is the main idea of the first paragraph?**
2. **What is the main idea of the second paragraph?**
3. **What details explain the features of southern Indiana's caves?**

WYANDOTTE CAVE

A Goose Named GILLIGAN

written by Jerry M. Hay
illustrated by Phyllis Pollema-Cahill

Hoosiers cherish the land and bodies of water of their state. A favorite spot for Hoosiers is the Wabash River. The Wabash River is the state's official river. Many people and groups, including the Indiana Waterways Association, work to protect the river. The following story about life on the Wabash River is true. Gilligan is the official mascot of the Indiana Waterways Association. Read now to learn Gilligan's story and more about Indiana's Wabash River.

One spring morning, Jerry was returning from a mission when he heard a terrible noise. Then he noticed frantic splashing near the shore.

"Wonder what's going on?" he thought, as he pulled his boat closer.

At first, he couldn't believe his eyes. A very large goose was in a lot of trouble.

The goose was tangled in a trotline and could not get free. In case you're wondering, a trotline is a number of fishing lines and hooks tied to a main cord and float and then anchored. Fishermen use them to catch fish without using a pole.

The goose was struggling to get away, but the more he fought the worse it got. His feet and wings were wrapped tight in the lines, and the hooks were caught in his feathers. The float was hanging from his neck, and if it hadn't been so serious, Jerry would have laughed out loud.

Jerry quickly tied up his boat, jumped into the water, and swam to where the goose was struggling. This made the goose even more frantic. Jerry swam around the goose, who was hissing, warning him to stay away.

"I know you're really scared, goose, but I can't leave you like this. You'll surely die," coaxed Jerry.

The goose was having none of it, and as the river man cut the lines he was pecked and slapped repeatedly for his efforts. Finally, all the lines attached to the anchor were cut, but there were still lines and hooks wrapped around the goose.

Holding the goose tightly, Jerry explained, "There's only one way to get you free. You and I are going to have to go ashore."

Jerry fought his way up the muddy bank, the goose pecking and slapping, and Jerry talking to him to calm him down. They wrestled in the deep mud and fell back into the river twice. But Jerry was determined to help this stubborn critter. Finally, the river man reached a firm spot on the bank, and he hugged the goose in an effort to quiet him.

"Things will go better if you'd just calm down," Jerry pleaded. "I'm trying to help you."

After what seemed like forever, the big goose stopped struggling. He finally understood that this human was trying to help him.

"Well, that's better," said Jerry, as he carefully removed the last line. Unexpectedly, the goose started talking back. "Honk, honk," he said, as if he understood that Jerry was his friend.

Jerry thought the goose would fly off as soon as he was let loose. Instead, the goose stood in the mud honking, as though to thank the river man.

"You're free now," Jerry explained.

The goose slowly slid into the river and began to thrash about, pecking at the globs of mud that covered him. "What a good idea," Jerry agreed, as he followed the goose into the water.

The two of them bathed and chatted about the predicament the goose had been in. When the goose still didn't leave, Jerry became concerned that he might be injured and couldn't fly.

By now it was getting late, so Jerry swam back to his boat. The goose followed him, swimming in circles and repeating his friendly, "Honk, honk."

"I won't leave 'til I see you fly, but I do have to get along home," explained the river man.

With that, the goose began to run along the water, flapping his huge wings. Then he lifted off. Jerry watched as the goose flew in a circle, honking his goodbyes. The river man waved one last time and headed home.

Neither the scratches and the welts on his head nor the mud and his torn clothes mattered. Jerry was grateful that he had happened along at just the right time.

Early the next day, Jerry was awakened by a now-familiar sound. A loud and insistent honking was coming from the direction of his dock. He threw on some clothes and hurried down to the river, where he was greeted by a visitor. It was the beautiful goose he had saved the day before!

"Well now, it really is nice to see you. I was hoping that I might run across you again someday," greeted Jerry.

"Honk, honk," answered the goose.

They visited for a while before the goose flew away. The next day the goose came by for another visit and stayed a little longer. He stopped by every day after that, staying longer each time. Soon the goose could be found at the dock almost any time of the day or night.

The goose became quite an attraction, and neighbors up and down the river stopped by to visit with him. Some folks were afraid of the goose, especially when he came hurrying up to the house to greet them with an enthusiastic, "Honk, honk."

"Don't worry, he won't hurt you. He's just being friendly," Jerry would explain.

One day a visitor asked, "What do you call your goose?"

Jerry was startled. The river man never claimed ownership of the goose, since he believed that all wild animals should be free to come and go as they please.

"I call him 'goose' or 'the goose,'" Jerry replied.

"But he has to have a name," insisted his friend.

Jerry thought about that for a minute. "Well, I guess it wouldn't hurt. Why don't you name him?"

She was very pleased to be asked. "I think Gilligan would be a good name for him, and your dock can be Gilligan's Landing."

From that day on, everyone on the river called the goose Gilligan. It didn't take long for the goose to recognize his name, and he would come when called. Some evenings Gilligan would be at his landing honking so loudly that the echo could be heard up and down the river.

Response Corner

1. **Main Idea and Details** What does Gilligan's story teach people about the Wabash River?

2. **Make It Relevant** Why is it important to keep bodies of water clean?

Lesson 1

The Geography of Indiana

WHAT TO KNOW
Where in the United States is Indiana located?

VOCABULARY

region p. 13

relative location p. 13

border p. 13

physical feature p. 14

plain p. 14

fertile soil p. 14

tributary p. 14

human feature p. 14

industry p. 16

PLACES

Indiana
United States
Midwest
Wabash River
White River
Ohio River
Lake Wawasee
Lake Michigan
Monroe Lake
Indianapolis
Fort Wayne
South Bend
Gary
Evansville

MAIN IDEA AND DETAILS

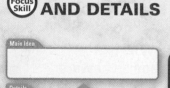

YOU ARE THERE "You have e-mail!" says your computer. The message is from your new pen pal in Germany. Like you, she's in fourth grade.

You sent your first e-mail to her yesterday. In it, you wrote that you live in **Indiana**. Now your pen pal is asking a lot of questions about your state. She wants to know where it is, what the land looks like, and what its cities are like. Do you know enough about Indiana's geography to answer all these questions?

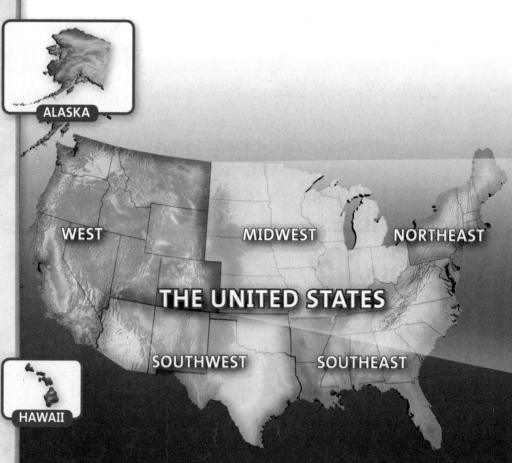

ALASKA

WEST
MIDWEST
NORTHEAST

THE UNITED STATES

SOUTHWEST
SOUTHEAST

HAWAII

Indiana in the United States

You could describe Indiana's location to your pen pal in different ways. You could start by writing that Indiana is one of the 50 states that make up the **United States**.

A Midwestern State

You could write that Indiana is in the **Midwest**. The Midwest is one of the five geographic regions of the United States. A **region** is an area with at least one feature that makes it different from other areas. The other four geographic regions are the Northeast, the Southeast, the Southwest, and the West. The states that make up each geographic region are all located in the same part of the United States.

Relative Location

You could describe Indiana's relative location to your pen pal, too. The **relative location** of a place is where it is in relation to other places on Earth.

Indiana shares its borders with four other states. A **border** is a line that divides one place from another. To the east of Indiana is Ohio, and to the south is Kentucky. To the west is Illinois. To the north is Michigan.

You can now answer your pen pal. Indiana is one of the 50 states that make up the United States. It is located in the Midwest region of the United States. In addition, Indiana is bordered by four states—Ohio, Kentucky, Illinois, and Michigan.

READING CHECK ⓞMAIN IDEA AND DETAILS
In which region is Indiana located?

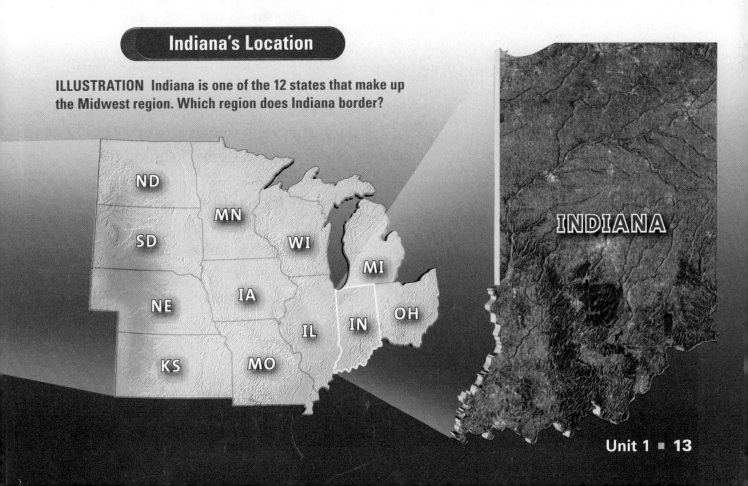

Indiana's Location

ILLUSTRATION Indiana is one of the 12 states that make up the Midwest region. Which region does Indiana border?

ND MN SD WI MI IA NE IL IN OH KS MO

INDIANA

Indiana's Land and Water

To describe what Indiana looks like, you need to know about its **physical features**, or features formed by nature. These features include the state's land-forms and bodies of water.

Plains and Hills

Most of Indiana's land lies between 500 and 1,000 feet above sea level. Sea level is the height of the ocean sur-face. Indiana's land has two main kinds of land-forms—plains and hills.

Wide **plains**, or areas of low, flat land, cover the northern two-thirds of Indiana. Their **fertile soils**, or soils good for growing crops, support much of the state's farming.

The southern one-third of Indiana has more variety than the rest of the state. As you travel from west to east, areas of plains follow areas of hills. The hills include features such as waterfalls, caves, and ridges. A ridge is a long chain of hills.

Describing Indiana to a friend in a letter, William Henry Harrison wrote in 1801,

❝I am much pleased with this country. Nothing can exceed its . . . fertility.❞

Rivers

The **Wabash River** is Indiana's longest river, flowing for 475 miles. Along its route, the Wabash is joined by several tributaries. A **tributary** is a smaller river that flows into a larger river. One major tributary of the Wabash River is the **White River**.

Indiana has other important rivers. These rivers include the St. Marys, St. Joseph, Maumee, and Kankakee Rivers. The **Ohio River** forms the border between Indiana and Kentucky.

▶ WATERFALL IN SOUTHERN INDIANA

Lakes

Many lakes are found in northern Indiana. Most are natural, or made by nature. **Lake Wawasee** is Indiana's largest natural lake. Northern Indiana also borders about 48 miles of **Lake Michigan**.

Some lakes in central and southern Indiana are **human features**, or fea-tures made by people. People build dams, or walls, across rivers. Water collects behind dams, forming lakes. A human-made lake is called a reservoir (REH•zuh•vwahr).

A dam built across Salt Creek formed **Monroe Lake**, Indiana's largest reservoir. Other reservoirs in central and southern Indiana include the Patoka, Brookville, Salamonie, and Mississinewa Lakes.

READING CHECK ŎMAIN IDEA AND DETAILS
What are two main landforms in Indiana?

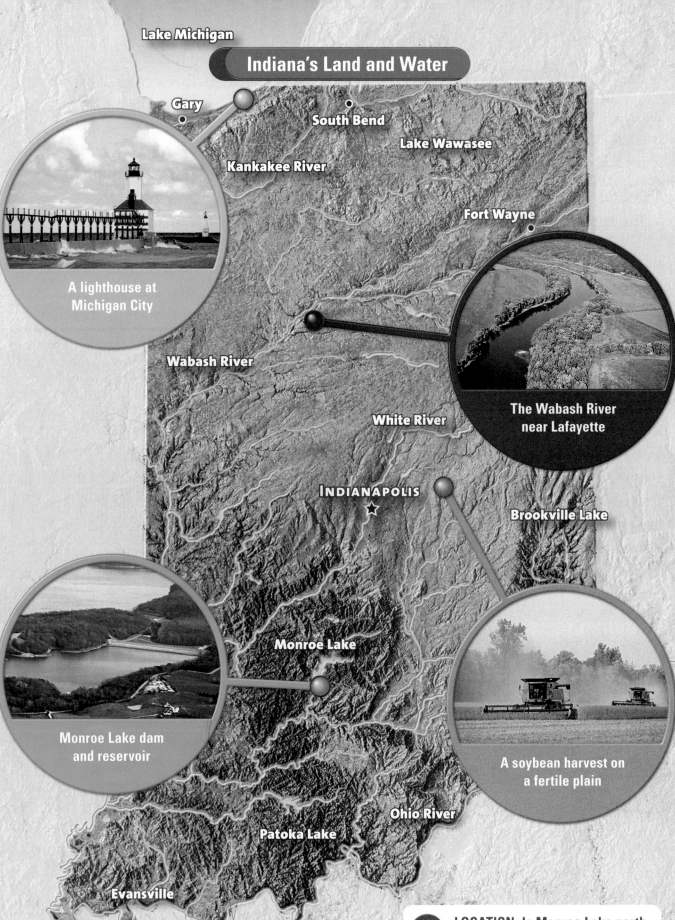

Indiana's Land and Water

Lake Michigan

Gary

South Bend

Lake Wawasee

Kankakee River

Fort Wayne

A lighthouse at
Michigan City

Wabash River

The Wabash River
near Lafayette

White River

INDIANAPOLIS

Brookville Lake

Monroe Lake

Monroe Lake dam
and reservoir

A soybean harvest on
a fertile plain

Ohio River

Patoka Lake

Evansville

MAP SKILL   **LOCATION** Is Monroe Lake north
or south of Indianapolis?

Indiana's Cities

Cities are another human feature of Indiana. Most of the state's cities are located near rivers and lakes.

The State Capital

Indianapolis is the state capital of Indiana. It is located in the center of the state, along the White River. With a population of nearly 800,000 people, it is Indiana's largest city.

Indianapolis is Indiana's center of business and transportation. Several large companies have their headquarters in or near the city. Also, five major interstate highways meet in Indianapolis. These highways contribute to the state's motto as "the Crossroads of America." Other cities in central Indiana include Muncie, Lafayette, Kokomo, and Anderson.

Cities in Northern Indiana

Fort Wayne is the second-largest city in Indiana. It is located in northeastern Indiana where the St. Joseph and St. Marys Rivers join to form the Maumee River. Fort Wayne has a growing healthcare industry. An **industry** is all the businesses that provide one kind of product or service.

Near the Indiana-Michigan border, **South Bend** is Indiana's fourth-largest city. Its name comes from its location on a southern bend of the St. Joseph River. South Bend is at the center of a region called Michiana.

West of South Bend is the city of **Gary**. It is located on Lake Michigan, a major transportation route. Gary is Indiana's fifth-largest city. Nearby is Hammond, the state's sixth-largest city. Both cities have strong ties with nearby Chicago, Illinois.

Indiana's Ten Largest Cities, 2006	
CITY	**POPULATION**
Indianapolis	785,597
Fort Wayne	248,637
Evansville	115,738
South Bend	104,905
Gary	97,715
Hammond	78,292
Bloomington	69,247
Muncie	65,287
Lafayette	61,244
Carmel	60,570

TABLE Lafayette (below) is located on the Wabash River. Which city has the larger population, Lafayette or Evansville?

Cities in Southern Indiana

Evansville is located on the Ohio River in southwestern Indiana. It is the state's third-largest city. Because of its location, Evansville is an important hub, or center of activity, for the area where Indiana, Illinois, and Kentucky meet. Other cities in southern Indiana include Bloomington and New Albany.

READING CHECK **DRAW CONCLUSIONS**
How is Gary's location different from Fort Wayne's location?

▶ **EVANSVILLE**, located on the Ohio River, is a hub for trade between Indiana, Illinois, and Kentucky.

Summary

Indiana is located in the Midwest region of the United States. The state has two main kinds of landforms—plains and hills. It also has major rivers and important lakes. Most of Indiana's cities are located near rivers and lakes.

REVIEW

1. **WHAT TO KNOW** Where in the United States is Indiana located?

2. **VOCABULARY** Use the terms **border** and **relative location** in a sentence that describes Indiana.

3. **GEOGRAPHY** What city is Indiana's state capital, and on which river is it located?

4. **CRITICAL THINKING** Why do you think many of Indiana's cities are located near rivers and lakes?

5. **MAKE A BOOK COVER** Make a book cover for an atlas of Indiana. On the cover, include a title and a map. On the map, show physical and human features of the state.

6. **MAIN IDEA AND DETAILS** On a separate sheet of paper, copy and complete this graphic organizer.

Main Idea

Three of Indiana's five largest cities are in northern Indiana.

Details

Use Latitude and Longitude

Why It Matters By stating latitude and longitude, you can describe the **absolute location**, or exact location, of a place.

❱ LEARN

Lines of latitude and longitude form a grid on a map or a globe. To describe a place's absolute location, you name the line of latitude and the line of longitude closest to it.

Lines of latitude run east and west on a map or a globe. The equator is a line of latitude. Find the equator on Map A. It is marked 0°, or zero degrees. All other lines of latitude are measured in degrees north or south of the equator.

Lines of longitude run north and south on a map or a globe, from the North Pole to the South Pole. The **prime meridian** is a line of longitude. Find the prime meridian on Map A. It is marked 0°. All other lines of longitude are measured in degrees east or west of the prime meridian.

Map A: Latitude and Longitude

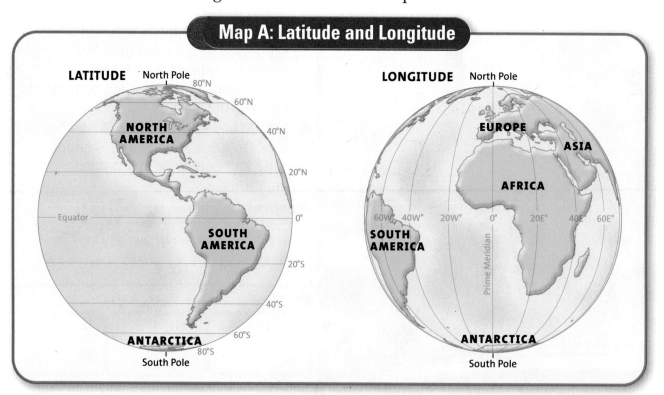

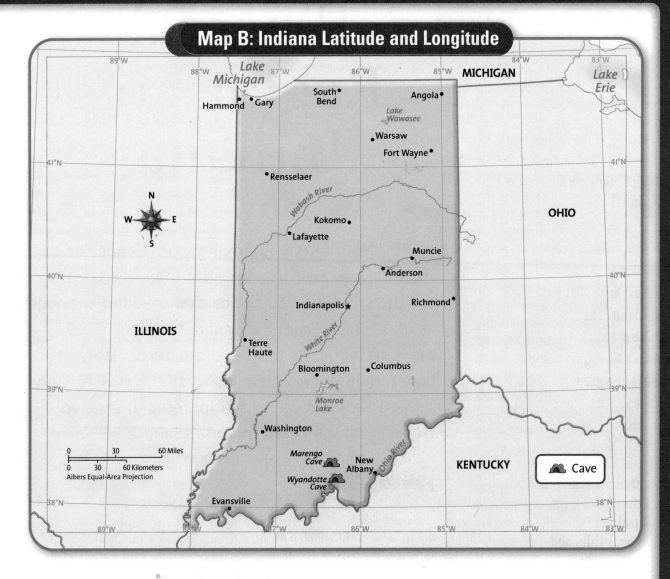

Map B: Indiana Latitude and Longitude

❯ PRACTICE

Use Map B to answer these questions.

❶ Which line of latitude is closest to Monroe Lake?

❷ What physical feature crosses 40°N near 86°W?

❸ Find the lines of latitude and longitude that are closest to Fort Wayne, Indianapolis, and Rensselaer.

❯ APPLY

Make It Relevant Use lines of latitude and longitude to describe your community's absolute location. Then use surrounding towns, landforms, or bodies of water to describe your community's relative location.

Map and Globe Skills

Lesson

Physical Regions of Indiana

WHAT TO KNOW
What is unique about each of Indiana's physical regions?

VOCABULARY
glacier p. 21
lithosphere p. 21
wetland p. 22
dune p. 22
till p. 23
elevation p. 23
canyon p. 23
sinkhole p. 24

PLACES
Northern Moraine and Lake
Central Till Plain
Southern Hills and Lowlands
Indiana Dunes National Lakeshore
Hoosier Hill
Hoosier National Forest
Brown County State Park

MAIN IDEA AND DETAILS

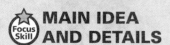

YOU ARE THERE Your family is driving from Evansville to Gary to visit your grandparents. Looking out the window, you notice that the land changes as you travel. From Evansville to Terre Haute, the land is mostly hilly. Around Terre Haute, it becomes flat, and it stays flat all the way to Gary. As you arrive at your grandparents' home, you wonder what shaped Indiana's land.

FAST FACT

Today, glaciers cover about one-tenth of Earth's land. If all of these glaciers melted, the level of the ocean would rise more than 200 feet!

Rivers of Ice

Earth's climate changes over time. In the past, Earth has had long periods of low temperatures called Ice Ages. During the Ice Ages, **glaciers** (GLAY•sherz), or slow-moving ice masses, covered much more of Earth than they do today.

Shaping Earth

The glaciers of long ago greatly affected parts of Earth's lithosphere. The **lithosphere** is the soil and rocks that form Earth's surface. Some landforms that glaciers created include plains, valleys, hills, and lakes.

As the glaciers spread over land, they flattened it, carved it out, or filled it in. They also moved rocks and soil, and they ground rocks into soil. As glaciers melted, they left behind rocks, soil, and water.

Shaping Indiana

During the last Ice Age, glaciers pushed into Indiana from the north three different times. Little is known about the first glacier. The second glacier covered all of Indiana except for the center of the southern part. The third glacier covered the northern two-thirds of the state.

The landscape and environment of Indiana today are related to the glaciers of the past. Glaciers flattened much of the state. In some places, they left behind soil that is fertile. They also created underground deposits of water and minerals. Glaciers formed not only the five Great Lakes to the north but also many of Indiana's rivers and lakes.

READING CHECK ⟳**MAIN IDEA AND DETAILS**
What shaped much of Indiana's landscape and environment?

❯ **GLACIERS** still cover and shape parts of Earth, just as they did in Indiana long ago (below). The photograph shows a present-day glacier in Alaska.

Glaciers of the Ice Age

PACIFIC OCEAN

ATLANTIC OCEAN

Northern Moraine and Lake

Geographers often divide Indiana into three physical regions. They are the **Northern Moraine and Lake**, the **Central Till Plain**, and the **Southern Hills and Lowlands**.

Lakes, Wetlands, and Dunes

The Northern Moraine and Lake region covers the northern one-third of Indiana. Glaciers flattened most of this region into a plain and formed many other land and water features.

In the eastern part of the region, glaciers created natural lakes. First, they scraped out holes in the land. Later, water from melting glaciers filled the holes. Lake Wawasee is one example. The glaciers also left hills of soil and rocks. Hills of this kind are called moraines (muh•RAYNZ).

To the west, glaciers left sandy soil and water. These deposits created **wetlands**, or areas where the water is near the land's surface. Marshes and swamps are examples of wetlands.

Along Lake Michigan are **dunes**, or hills of sand built up by wind. Long ago, the water level of Lake Michigan fell. This process created a series of sandy shorelines that became dunes. Today, these dunes can be seen at **Indiana Dunes National Lakeshore.**

READING CHECK Ŏ**MAIN IDEA AND DETAILS**
What are Indiana's three physical regions?

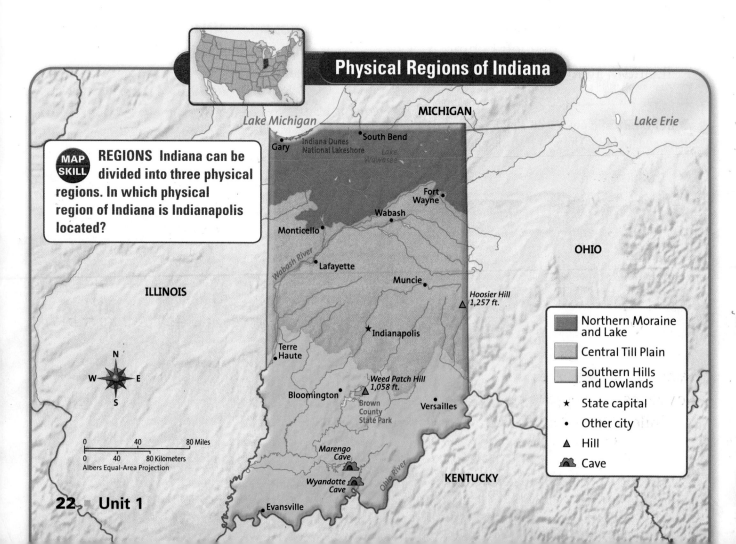

Physical Regions of Indiana

MAP SKILL **REGIONS** Indiana can be divided into three physical regions. In which physical region of Indiana is Indianapolis located?

Legend:
- Northern Moraine and Lake
- Central Till Plain
- Southern Hills and Lowlands
- ★ State capital
- • Other city
- ▲ Hill
- Cave

MICHIGAN
Lake Michigan
Lake Erie
South Bend
Gary
Indiana Dunes National Lakeshore
Lake Wawasee
Fort Wayne
Wabash
Monticello
OHIO
Wabash River
Lafayette
Muncie
ILLINOIS
Hoosier Hill 1,257 ft.
Indianapolis
Terre Haute
Weed Patch Hill 1,058 ft.
Bloomington
Brown County State Park
Versailles
N
W E
S
0   40   80 Miles
0   40   80 Kilometers
Albers Equal-Area Projection
Marengo Cave
Wyandotte Cave
Ohio River
KENTUCKY
Evansville

▶ **LANDSCAPES** Indiana Dunes National Lakeshore (left) is in the Northern Moraine and Lake region. Fertile farmland (right) covers much of the Central Till Plain.

Central Till Plain

South of the Northern Moraine and Lake region is the Central Till Plain. This region is named for the fertile **till**, or mixture of clay, sand, and small stones, that the glaciers left behind.

Flat, Fertile Land

Glaciers that flattened the Northern Moraine and Lake region also created the Central Till Plain. Together, the flat land and fertile till of the Central Till Plain provide Indiana with its best farmland. Here, farmers grow corn, soybeans, and other crops.

While most of the Central Till Plain is low, flat land, the region also has low, rolling hills and small valleys.

These landforms are found mostly in the eastern part of the region. Near the Indiana–Ohio border is **Hoosier Hill**. With an elevation of 1,257 feet, Hoosier Hill is Indiana's highest point. **Elevation** is the height of land above or below sea level.

In several valleys of the Central Till Plain, rivers flow through canyons. A **canyon** is a deep, narrow valley with steep sides. Scenic canyons lie along the Wabash River and many of its tributaries. At the end of the last Ice Age, the water from melting glaciers carved out these canyons.

READING CHECK **CAUSE AND EFFECT**
How are Ice Age glaciers and Indiana's best farmland connected?

Southern Hills and Lowlands

The Southern Hills and Lowlands region covers the southern one-third of Indiana. This region looks different from the other two regions. Glaciers that reached the region covered only some of its western and eastern parts. As a result, the region kept most of its hills and formed other features.

Lowlands and Uplands

The land of the Southern Hills and Lowlands region mostly follows a pattern. From west to east is a strip of lowland, or low land, followed by a strip of upland, or high land. Another strip of lowland follows, then a strip of upland, and so on.

Caves, Sinkholes, and Knobs

The westernmost lowland area is about 500 feet above sea level. Here, dunes can be found along parts of the Wabash and Ohio Rivers.

To the east, the first upland has the state's largest caves, including Wyandotte and Marengo Caves. **Hoosier National Forest** also covers much of this area.

Sinkholes are a main feature of the next lowland. **Sinkholes** are large, bowl-shaped holes that form when limestone layers above underground holes collapse. Underground water flowing through limestone cracks creates the underground holes. This lowland has about 300,000 sinkholes.

The next upland has some of the state's most rugged land. Crossing the

Children IN HISTORY

The Hiestand Children

In September 1883, 15-year-old Blanche Hiestand and her 11-year-old brother, Orris, decided to explore a nearby sinkhole. Using only candles for light, they entered a small hole in the sinkhole. Inside, they found a large cave full of beautiful formations. Excited but nervous, Blanche and Orris left the cave, both covered in mud. News of their discovery quickly reached the owner of the land around the cave. Soon the landowner began giving tours of what became known as Marengo Cave.

Make It Relevant What were some of the dangers Blanche and Orris probably faced?

upland is a long, high cliff made up of steep hills called knobs. The highest, Weed Patch Hill, is 1,058 feet tall. It is in **Brown County State Park**, Indiana's largest state park.

The easternmost lowland and upland have their own features. The lowland shows evidence that the area was once covered by an ocean. The upland has some of Indiana's higher elevations.

READING CHECK **CAUSE AND EFFECT**
What causes sinkholes to form?

Summary

Glaciers affected much of Indiana. To understand these effects, geographers often divide the state into three physical regions—the Northern Moraine and Lake, the Central Till Plain, and the Southern Hills and Lowlands.

▶ **SINKHOLES** dot part of the landscape of the Southern Hills and Lowlands region.

REVIEW

1. **WHAT TO KNOW** What is unique about each of Indiana's physical regions?

2. **VOCABULARY** Use the term **glacier** in a sentence about Indiana's land and water.

3. **GEOGRAPHY** How many times did glaciers cover parts of Indiana during the last Ice Age?

4. **CRITICAL THINKING** How might Indiana's land look different today if glaciers had not covered much of the state?

5. ✏️ **WRITE A REPORT** Draw a map of Indiana's physical regions. Then choose one of the regions, and write a report about it. Explain how glaciers affected that region.

6. ⭐ (Focus Skill) **MAIN IDEA AND DETAILS**
On a separate sheet of paper, copy and complete this graphic organizer.

Main Idea

Geographers often divide Indiana into three physical regions.

Details

How Should Lake Michigan Be Used?

Lake Michigan is important to the lives of Hoosiers and others. People use the lake in many ways. They use it for recreation, such as boating, fishing, and swimming, and for transportation. They use it as a source of water for homes, businesses, and industries.

Not everyone agrees on how Lake Michigan should be used. Some people want to allow growing industries to use more of the lake's water. These industries provide much-needed products and jobs, but their activities would add pollution to the lake. Others do not want the industries to use more of the lake's water.

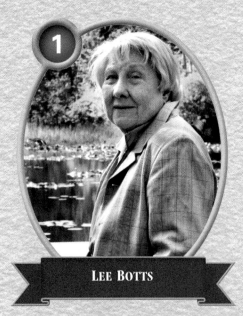

1

LEE BOTTS

Lee Botts is an environmentalist who lives in Gary, Indiana.

"This is the source of drinking water for nearly 8 million people here at the south end of Lake Michigan."

2

STEPHEN JOHNSON

Stephen Johnson is an administrator of the Environmental Protection Agency.

"We want to work with companies to do what we can to improve the condition of Lake Michigan."

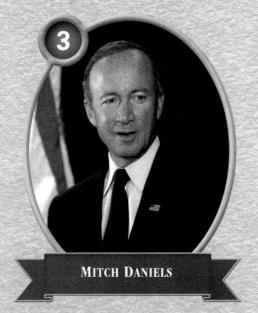

③

MITCH DANIELS

Mitch Daniels is the forty-ninth governor
of Indiana.

66 It's [the government's] responsibility to keep Lake Michigan clean
and people at work. 99

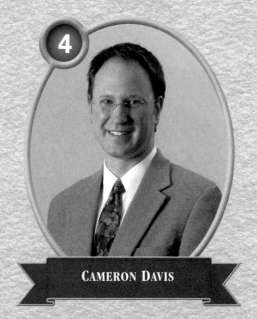

④

CAMERON DAVIS

Cameron Davis is the president of
the Alliance for the Great Lakes.

66 At a time when we've spent
billions and billions of dollars invest-
ing in the rehabilitation [restoring to
good condition] of the Great Lakes,
we should not be taking a step
backward. 99

It's Your Turn

Compare Points of View
Summarize each person's point of view. Then answer the
questions.

1. How are the views of Stephen Johnson and Mitch
Daniels alike?

2. How are the views of Mitch Daniels and Stephen
Johnson like those of Lee Botts and Cameron Davis?
How are they different?

3. What might be affecting the opinion of each person?

Make It Relevant Why might you and a classmate have
different points of view about an event or idea?

Climate and Wildlife of Indiana

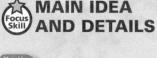
WHAT TO KNOW
What are Indiana's climate and wildlife like?

VOCABULARY

climate p. 29
tornado p. 29
precipitation p. 29
drought p. 29
hydrosphere p. 31
biosphere p. 32

PLACES
Lake Michigan
Hoosier National Forest

MAIN IDEA AND DETAILS

Main Idea

Details

YOU ARE THERE It's a chilly morning in fall, a nice change from the hot, humid summer. You and your family are hiking on a trail in southern Indiana. Here, the forests are a mix of bright reds, golds, and oranges. Earlier, you spotted a family of white-tailed deer crossing the trail ahead of you. Now, you're watching wild turkeys search for food around the trunk of a rare yellow-wood tree. You wonder whether Indiana's climate and wildlife are the same across the state.

Fall

Winter

Indiana's Climate

The kind of weather a place has over a long period of time is its **climate**. Indiana has a temperate climate—it is usually neither very hot nor very cold. Still, temperatures can be extreme at times, depending on the season.

Varied Seasons

Indiana has four very different seasons. Summer is hot and humid because warm air pushes up from the Gulf of Mexico. Fall, or autumn, is pleasant, with lower humidity, mild temperatures, and sunny skies. During winter, icy air sweeps down from Canada and the Great Lakes. This cold air can bring snow to the state. Spring brings warmer temperatures and plentiful rainfall.

Both spring and summer also bring **tornadoes**, or funnel-shaped, spinning windstorms. Tornadoes form when masses of warm air and cold air meet over the plains. They move over the land quickly, destroying everything in their path. Some have wind speeds of up to 300 miles per hour!

Indiana's precipitation also varies with its seasons. **Precipitation** is water that falls to Earth as rain, sleet, hail, or snow. Precipitation is highest during late spring and early summer. It is lowest in winter. At times, areas of southern Indiana has floods because of too much rainfall. At other times, it has **droughts**, or long periods of little or no precipitation.

READING CHECK ⚫**MAIN IDEA AND DETAILS**
What kind of climate does Indiana have?

▶ **FOUR SEASONS** People can enjoy Indiana's seasons by viewing the scenery or by taking part in outdoor activities.

Spring

Summer

Earth and Sun

In Indiana, temperatures and the amount of daylight both vary with the changing seasons. Seasons change because of the relationship between Earth's tilt and the sun.

The Science of Seasons

Earth's axis is tilted in relation to the sun. The tilt never changes, but the relationship between Earth's tilt and the sun does change.

As Earth rotates on its axis, it also travels around the sun. It completes a trip in one year. During the trip, the Northern and Southern Hemispheres are tilted toward or away from the sun at different times of the year.

When the Northern Hemisphere is tilted toward the sun, it is summer there. Indiana and other places in the hemisphere get more direct sun rays and more hours of daylight. As a result, temperatures are warmer.

When the Northern Hemisphere is tilted away from the sun, it is winter there. Places in the hemisphere are cooler because they get indirect sun rays and fewer hours of daylight.

In spring and fall, sun rays strike the equator directly. Places away from the equator, such as Indiana, have temperatures and hours of daylight between those of summer and winter.

READING CHECK **CAUSE AND EFFECT**
What causes summer in Indiana?

DIAGRAM When does winter begin in the Northern Hemisphere?

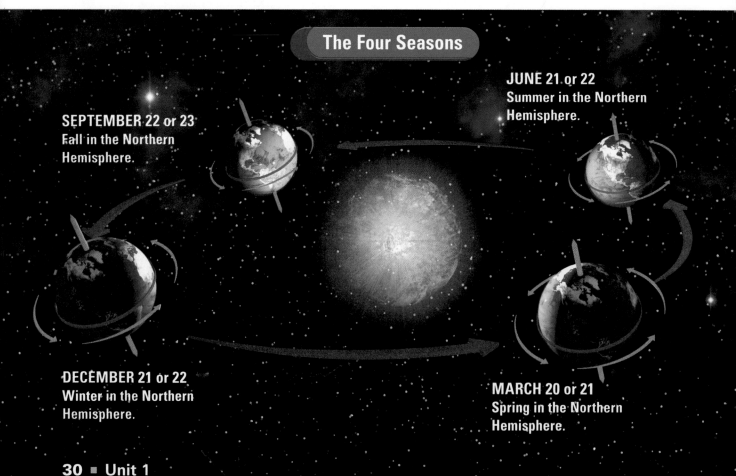

The Four Seasons

SEPTEMBER 22 or 23
Fall in the Northern Hemisphere.

JUNE 21 or 22
Summer in the Northern Hemisphere.

DECEMBER 21 or 22
Winter in the Northern Hemisphere.

MARCH 20 or 21
Spring in the Northern Hemisphere.

PRECIPITATION Clouds release water as rain, sleet, hail, or snow.

CONDENSATION Water vapor cools and forms clouds.

Stream

Ocean

Lake

EVAPORATION The sun heats water in the ocean and turns it into water vapor.

COLLECTION Precipitation that falls onto land eventually flows toward the ocean.

The Water Cycle

DIAGRAM Which part of the water cycle occurs after evaporation?

Precipitation

Precipitation in Indiana and other places is part of the water cycle. The water cycle is water's movement in the **hydrosphere**, or the system of water below, on, and above Earth's surface.

The Lake Effect

Large bodies of water, such as the Great Lakes, affect the weather of areas that border them. For example, **Lake Michigan** affects the weather of Indiana. In summer, Lake Michigan takes in heat. It then releases this heat in winter. When cold winds from the north blow across the warmer water of the lake, they pick up moisture and form clouds. As the clouds move over the colder land, they release snow. This process is called the lake effect.

Precipitation Varies

Indiana gets plenty of precipitation—an average of 40 inches each year. However, amounts and kinds of precipitation vary from north to south. The lake effect gives northern Indiana more snow than southern Indiana. Warm, moist air from the Gulf of Mexico gives southern Indiana more rainfall than northern Indiana.

READING CHECK SUMMARIZE
How does Lake Michigan affect Indiana's weather?

Indiana's Wildlife

Indiana's biosphere is rich in plant and animal life. A **biosphere** includes living things and their environment. Many plants and animals can be found throughout the state. Others live only in some places.

Plants

Today, forests cover about one-fifth of Indiana. Larger forests are found in southern Indiana and smaller ones in northern Indiana. In south-central Indiana is **Hoosier National Forest,** one of the state's largest forests.

Many kinds of trees grow in the forests of Indiana. The most common hardwood trees are beech, hickory, maple, oak, poplar, walnut, and sycamore. The yellow poplar, or tulip tree, is Indiana's state tree. Ash, aspen, dogwood, elm, and cedar are also common trees.

Indiana has a variety of wildflowers and shrubs. Wildflowers include the violet, lupine (LOO•puhn), peony (PEE•uh•nee), goldenrod, wild carrot, and sunflower. The elderberry, wild rose, and sumac (SOO•mak) are all common shrubs.

Indiana Wildlife

ILLUSTRATION What birds are labeled in the illustration?

❶ Eastern box turtle
❷ Bobwhite
❸ Yellow poplar
❹ Northern scarlet snake
❺ White-tailed deer
❻ Peony
❼ Long-tailed weasel
❽ Northern cardinal
❾ Five-lined skink

Certain plants can grow in only some areas of Indiana. In the sand dunes of northern Indiana are cactuses, ferns, and orchids. Along the Wabash and Ohio Rivers of southwestern Indiana are cypress trees, bamboo, and mistletoe. Blueberries and cranberries grow in some wetlands of northern Indiana.

Animals

Indiana has many kinds of animals. The white-tailed deer is one of the larger ones. Smaller animals include the gray squirrel, raccoon, opossum, and rabbit. The state also has about 200 kinds of birds, including the blue jay, the bobwhite, and the cardinal, the state bird. Large numbers of migrating birds stop in the state during spring and fall.

READING CHECK Ⓞ **MAIN IDEA AND DETAILS**
In what part of Indiana are its larger forests found?

▶ **CHIPMUNKS** are among the many smaller animals found across Indiana.

Summary

Indiana has a temperate climate with four very different seasons. As in all places, seasons in Indiana are affected by the relationship between Earth's tilt and the sun. The state is rich in plant and animal life.

REVIEW

1. **WHAT TO KNOW** What are Indiana's climate and wildlife like?

2. **VOCABULARY** Use the term **biosphere** in a sentence about Indiana's wildlife.

3. **GEOGRAPHY** How does the relationship between Earth's tilt and the sun affect temperatures in Indiana?

4. **CRITICAL THINKING** If it is summer in the Northern Hemisphere, what is the season in the Southern Hemisphere?

5. **DESIGN A PARK** Design a park for your community by researching plants and trees that grow well there.

6. **MAIN IDEA AND DETAILS**
(Focus Skill) On a separate sheet of paper, copy and complete this graphic organizer.

Main Idea

Details		
water below Earth's surface	water on Earth's surface	water above Earth's surface

Lesson 4

People and Resources of Indiana

WHAT TO KNOW
What is the relationship between Indiana's people and its natural resources?

VOCABULARY
natural resource p. 35
agriculture p. 35
mineral p. 35
canal p. 36
rural p. 37
urban p. 37
suburb p. 38

PEOPLE
Gene Stratton-Porter

PLACES
Loblolly Marsh

MAIN IDEA AND DETAILS
Focus Skill

Main Idea

Details

YOU ARE THERE You're visiting **Loblolly Marsh**, a wetland in eastern Indiana. A guide explains that 100 years ago it was part of the Limberlost Swamp. Author **Gene Stratton-Porter** wrote about and photographed the swamp. Then people began changing the land. They drained the swamp, removed trees, drilled for oil, and planted crops. You are glad to learn that people have helped a small part of the swamp return. Their efforts created Loblolly Marsh.

▶ LOBLOLLY MARSH was once part of the Limberlost Swamp that Gene Stratton-Porter (left) explored.

▶ **FARMLAND** Corn is one of Indiana's major crops. It is used in food products, including popcorn, and as animal feed.

▶ **MINERALS** Limestone is made into many products. This sculpture of a race car was carved from limestone.

Indiana's Resources

Indiana is rich in natural resources. A **natural resource** is something found in nature that people can use. Hoosiers work together to use their natural resources wisely.

Crop Regions

Fertile soil and flat land are important natural resources in Indiana. Together, they make much of Indiana good for **agriculture**, or farming. Crop regions can be found across the Northern Moraine and Lake and Central Till Plain regions. Major crops include corn, soybeans, and wheat.

Crop regions can also be found in the lowlands of the Southern Hills and Lowlands region. In its westernmost lowland are crops of corn, soybeans, strawberries, and melons. In its easternmost lowland is tobacco.

From Fuels to Forests

The Southern Hills and Lowlands region has other natural resources. Coal, oil, and natural gas are found in the western part. People burn these fossil fuels for heat or energy. The region also has valuable deposits of **minerals**, or natural nonliving substances. Limestone is found in the central part of the region. It is used in the construction of buildings and roads.

Forests are another important natural resource of the Southern Hills and Lowlands region. People use trees such as oak, hickory, and pine for lumber, paper, and other products.

READING CHECK ⚫**MAIN IDEA AND DETAILS**
Where are Indiana's major crop regions?

Modifying the Land

To meet their needs, people modify, or change, their environment. Over the past 200 years, people in Indiana have modified the landscape in many ways.

Farmland

During the 1800s, more and more settlers arrived in Indiana. Soon they began to modify the land.

As the population grew, settlers cleared forests to create farmland. In 1800, forests covered more than four-fifths of Indiana. At that time, fewer than 20,000 Native Americans and 3,000 settlers lived in the region. By 1900, Indiana's population had grown to more than 2½ million people, and forests covered less than one-tenth of the state.

People also gained farmland by draining wetlands. They drained many of the wetlands in the Northern Moraine and Lake region.

Transportation

Hoosiers soon modified the land to provide more transportation routes. In the early 1800s, rivers provided the best transportation routes. However, most of the rivers that were deep and wide enough for boats were in southern Indiana.

In the 1820s, Hoosiers began building roads across the state. Early dirt roads were later paved with stones.

Hoosiers began building **canals**, or human-made waterways in the 1830s. Canals made it easier to move the state's crops and products to markets and also for people to travel.

Hoosiers Modify Indiana's Land

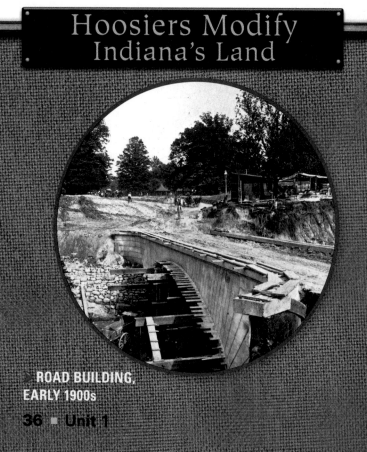

> ROAD BUILDING, EARLY 1900s

> FARMING, 1910

The arrival of railroads in the 1850s helped Hoosiers overcome their earlier transportation problems. Travel on roads was rough, and building canals was expensive. Trains moved people and goods more easily, helping Indiana's businesses grow.

Fuels, Dams, and Forests

Into the 1900s, Hoosiers continued to modify Indiana's environment. They mined for coal and drilled for oil and natural gas. They built large dams to control flooding on rivers and to generate electricity. These dams created huge new lakes, including Monroe Lake, the state's largest lake.

Hoosiers also replanted many of the state's forests that had been cleared in the 1800s. Today, forests cover about one-fifth of Indiana's land.

The Growth of Cities

In the early 1800s, settlers cleared forests along Indiana's rivers to build the first towns. Since most people were farmers living in **rural** areas, or in the countryside, towns were small. As transportation improved, some towns grew into cities.

In the late 1800s, many Indiana cities began to grow rapidly. Then, farmers used new machines that helped them produce more crops with fewer workers. At the same time, factories in cities needed more workers. Many Hoosiers moved from rural areas to **urban** areas, or cities. By 1921, about half of all Hoosiers lived in urban areas.

READING CHECK **CAUSE AND EFFECT**
What caused Indiana's early settlers to clear forests and drain wetlands?

MAP SKILL **MOVEMENT** By 1860, different kinds of transportation routes crossed Indiana. What two major roads crossed in Indianapolis?

INDIANA
— MAJOR ROADS
+++ RAILROADS
⌣⌣⌣ CANALS

INDIANAPOLIS, 1920s

Urban Challenges

Hoosiers have continued to move to cities. Today, nearly three out of every four Hoosiers live in a city or a suburb. A **suburb** is a smaller community near a city.

Growing cities present Hoosiers with challenges. People clear forests around growing cities. Suburbs spread out farther from city centers, so people must travel farther to reach their jobs. More cars on the roads cause traffic jams and air pollution.

The growth of cities also causes greater demand for services. People need more water, electricity, schools, and trash removal. They need more roads, bridges, and sewer systems. Hoosiers must look for ways to meet these challenges.

READING CHECK ⏱**MAIN IDEA AND DETAILS**
What are some challenges Hoosiers face because of their growing cities?

▶ **SUBURBS are growing rapidly in Indiana.**

Summary

Hoosiers use many of Indiana's natural resources. Over time, people in Indiana have modified the environment to meet different challenges. Today, they face many challenges caused by growing cities.

REVIEW

1. **WHAT TO KNOW** What is the relationship between Indiana's people and its natural resources?

2. **VOCABULARY** Use the term **agriculture** in a sentence about Indiana's regions.

3. **HISTORY** How have people in Indiana modified their environment over time?

4. **CRITICAL THINKING** Make It Relevant How have people modified the environment of your community?

5. 🖌 **MAKE A MAP** Make a map of one form of transportation in Indiana in 1860. Include a map key.

6. ⭐ **MAIN IDEA AND DETAILS**
   (Focus Skill) On a separate sheet of paper, copy and complete this graphic organizer.

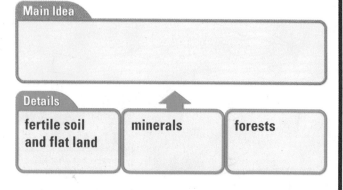

Main Idea

Details

| fertile soil and flat land | minerals | forests |

Gene Stratton-Porter

Biography

Trustworthiness
Respect
Responsibility
Fairness
Caring
Patriotism

"*It is my belief that to do strong work any writer must stick to the things he truly knows. . . . So I stick to Indiana.*"

Gene Stratton-Porter grew up in Wabash County, Indiana. As a child, she explored the outdoors near her rural home. From this, she developed a love of nature.

In 1895, Stratton-Porter moved to Geneva, Indiana, near the Limberlost Swamp. There she began to take notes, draw sketches, and photograph the plants and animals of Limberlost. She also began writing poetry, short stories, and articles for magazines.

The time Stratton-Porter spent in nearby swamps, meadows, and woods inspired her to write novels. She often used Indiana settings in her stories. In 1903, her first novel, *The Song of the Cardinal*, was published. Stratton-Porter went on to write more than 20 novels. Today, her home in Geneva is part of the Limberlost State Historic Site.

Why Character Counts

How did Stratton-Porter's work as an author show her respect for Indiana's land?

Time

1863
Born

1924
Died

1901 Stratton-Porter's first short story is published

1909 *A Girl of the Limberlost*, her most popular novel, is published

Read a Land Use and Resources Map

Why It Matters A land use and resources map shows how land is used and where resources are located.

❱ LEARN

Follow these steps to use the land use and resources map on page 41.

Step 1 Use the colors in the map key to see how the land is used in each place shown on the map.

Step 2 Use the symbols in the map key to see where different resources are grown, raised, or found.

❱ PRACTICE

Use the map to answer these questions.

1 How is most of the land in Indiana used?

2 In which area of Indiana is coal found?

3 Which color shows the areas where land is used for manufacturing? In and around which cities does manufacturing take place?

4 Which resources are found near Fort Wayne?

❱ APPLY

Make It Relevant Use the library, the Internet, or other reference sources to find out how people use the land in your community. Then draw a land use and resources map of your community. Use the map on page 41 as a model. Include a title and a map key.

❱ MINT LEAVES

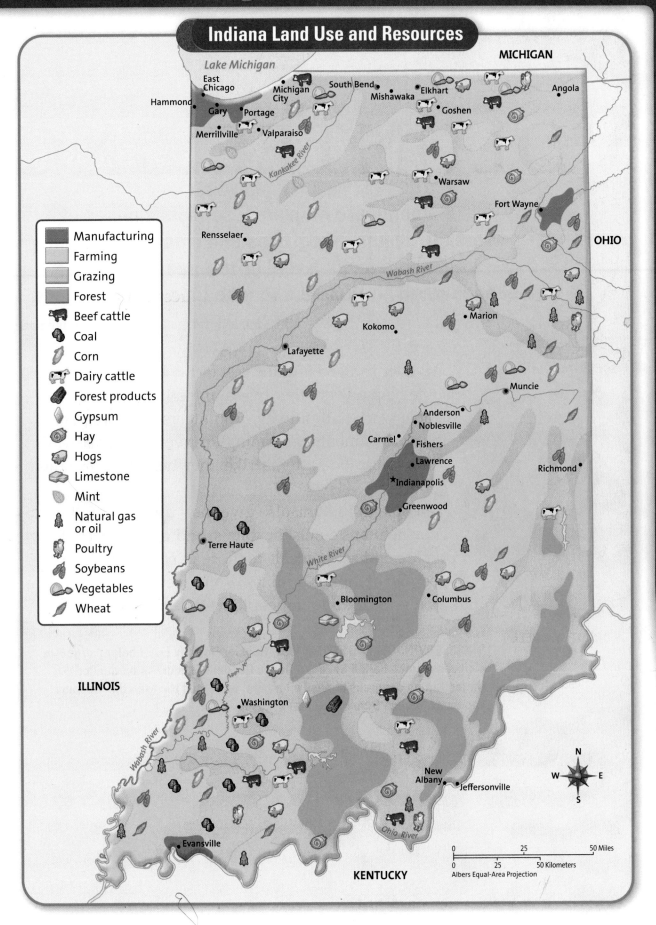

Indiana Land Use and Resources

Legend:
- Manufacturing
- Farming
- Grazing
- Forest
- Beef cattle
- Coal
- Corn
- Dairy cattle
- Forest products
- Gypsum
- Hay
- Hogs
- Limestone
- Mint
- Natural gas or oil
- Poultry
- Soybeans
- Vegetables
- Wheat

MICHIGAN

Lake Michigan

East Chicago • Michigan City • South Bend • Mishawaka • Elkhart • Angola
Hammond • Gary • Portage • Goshen
Merrillville • Valparaiso
Kankakee River
Warsaw
Fort Wayne
OHIO
Rensselaer
Wabash River
Kokomo • Marion
Lafayette
Muncie
Anderson • Noblesville
Carmel • Fishers
Lawrence • Richmond
★Indianapolis
Greenwood
White River
Terre Haute
Bloomington • Columbus
ILLINOIS
Washington
Wabash River
New Albany • Jeffersonville
Evansville
Ohio River
KENTUCKY

N
W E
S

0   25   50 Miles
0   25   50 Kilometers
Albers Equal-Area Projection

Map and Globe Skills

VOLUNTEERING

"People are helping in schools, houses of worship, community groups and many other places. Volunteers make a real difference in our state. I encourage all Hoosiers to take time to help others."

Mitch Daniels, forty-ninth governor of Indiana

All over Indiana and the rest of the United States, people help one another by volunteering. All these people work without pay. Volunteers help preserve the environment by cleaning up rivers and roadways. After natural disasters strike, they help communities rebuild.

People in Indiana also give their time in other ways. They help at schools, hospitals, and other places. They prepare and serve meals to those in need. They build houses for homeless families. Volunteers collect and give out food and clothing to people who need them.

❯ DOROTHY BUELL

❯ **PRESERVING THE DUNES** In 1952, Hoosier Dorothy Buell helped organize a citizens' group called Save the Dunes Council. This group persuaded the United States Congress to pass a law that protected the area that became known as Indiana Dunes National Lakeshore.

In Indiana, different kinds of volunteer organizations exist in every part of the state. For example, many communities have volunteer centers. Workers in these centers find and train new volunteers. They also work to identify people who need help. Then they connect these people with volunteers.

In a recent year, more than one-third of Indiana's people volunteered. They helped their neighbors and worked to improve life in Indiana.

Make It Relevant How do volunteers help improve life in your community?

❯ A VOLUNTEER helps improve a playground.

❯ A VOLUNTEER teaches a young boy about art.

❯ VOLUNTEERS work to build a new home.

Lesson 5

People of Indiana

WHAT TO KNOW
What are the people of Indiana like today?

VOCABULARY
culture p. 44
population density p. 45
population distribution p. 45
immigrant p. 46
heritage p. 46
ethnic group p. 46

PLACES
Indianapolis
Benton County

MAIN IDEA AND DETAILS
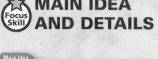

YOU ARE THERE

Today is World Culture Day at your school. First, some of your classmates showed on a map the countries from which their families came to the United States. Then, they shared parts of their **cultures**, or ways of life. Mika showed a Japanese kimono. Mark brought a Mexican blanket. Rachel wore African earrings. John sang an Irish folk song. You enjoy learning new things about other cultures.

▶ **DIVERSITY** Students in Indiana may have different backgrounds and cultures, but all of them are Hoosiers.

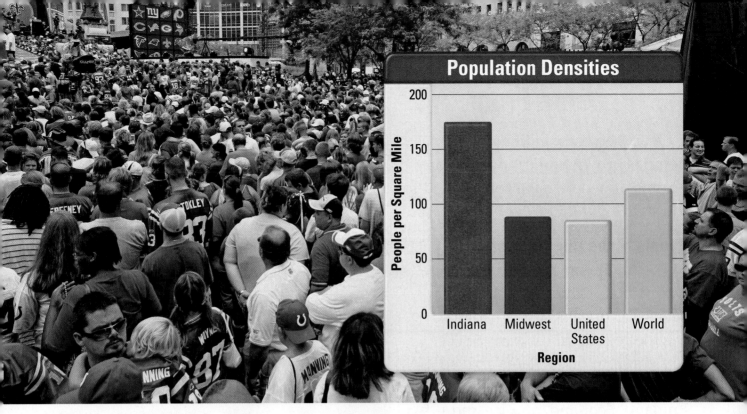

Population Densities

(bar graph — People per Square Mile vs. Region: Indiana, Midwest, United States, World)

GRAPH Indianapolis has a population density of about 2,167 people per square mile. Which has the greater population density, Indiana or the United States?

Indiana's Population

Today, more than 6 million people live in Indiana. From 2000 to 2007, the state's population grew from about 6,080,000 to about 6,345,000. That is an increase of 265,000 people. The population of the state is still growing.

Population Density

To understand populations better, geographers study different numbers. One important number is **population density**. That is the number of people living in an area of a certain size, usually 1 square mile.

Over the years, the population density of Indiana has increased. In 1900, it was about 68 people per square mile. Today, it is about 170 people per square mile.

Population Distribution

Population densities within Indiana vary greatly. They vary because of **population distribution**, or the way population is spread out over an area. In Indiana, more people live in cities and their suburbs than in rural areas.

Throughout Indiana, the population densities of the state's cities are higher than those of its rural areas. For example, **Indianapolis** has about 780,000 people living in about 360 square miles. Its population density is about 2,167 people per square mile. In contrast, **Benton County** has about 9,000 people living in about 400 square miles. Its population density is only about 23 people per square mile.

READING CHECK ☼**MAIN IDEA AND DETAILS**
Why do population densities vary greatly within Indiana?

Where Hoosiers Come From

Over the years, Indiana's population has grown and changed. Many groups of people have contributed to the state's diversity.

People of the Distant Past

The first people in Indiana were Native Americans. In the 1600s, Europeans began exploring the region. In the early 1800s, settlers from other states arrived to farm. Many had ancestors from England, Scotland, and Ireland. Free and enslaved African Americans also arrived.

In the early 1900s, Indiana's population continued to grow. People came to work in the state's mills and factories. Some were **immigrants**, or people who come from one country to live in another country. The immigrants came mostly from Germany, Hungary, Italy, Poland, and Mexico. More and more African Americans also arrived from the southern United States.

People of the Recent Past

Since the 1950s, the arrival of European immigrants to Indiana has slowed. However, people from other places have continued to move to Indiana. More Hispanics have come for job opportunities. The opening of Asian-owned factories has brought more Asians, especially Japanese.

> **MANDOLIN**

Hoosiers Today

Today, most people who live in Indiana were born in the state. Most are white people with European backgrounds. Nearly 1 out of 10 is African American. About 1 out of 20 is Hispanic, and about 1 out of 100 is Asian American.

Heritage

Hoosiers share both their history and their heritage with others. **Heritage** is a way of life, including customs and traditions, that is passed down through a family or group.

Festivals all over Indiana are one way people share their heritage. Many festivals are held by **ethnic groups**, or people from the same country, race, or culture. The festivals celebrate the customs of many cultures, including African American, German, Polish, Italian, Mexican, Scottish, Amish, and Native American.

Other festivals in the state cover a wide range of interests. They feature music, such as blues, bluegrass, and jazz. They celebrate car racing, a longtime sport in the state. They highlight covered bridges, a tradition in parts of Indiana.

Indiana's museums and state parks also provide places for people to experience the state's heritage. Many provide displays, performances, and living history reenactments.

READING CHECK **DRAW CONCLUSIONS**
Why do you think it is important for people to celebrate one another's heritage?

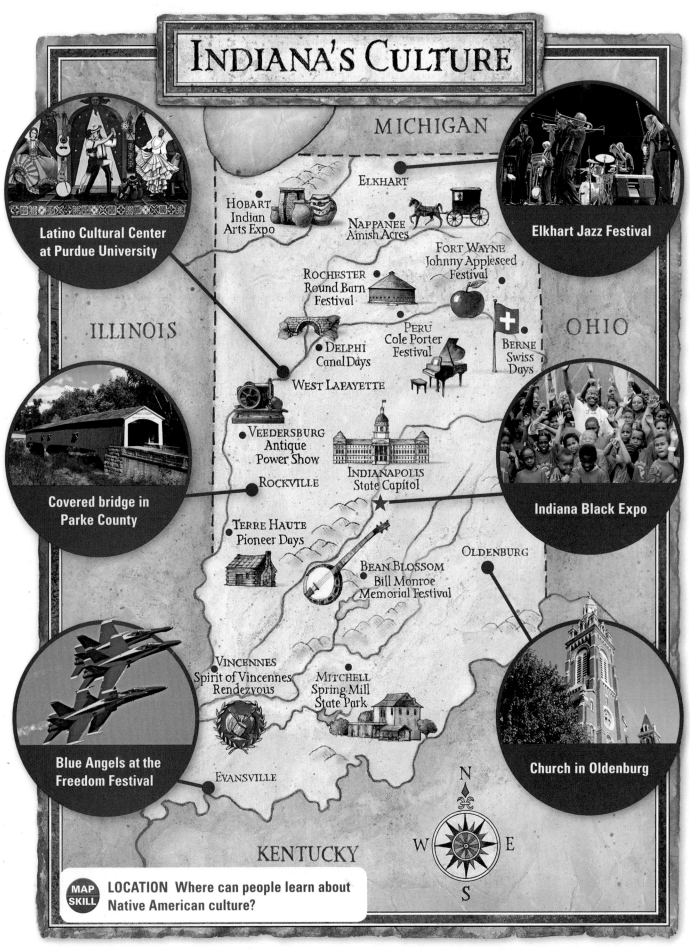

INDIANA'S CULTURE

MICHIGAN

Latino Cultural Center at Purdue University

Elkhart Jazz Festival

ELKHART

HOBART Indian Arts Expo

NAPPANEE Amish Acres

FORT WAYNE Johnny Appleseed Festival

ILLINOIS

ROCHESTER Round Barn Festival

DELPHI Canal Days

PERU Cole Porter Festival

BERNE Swiss Days

OHIO

WEST LAFAYETTE

Covered bridge in Parke County

VEEDERSBURG Antique Power Show

ROCKVILLE

INDIANAPOLIS State Capitol

Indiana Black Expo

TERRE HAUTE Pioneer Days

BEAN BLOSSOM Bill Monroe Memorial Festival

OLDENBURG

Blue Angels at the Freedom Festival

VINCENNES Spirit of Vincennes Rendezvous

MITCHELL Spring Mill State Park

Church in Oldenburg

EVANSVILLE

KENTUCKY

N
W E
S

MAP SKILL LOCATION Where can people learn about Native American culture?

Religion in Indiana

Religion is an important part of the heritage of many people in Indiana. Hoosiers follow many religions, including Christianity, Judaism, Islam, Buddhism, and Hinduism.

Religion in the Past

Christianity arrived in Indiana with early Europeans. The French brought Roman Catholic priests in the 1700s. The priests hoped to introduce Christianity to Native Americans.

Later, settlers brought Protestant beliefs to the region. In 1801, Baptists founded the first Protestant church. Soon people from Kentucky spread the beliefs of the Methodists. Other early Protestant groups included Presbyterians, Disciples of Christ, and Quakers. Over the years, many other Protestant groups, as well as other religions, gained followers in Indiana.

Religion Today

Christianity is the most common religion in Indiana today. Roman Catholics are the largest single group of Christians. They make up about one-fifth of all of Indiana's church members.

Different groups of Protestants make up more than one-half of Indiana's church members. They include Baptists, Methodists, and Lutherans.

People who follow other religions also live in Indiana. Jewish people follow the customs of Judaism at synagogues. Muslims, or followers of

▶ HOUSES OF WORSHIP Most religions have places of worship.

Protestant Church

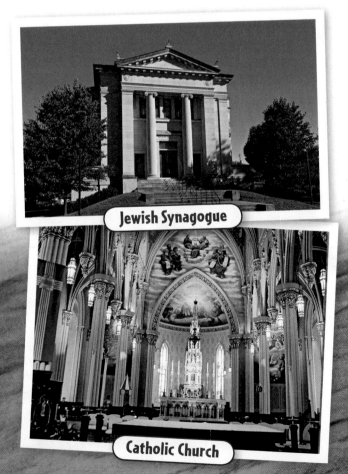

Jewish Synagogue

Catholic Church

Muslims

Hindus

Buddhists

▶ **WORSHIPPERS** People practice different religions throughout Indiana.

Islam, worship at mosques in many Indiana cities. Buddhists and Hindus practice their religions in temples around the state.

READING CHECK 🅾 **MAIN IDEA AND DETAILS**
What are some of the religions that people in Indiana follow?

Summary

More than 6 million people live in Indiana. They include people with European backgrounds, African Americans, Hispanics, and Asians. People in Indiana share their cultures and heritages with others.

REVIEW

1. **WHAT TO KNOW** What are the people of Indiana like today?

2. **VOCABULARY** Use the term **heritage** in a sentence about Indiana's people.

3. **HISTORY** What caused Indiana's population to grow in the early 1900s?

4. **CRITICAL THINKING** How are Indiana's population today and its population of long ago alike and different?

5. 🖌 **GIVE A SPEECH** Choose an ethnic group that has had an effect on Indiana. Find out more about that group's role in the state. Use your findings to plan and give a speech.

6. ⭐ Focus Skill **MAIN IDEA AND DETAILS** On a separate sheet of paper, copy and complete this graphic organizer.

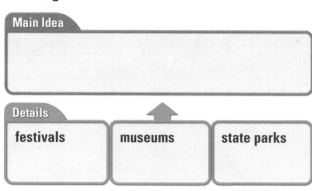

Main Idea

Details
| festivals | museums | state parks |

Read a Population Map

Why It Matters Reading a population map helps you understand where in a city, state, or country people live.

❯ LEARN

The map on page 51 is a population map of Indiana. It uses different colors to show population densities. The map key shows the range of population densities for each color.

To find the population density of an area, look to see what color that area is on the map. Then look at the map key to find that color. It tells you about how many people live in each square mile and square kilometer. For example, the area around Indianapolis is red. This means that more than 1,000 people live in each square mile of that area.

❯ PRACTICE

Use the map to answer these questions.

1 Which color on the map shows the areas that are the most crowded? the least crowded?

2 Which city—Terre Haute or Angola—has the higher population density?

3 What is the population density of the area around Bloomington?

❯ APPLY

Make It Relevant Using the map, find the approximate location of your community and its population density. Then write about how you think population densities affect the way people live.

THE PEOPLE OF
INDIANA
WELCOME YOU

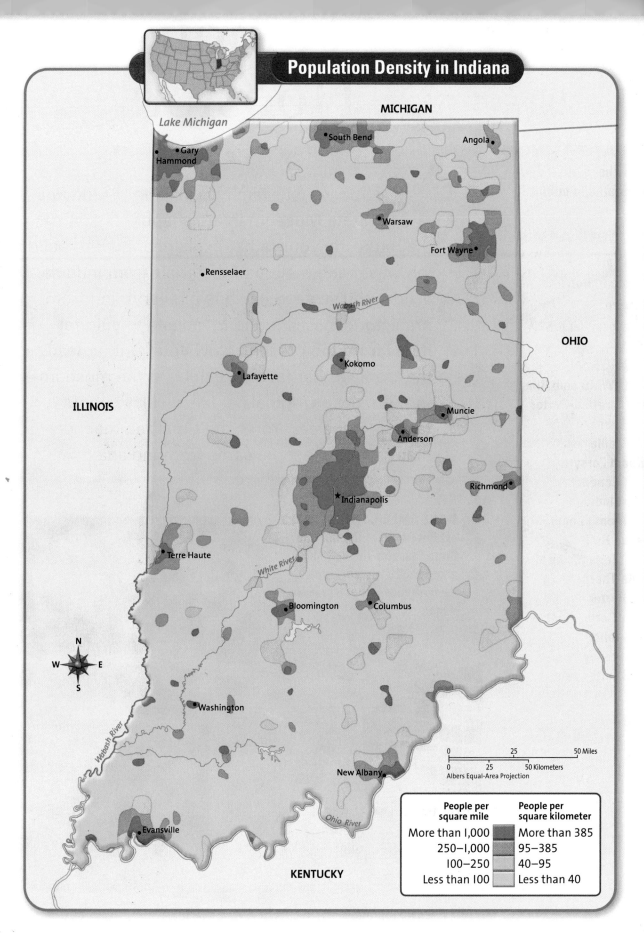

Population Density in Indiana

MICHIGAN

Lake Michigan

• South Bend

Angola •

• Gary
Hammond

• Warsaw

Fort Wayne •

• Rensselaer

OHIO

Wabash River

• Kokomo

• Lafayette

ILLINOIS

• Muncie

• Anderson

Richmond •

★ Indianapolis

• Terre Haute

White River

• Bloomington

• Columbus

N
W   E
S

Wabash River

• Washington

0   25   50 Miles
0   25   50 Kilometers
Albers Equal-Area Projection

New Albany •

People per square mile		People per square kilometer
More than 1,000		More than 385
250–1,000		95–385
100–250		40–95
Less than 100		Less than 40

• Evansville

Ohio River

KENTUCKY

Famous Hoosiers

 WHAT TO KNOW
How have Hoosiers contributed to culture?

VOCABULARY
dialect p. 54
science fiction p. 55
pop art p. 55
choreographer p. 57

PEOPLE
James Whitcomb Riley
Gene Stratton-Porter
Mari Evans
T. C. Steele
William Forsyth
Janet Scudder
Robert Indiana
Wes Montgomery
Joshua Bell
John Mellencamp
Twyla Tharp
Cole Porter
Hoagy Carmichael
Red Skelton
Jane Pauley
David Letterman

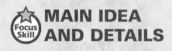 **MAIN IDEA AND DETAILS**

Main Idea

Details

YOU ARE THERE

Today, your family is visiting the Indiana State Museum in Indianapolis. Outside the museum, your father explained that the building was made mostly of materials from Indiana. Inside, you've seen exhibits of everything from prehistoric fossils found in Indiana to cultural items from the present. Now your mother leads the family to her favorite exhibit at the museum—the American Originals. It has displays about famous Hoosiers. You hadn't realized that so many famous people came from Indiana.

❯ **THE AMERICAN ORIGINALS** exhibit (right) at the Indiana State Museum (below) shows photographs, posters, and memorabilia of many famous Hoosiers.

Basketball

Football

Car Racing

Sports

Sports are an important pastime for Hoosiers. Indiana has given the world many famous sports figures.

Basketball

Some of basketball's best-known coaches and athletes have been from Indiana. Oscar Robinson grew up in Indianapolis. He became one of the NBA's top players in the 1960s and 1970s. Larry Bird, born in West Baden, was an NBA star in the 1980s. He went on to coach the Indiana Pacers from 1997 to 2000. Reggie Miller played for the Indiana Pacers for 18 years before retiring in 2005.

Indiana is also known for its college basketball teams. The Hoosiers of Indiana University and the Fighting Irish of Notre Dame are two well-known teams.

Car Racing and More

The Indianapolis 500, or Indy 500, is one of the oldest motor sports events. The race has been held in Indianapolis over the Memorial Day weekend since 1911. Over the years, several Hoosiers have won the race.

Indiana has contributed to football as well. Former Notre Dame coach Knute Rockne (NOOT RAHK•nee) was one of football's greatest coaches. In 2007, the Indianapolis Colts, led by coach Tony Dungy and quarterback Peyton Manning, won the Super Bowl.

Indiana has other famous sports figures. Great baseball players include Carl Erskine, Don Larsen, and Don Mattingly. Both Olympic swimmer Mark Spitz and NASCAR driver Jeff Gordon have lived in Indiana.

READING CHECK 🔄 **MAIN IDEA AND DETAILS**
When was the first Indianapolis 500 held?

Literature and Art

Many famous authors and artists are from Indiana. Their works are known around the nation and the world.

Golden Age of Literature

Many Indiana writers were part of the Golden Age of Indiana Literature. This period lasted from 1870 to 1920. The writers include **James Whitcomb Riley, Gene Stratton-Porter**, Booth Tarkington, Theodore Dreiser, and Meredith Nicholson.

James Whitcomb Riley wrote poems about everyday rural life in Indiana. He published his first poems while working for the *Indianapolis Journal*. In many of his poems, Riley used Indiana rural **dialects**, or ways of speaking. During his career, Riley became known as "the Hoosier Poet" and "the Children's Poet."

Gene Stratton-Porter worked as a nature photographer before becoming a writer. Between 1895 and 1913, she explored and photographed Limberlost Swamp. After her success at nature photography, she wrote her first novel, *The Song of the Cardinal*.

Booth Tarkington was an award-winning writer. His best-known work is *The Magnificent Ambersons*. This novel is the second of three novels he wrote about social change after the Civil War.

Theodore Dreiser (DRY•ser) wrote about hardships in life, including unfairness in society. Among his most successful novels is *An American Tragedy*, published in 1925.

Indiana's
Writers, Poets, and Artists

▶ **MARI EVANS wrote** *Tell Somebody!*

▶ **KURT VONNEGUT** wrote *A Man Without a Country*.

Meredith Nicholson was not only a best-selling author but also a politician. He published several novels and poems from 1891 to 1928.

Recent Writers

Indiana has had other writers. Kurt Vonnegut wrote **science fiction**, or fiction about how real or imagined science affects people. **Mari Evans** wrote poems, children's stories, and plays. She also worked in education and in television.

Artists

Indiana artists **T. C. Steele** and **William Forsyth** were members of the Hoosier Group. During the late 1800s and early 1900s, this group of painters focused on Indiana's landscapes. One of Forsyth's paintings is called *The Constitutional Elm*. It shows the elm under which state leaders wrote the state constitution.

Artist **Janet Scudder** created garden sculptures and fountains in the late 1800s and early 1900s. Most of her work included children, animals, and fairies. Scudder is also known for her support of women's rights.

Indiana has other famous artists, too. Jim Davis created the popular *Garfield* cartoon strip, which appears in newspapers across the country. **Robert Indiana** became famous for his **pop art**, an art style that uses common objects. His best-known work is the word *LOVE* arranged in a square shape with the letter *O* tilted.

READING CHECK ⚙ **MAIN IDEA AND DETAILS**
Who became known as "the Hoosier Poet"?

▶ **T. C. STEELE** painted *Selma in the Garden*.

▶ **JANET SCUDDER** designed a medal for Indiana's 100-year anniversary.

THE SENSATIONAL BASE BALL SONG

TAKE ME OUT TO THE BALL GAME

WORDS BY JACK NORWORTH MUSIC BY ALBERT VON TILZER

THE YORK MUSIC CO.

SHEET MUSIC BY ALBERT VON TILZER

THE JACKSON FIVE

JOHN MELLENCAMP

Music

Many famous musicians have connections with Indiana. They have worked in many musical styles.

Great American Songwriters

Paul Dresser and Albert Von Tilzer were two great American songwriters. Dresser wrote Indiana's official state song, "On the Banks of the Wabash, Far Away." Von Tilzer wrote the popular song "Take Me Out to the Ball Game," which is played during many baseball games.

From Jazz to Opera

Guitarist **Wes Montgomery** was born in Indianapolis in 1925 and grew up in a musical family. He was one of the greatest modern jazz guitarists.

Opera singer James McCracken first began singing in his church choir as a child in Gary. He went on to perform with the Metropolitan Opera in New York City for more than 30 years before retiring in 1978.

Joshua Bell of Bloomington began playing the violin in 1971 at the age of four. He performed with a major orchestra at the age of 14. Since then, Bell has played with most of the major orchestras around the world.

Pop Stars

Pop music stars from Indiana have entertained millions of people around the world. These stars include Deniece Williams, **John Mellencamp**, and the Jackson Five. As a solo artist, Michael Jackson of the Jackson Five, recorded one of the best-selling albums of all time. His sister, Janet Jackson, has also had many hit albums.

Festivals and Concerts

Many Hoosiers have cultural ties to the southern states of Kentucky and Tennessee. Many of them enjoy bluegrass music. Every year, people gather at the Bill Monroe Memorial Bluegrass Festival. It is held in the community of Bean Blossom, just north of Nashville, Indiana. Hoosiers also enjoy festivals that celebrate other musical styles, such as blues, jazz, rock, and pop.

The Indianapolis Symphony Orchestra was founded in 1930. It is one of the few orchestras in the nation that plays all year round. It performs many concerts at the Hilbert Circle Theatre. Butler University's famous Clowes Memorial Hall features its own symphony orchestra, as well as touring musicals.

Dance

Hoosiers enjoy dancing as exercise and as entertainment. They take part in different styles of dancing, including swing, ballroom, tap, jazz, ballet, clogging, salsa, and more.

Dancer and choreographer **Twyla Tharp** was born in Portland, Indiana. A **choreographer** is a person who creates dances. Tharp later lived in California and New York City. In her work, Tharp combines classical ballet, tap, and social dances. She creates dances to many styles of music, such as classical, jazz, and pop. Tharp has won many awards for her work and continues to choreograph new dances.

READING CHECK ⚫**MAIN IDEA AND DETAILS**
How is songwriter Albert Von Tilzer connected to the sport of baseball?

❱ **TWYLA THARP**

❱ **DANCERS perform in a show choreographed by Twyla Tharp.**

▶ **DAVID LETTERMAN** is best known for hosting his late-night talk show on television.

Broadway and Hollywood

Many Hoosiers have contributed to film, television, radio, and theater. In the early 1900s, **Cole Porter** of Peru, Indiana, wrote musicals for Broadway, an area of theaters in New York City. At about the same time, **Hoagy Carmichael** of Bloomington wrote songs, hosted radio shows, and appeared in films and on television. From 1937 to 1971, comedian **Red Skelton** of Vincennes performed on radio and television.

Other Hoosiers have contributed as well. They include film director Robert Wise and actors James Dean and Brendan Fraser. **Jane Pauley** has worked as a television host and jounalist since 1976. **David Letterman** of Indianapolis is an award-winning comedian and talk show host.

READING CHECK ☼**MAIN IDEA AND DETAILS**
Which Hoosier wrote musicals for Broadway in the early 1900s?

Summary

Over the years, Hoosiers have contributed to sports, literature, art, and entertainment. Many of these Hoosiers are known throughout the United States and around the world.

REVIEW

1. **WHAT TO KNOW** How have Hoosiers contributed to culture?

2. **VOCABULARY** Use the term **dialect** in a sentence about a famous Hoosier.

3. **CULTURE** What was the Hoosier Group?

4. **CRITICAL THINKING** Why are sports and the arts important to cultures?

5. **WRITE A POEM** Write a short poem about a famous person from Indiana.

6. **MAIN IDEA AND DETAILS** (Focus Skill) On a separate sheet of paper, copy and complete this graphic organizer.

Main Idea
Many well-known literary figures have lived in Indiana.

Details

James Whitcomb Riley

Biography

Trustworthiness
Respect
Responsibility
Fairness
Caring
Patriotism

"*I could not resist the inclination [desire] to write. It was what I most enjoyed doing.*"

James Whitcomb Riley was born in 1849 in Greenfield, Indiana. As a child, he learned about the lives of people who lived in the rural areas of Indiana. Riley felt so close to rural people that he later wrote poems about them.

In 1875, Riley began publishing his poems, first in newspapers and later in books. His most popular poems include "When the Frost Is on the Punkin," "Little Orphant Annie," and "The Raggedy Man." Riley's first collection of poetry, *The Old Swimmin' Hole and 'Leven More Poems*, was published in 1883.

In many poems, Riley used humor and Hoosier dialects to describe everyday rural life. At poetry readings across the United States, he entertained audiences with these poems. Known as "the Hoosier Poet," Riley gained popularity around the world.

Why Character Counts

How did Riley show that he cared about the people of Indiana?

Time

1849		1916
Born		Died

1883 Riley's *The Old Swimmin' Hole and 'Leven More Poems* is published

1915 Indiana celebrates Riley Day on October 7

Fun with Social Studies

My state is right in the middle of the United States. It's on the Great Plains. You should see some of our huge cattle ranches!

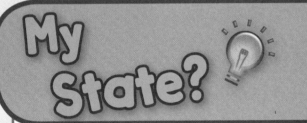

My State?

Which one lives in Indiana?

My Midwestern state borders Lake Michigan. Our cities have lots of factories. Other land is used for farming.

I go to the beach a lot because I live on the Atlantic coast. A part of my state has mountains. Most of the state has a warm climate, and it almost never snows.

Picture This!

Can you figure out which words are shown? Each word fits one of the clues on the right.

 + al

It's a smaller community near a city.

sink +

Humans made this waterway.

 + urb

This is a large, bowl-shaped hole.

Statue Scramble

Which plaque should the sculptor put on each statue?

Stratton-Porter

Riley

Tharp

Letterman

Let's dance!

I can make you laugh!

The Hoosier Poet

Nature lover and writer

Online Adventures

GO ONLINE

Oh, no! There's a branch blocking the path! I think I see a sign here. Let's take a look.

Join Eco on a journey through a spooky forest. The two of you are on your way to an old house, but there are wild animals and branches blocking your path! To get around them, you must use what you have learned about Indiana's geography and culture. Play now at www.harcourtschool.com/ss1

Visual Summary

Plains and hills are two of Indiana's main landforms

Summarize the Unit

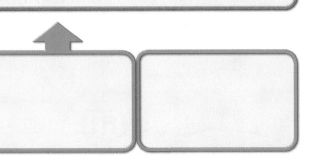

Main Idea and Details Complete this graphic organizer to show that you understand the main idea and details about Indiana's geography.

Main Idea

Each of Indiana's physical regions has its own unique features.

Details

 Vocabulary

Identify the term from the word bank that correctly matches each definition.

1. the height of land above or below sea level

2. the kind of weather a place has over a long period of time

3. a way of life

4. where a place is in relation to other places on Earth

5. a smaller community near a city

6. a slow-moving ice mass

7. a way of speaking

8. something found in nature that people can use

Word Bank

relative location p. 13   natural resource p. 35

glacier p. 21   suburb p. 38

elevation p. 23   culture p. 44

climate p. 29   dialect p. 54

Indiana is rich in natural resources

People from many different backgrounds live in Indiana

Facts and Main Ideas

Answer these questions.

9. On which river is Indianapolis located?

10. How did glaciers shape Indiana's landscape?

11. What are some important natural resources in Indiana?

12. How have ethnic and cultural groups affected Indiana?

Write the letter of the best choice.

13. Which term describes the soil and rocks that form Earth's surface?
    A atmosphere
    B biosphere
    C hydrosphere
    D lithosphere

14. What kind of landform can be found near Lake Michigan?
    A canyons
    B dunes
    C hills
    D sinkholes

15. From where did many of Indiana's first settlers come?
    A England, Scotland, Ireland
    B Asia
    C Germany, Italy, Hungary
    D Mexico

Critical Thinking

Answer these questions.

16. Why are rivers and lakes important to Indiana's cities?

17. **Make It Relevant** How do people modify the environment of your community?

Skills

Use Latitude and Longitude

Use the map on page 19 to answer these questions.

18. Which lines of latitude and longitude are closest to the city of Rensselaer?

19. Which lines of latitude and longitude are closest to Wyandotte Cave?

20. What river crosses 38°N, 88°W?

writing

Write a Report Write a report that explains the effects of the Earth-sun relationship on the climate of Indiana.

Write an Obituary Choose a writer from Indiana's Golden Age of Literature. Then write an obituary for that person, performing research if necessary. Include how the writer contributed to the culture of Indiana.

Unit 1 Activities

Show What You Know

Unit Writing Activity

Write an Information Report Write a brief report about Indiana's people.

- Tell about the different groups of people who lived in Indiana in the past.
- Tell about the different groups of people who live in Indiana today.
- Explain how Hoosiers share their history and heritage with others.

Unit Project

Make an Indiana Atlas Make an atlas that includes information and maps.

- Research the regions of Indiana.
- Write about the physical and human features of Indiana.
- Draw maps of Indiana.

Read More

- *H is for Hoosier* by Cynthia Furlong Reynolds. Thomson Gale.

- *Indiana* by Bettina Ling. Children's Press.

- *Legendary Hoosiers* by Nelson Price. Hawthorne Publishing.

For more resources, go to
www.harcourtschool.com/ss1

1747 FRANCIS VIGO

Start with the Standards

INDIANA'S ACADEMIC STANDARDS FOR SOCIAL STUDIES

History 4.1.1, 4.1.2, 4.1.3, 4.1.4, 4.1.6, 4.1.17

Civics and Government 4.2.1, 4.2.2, 4.2.5, 4.2.6

Geography 4.3.11

Economics 4.4.3

The Big Idea

Exploration and Settlement

Exploration and settlement of North America led to changes in the area that is now Indiana.

What to Know

- How did life change for the early people of Indiana?

- Who were some of the early Native American groups of Indiana, and how did they live?

- Why did Europeans explore and settle what is now Indiana?

- How did the American Revolution affect Indiana?

- How did the Northwest Ordinance affect settlers and Native Americans?

- How did the people of Indiana work to set up their new state?

NATIVE AMERICANS IN INDIANA

DID YOU KNOW?

Indiana means "land of the Indians."

Mississinewa Lake, in Frances Slocum State Park

The first people to live in what is now Indiana were ancestors of Native Americans. Later, Native Americans hunted, fished, and farmed in the area. When Europeans arrived, they met the Native Americans and traded with them. Today, Hoosiers can learn about Native Americans from Indiana through artifacts, museums, folktales, festivals, and historic sites.

Mounds State Park is a Native American site in Anderson. The site has ten mounds that were made by the Adena and Hopewell peoples. These groups of people lived more than 1,000 years ago. Their mounds were most likely used for ceremonies. Inside the mounds, archaeologists have found artifacts that belonged to Native Americans.

At powwows, visitors can learn about the culture of Native Americans of Indiana.

The Great Mound is the oldest mound in Mounds State Park.

The Evansville Museum of Arts, History and Science has an exhibit that shows the culture of the Native Americans who lived near Evansville. Another exhibit tells about Native American legends. The legends helped Native Americans explain their beliefs and their past. "Rabbit and Possum," a legend from the Miami, tells how the native people believed daylight came to be. Many Potawatomi legends tell about a spirit named Nanabozho. The Potawatomi tell that Nanabozho made the world. He often appears as a rabbit.

Many places in Indiana are named for Native Americans. The city of Kokomo was named after a Miami chief. The city of Mishawaka was named for a Shawnee princess. The Lost Sister Trail is named for Frances Slocum.

The Evansville Museum shows Native American clothing and other artifacts.

 INDIANA *TEST PREP*

❶ Who were the first people to live in Indiana?
A ancestors of Native Americans
B ancestors of Europeans
C ancestors of Africans
D the Miami

❷ For what did the Adena and Hopewell use mounds?
A farming
B building villages
C ceremonies
D hunting

❸ Which tribe tells stories about a spirit named Nanabozho?
A the Miami
B the Lenape
C the Potawatomi
D the Shawnee

❹ Writing How do people learn about Native Americans who lived long ago?

1747 FRANCIS VIGO 1836

Time

Indiana Long Ago

Late 1600s The Miami arrive in what is now Indiana, p. 84

1679 René-Robert Cavelier, Sieur de La Salle, explores what is now Indiana for France, p. 94

1754 The French and Indian War begins, p. 96

1400

1550

Indiana Long Ago

1776 The colonies declare their independence from Britain, p. 101

1800 The Indiana Territory is formed, p. 111

1816 Indiana becomes the nineteenth state, p. 120

1700

1850

Miami

- Farmed and hunted animals
- Built dome-shaped houses called wigwams
- Lived in area that became Indiana and Ohio; now live in Indiana and Oklahoma

Shawnee

- First lived in the Ohio Valley along the Ohio River
- Later, many settled near the White River in area that is now Indiana
- Used canoes to travel for trade

People

1600	1650	1700

The Miami people interact with settlers in what is now Indiana

The Shawnee people interact with settlers in what is now Indiana

1643 • René-Robert Cavelier (Sieur de La Salle) 1687

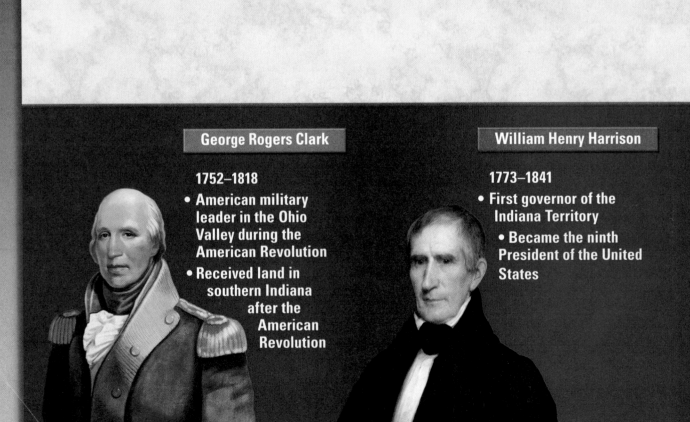

George Rogers Clark

1752–1818
- American military leader in the Ohio Valley during the American Revolution
- Received land in southern Indiana after the American Revolution

William Henry Harrison

1773–1841
- First governor of the Indiana Territory
- Became the ninth President of the United States

René-Robert Cavelier (Sieur de La Salle)

1643–1687

- First European to visit area that is now Indiana
- Wanted to find a water route to the Pacific Ocean
- Wanted to expand the fur trade and claim new lands for France

Michikinikwa (Little Turtle)

1752?–1812

- Miami leader who defeated United States forces in what are now Ohio and Indiana in the early 1790s
- Urged Native American leaders to seek peace with the United States before the Battle of Fallen Timbers

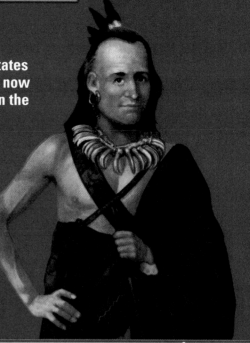

1750   1800   1850

1752? • Michikinikwa (Little Turtle)   1812

1752 • George Rogers Clark   1818

1773 • William Henry Harrison   1841

1773 • Frances Slocum   1847

1784 • Jonathan Jennings   1834

Frances Slocum

1773–1847

- Kidnapped by Native Americans when she was five years old
- Married a Miami chief and lived among Native Americans all her life

Jonathan Jennings

1784–1834

- Led the movement for statehood in Indiana
- First governor of the state of Indiana

Unit 2

Place

Indiana in the United States, 1787

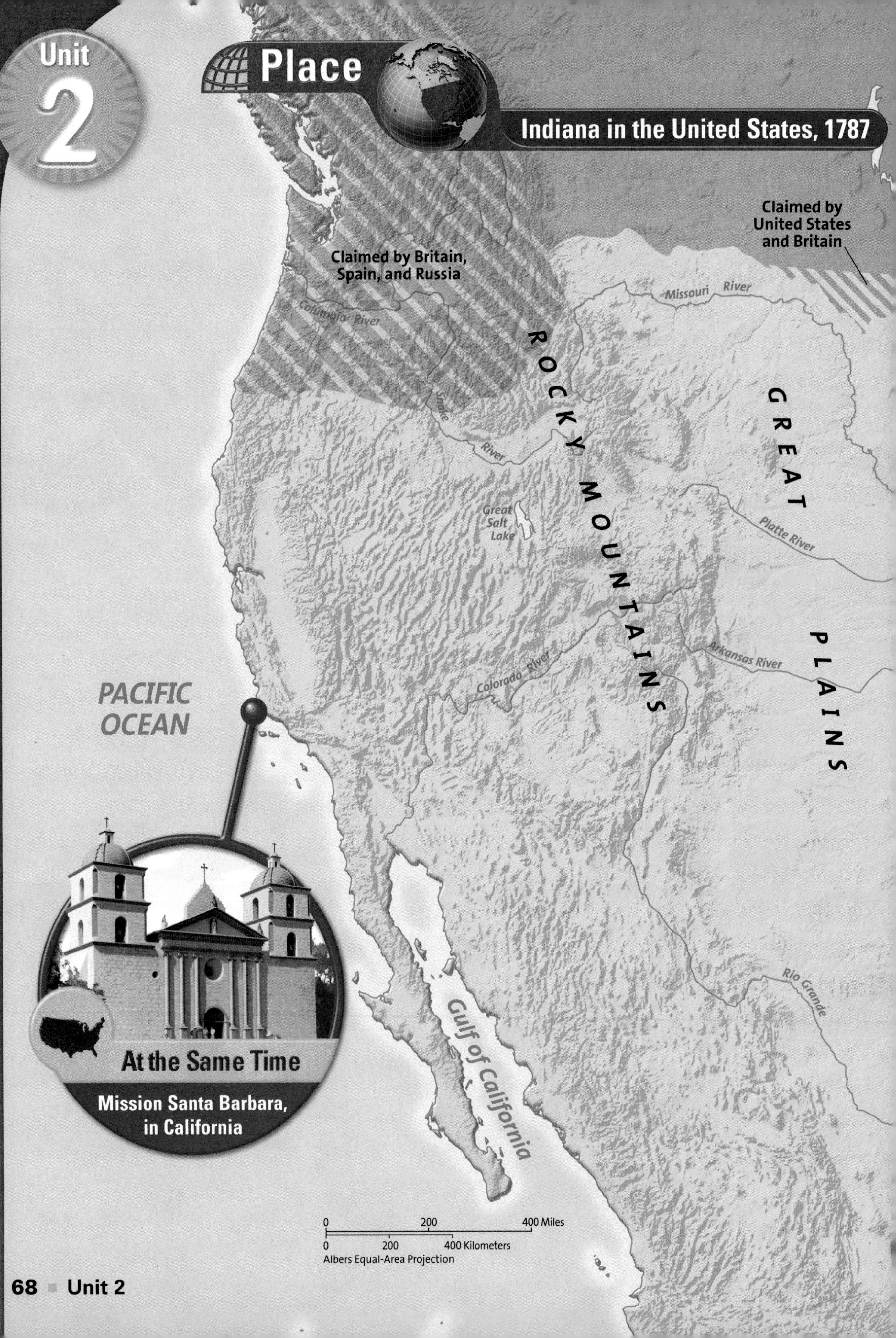

Claimed by United States and Britain
Claimed by Britain, Spain, and Russia
Missouri River
Columbia River
ROCKY MOUNTAINS
GREAT PLAINS
Snake River
Great Salt Lake
Platte River
Arkansas River
Colorado River
PACIFIC OCEAN
Gulf of California
Rio Grande
0 200 400 Miles
0 200 400 Kilometers
Albers Equal-Area Projection

At the Same Time

Mission Santa Barbara, in California

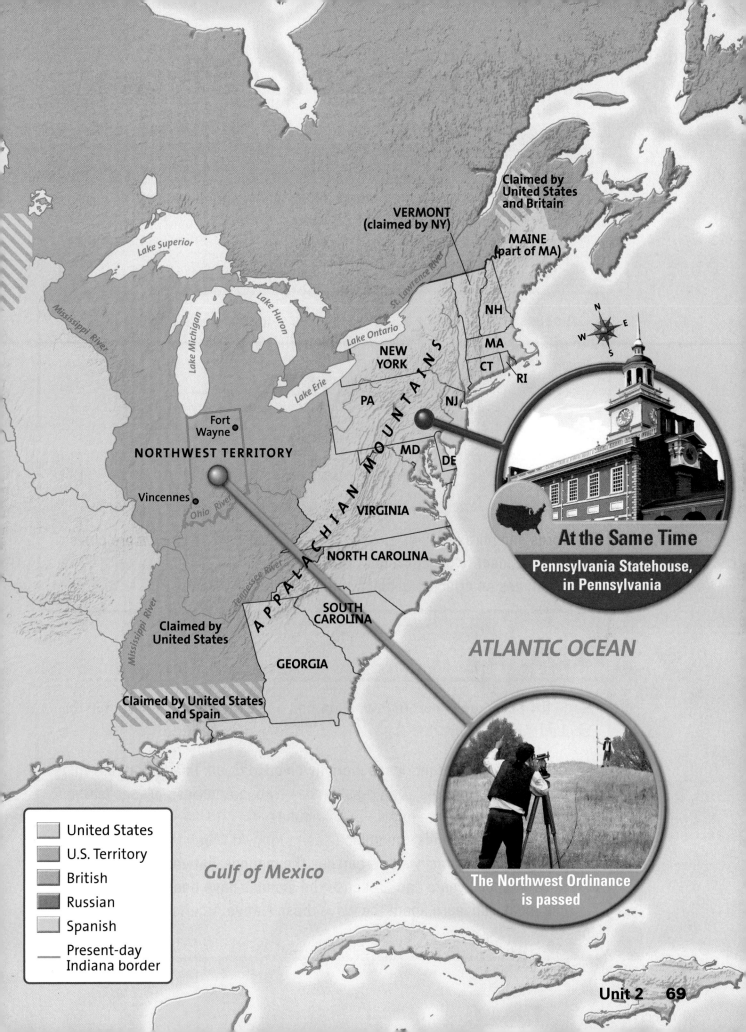

Claimed by
United States
and Britain

VERMONT
(claimed by NY)

MAINE
(part of MA)

NH

MA

CT

RI

Lake Superior

Lake Michigan

Lake Huron

Lake Ontario

Lake Erie

Mississippi River

St. Lawrence River

NEW
YORK

PA

NJ

Fort
Wayne

NORTHWEST TERRITORY

MD

DE

Vincennes

Ohio River

VIRGINIA

NORTH CAROLINA

Tennessee River

A P P A L A C H I A N   M O U N T A I N S

Claimed by
United States

Mississippi River

SOUTH
CAROLINA

GEORGIA

Claimed by United States
and Spain

At the Same Time

Pennsylvania Statehouse,
in Pennsylvania

ATLANTIC OCEAN

The Northwest Ordinance
is passed

Gulf of Mexico

United States

U.S. Territory

British

Russian

Spanish

Present-day
Indiana border

Reading Social Studies

(Focus Skill) Cause and Effect

Why It Matters Understanding cause and effect can help you see why events and actions happen.

▶ LEARN

A **cause** is an action or event that makes something else happen. An **effect** is what happens as the result of that action or event.

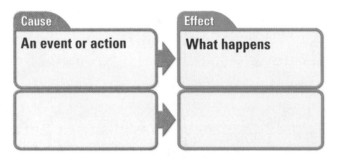

Cause		Effect
An event or action	→	What happens
	→	

- Words and phrases such as *because, since, so*, and *as a result* are clues that help identify causes and effects.
- Sometimes an effect may be stated before its cause.

▶ PRACTICE

Read the paragraphs that follow. Then find one cause and one effect in the second paragraph.

Many early Native Americans were involved in trade. In addition to trading goods, they traded ideas. As a result, many Native American groups learned from other native people how to build mounds.

> Cause
> Effect

Some of these mounds can still be seen today. At Mounds State Park, near Anderson, Indiana, visitors can see the mounds Native Americans built there about 2,000 years ago. Because the mounds have been preserved, people today can learn about the ways these Native Americans lived in the past.

Read the paragraphs, and answer the questions.

The Mississippians

About 1,300 years ago, a group of people lived along the Mississippi River and in what is now Indiana. These Native Americans, called the Mississippians, built mounds.

The Mississippians lived near rivers because rivers provided water for drinking and for watering crops. They became farmers and planted corn, beans, and squash.

Over time, the Mississippians began to grow more food than they needed to survive. This extra food allowed Mississippian communities to grow into large cities.

As a result, people could work on activities other than farming. One popular activity was making art, such as pottery or jewelry.

By 1450, the Mississippian culture had started to decline. Some archaeologists think the culture declined because the Mississippian cities had grown to be too large and the natural resources were used up. Diseases brought by Europeans and fighting between groups also may have killed many Mississippians. By the 1700s, the Mississippian culture had vanished.

 Focus Skill ## Cause and Effect

1. Why did the Mississippians live near rivers?
2. What led to the Mississippians' having the opportunity to make art?
3. What may have caused the Mississippian culture to decline?

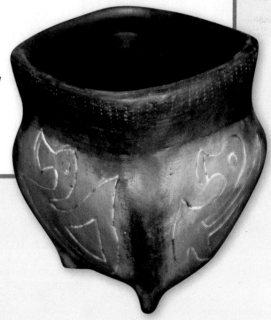

Woodpecker & Sugar Maple

A Lenape Legend
retold by Jane Louise Curry
illustrated by Naomi Mariou

The Lenape (len•ah•pay) people, also known as the Delaware, arrived in Indiana in the 1770s. They had slowly moved west from their homeland, located in the area that is now Pennsylvania, New Jersey, New York, and Delaware.

The Lenape and other Native Americans had many stories about the world long ago, which they believed was remade several times. Some of these stories had a lesson. Read now to find out how the Lenape believed maple syrup was made. Maple syrup is still made in Indiana today.

Not long after the world was made new, after the animals chose their new homes, and the trees and plants grew strong and green, Sugar Maple began to itch. Dozens of little beetles had decided to make their homes under his bark. They nibbled their way in, and tunneled in all directions. When their eggs hatched into grubs, the grubs tunneled, too. The itch was so bad that Sugar Maple moaned and swayed and twisted in torment. When he tried to scratch his itch, all he could do was shake his branches and shiver his leaves. The dozens of beetles became hundreds, then hundreds more, and they nibbled away busily.

"Help!" cried Sugar Maple when he could stand it no longer. "Someone—anyone—everyone—*help!*"

Many animals passed through the forest as they went about their daily business, but none offered to help.

"Itches are terrible," said Squirrel, "but I am too busy. My storeroom is only half full of nuts."

Porcupine shook his head. "You must be miserable," he said. "Because of my spines, I cannot scratch my back when it itches, either, but I cannot help you now. I am late home for dinner."

"You'll feel better tomorrow," Beaver called as he bustled by. "Keep busy. Try not to think of it."

Sugar Maple groaned. Perhaps, if the animals could not help, the birds would. "Help!" he called. "You feathered people—Hummingbird—Hawk— oh, *help!*"

But the birds, when they came, were no help. "What can we do?" they asked. "If you had lice, we could pick them off. If you had feathers, we could <u>preen</u> them. But you do not, so what can we do?"

<u>**preen**</u> to clean with a beak

Then Woodpecker came.

"Grubs? Under your bark?" He cocked a bright eye. "Yes, I can help. So can my cousins." So he flew away, and returned with Flicker and Downy Woodpecker.

They pecked away busily at Sugar Maple's bark. They picked out grub after grub and beetle after beetle. *Tap-tap-ta-ta-ta-tap. Tap-tap-ta-ta-ta-ta-tap!* They pecked and pecked until Sugar Maple's itch was completely gone.

"*Wonderful!*" cried Sugar Maple. "I thank you all, good friends."

"We thank you for the beetle feast," Woodpecker and his cousins replied.

Long afterward, there came a time of drought. There was not a stream or pond or puddle to be found in the forest. The animals and birds searched far and wide for a drop of water to drink. Poor Woodpecker, half dead with thirst, came to rest on one of Sugar Maple's boughs. "*Help!*" he croaked.

"Quickly, good friend," cried Sugar Maple. "Hop to my trunk and make a hole. Make as many as you like, so that you can drink my sap when it begins to drip."

Tap-tap-tap-ta-ta-ta-tap! tapped Woodpecker. As the sweet sap dripped, he drank and drank until he was full—and found it so good that woodpeckers have been drinking it ever since.

Later, in the Second World, when men and women like us were made, Woodpecker taught them about Sugar Maple's sweet sap—and we have made it into syrup and sugar ever since.

Response Corner

1. **Focus Skill** **Cause and Effect** What was the result of Woodpecker's helping Sugar Maple?

2. **Make It Relevant** Why do you think people pass down legends over time?

Time

| 15,000 years ago | | 1,000 years ago |

About 12,000 years ago
People arrive in what is now Indiana

About 3,000 years ago
Farming begins in North America

About 1,000 years ago
Mississippians build mounds in Indiana

WHAT TO KNOW
How did life change for the early people of Indiana?

VOCABULARY
nomad p. 77
ancestor p. 77
extinct p. 78
mound p. 78
permanent p. 78
barter p. 78

PEOPLE
Paleo-Indians
Archaic Indians
Woodland Indians
Adena
Hopewell
Mississippians

PLACES
Evansville
Angel Mounds
Ohio River

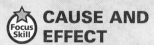

CAUSE AND EFFECT

Early People of Indiana

YOU ARE THERE
"Shhh! I see one," a hunter near you whispers. Down the hill, by the watering hole, stands a woolly mammoth. A successful hunt is important to your people. For the first time in weeks, you will have a source of meat that will feed your family for many days. The mammoth's skin will keep you warm and provide shelter for the winter. Very, very slowly you move toward it, spear in hand.

Long, Long Ago

During the Ice Ages, much of Earth's water was frozen in glaciers. As a result, the water level of the oceans dropped. At times, a "bridge" of dry land appeared between Asia and what is now Alaska in North America.

Early People Arrive

Many scientists think that people first reached North America by crossing that land bridge. They were **nomads**, or people who moved from place to place in search of food. We now call these early people **Paleo-Indians**. However, Native Americans today believe that their people have always lived in the Americas.

Over thousands of years, early people spread out over North America and South America. They were the **ancestors**, or early family members, of present-day Native Americans. Native Americans are also sometimes called American Indians.

MAP SKILL MOVEMENT Groups of Paleo-Indians used spears to hunt mammoths. In which direction did early people travel from Asia to reach what is now Indiana?

Early People of Indiana

Paleo-Indians may have reached present-day Indiana more than 12,000 years ago. They used spears tipped with stone points to hunt mastodons and woolly mammoths. They used the animals' bones to make tools. They also gathered wild plants for food.

READING CHECK ☼CAUSE AND EFFECT
Why did a land bridge appear between Asia and North America?

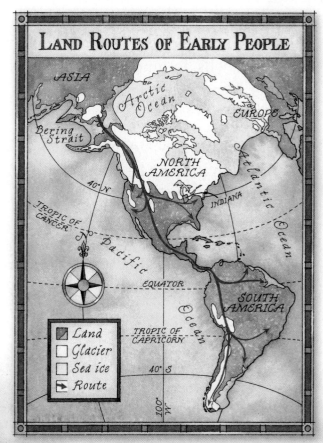

LAND ROUTES OF EARLY PEOPLE

ASIA
Arctic Ocean
EUROPE
Bering Strait
NORTH AMERICA
40°N
Atlantic Ocean
INDIANA
TROPIC OF CANCER
N
Pacific
EQUATOR
Ocean
SOUTH AMERICA
TROPIC OF CAPRICORN
40°S
100°W

☐ Land
☐ Glacier
☐ Sea ice
➤ Route

New Ways of Life

About 10,000 years ago, the last Ice Age ended. The warmer climate caused the larger animals to become **extinct**, or die out. People had to change their ways of life to survive.

New Foods

The people who lived during this period are called **Archaic Indians**. They hunted smaller animals, such as deer, and gathered plants, nuts, and berries. The Archaic Indians ate mussels from the rivers. They threw away the shells, in time forming shell mounds. **Mounds** are large piles.

Settling Down and Trading

About 3,000 years ago, Native Americans in Indiana began to farm. They found that if they planted seeds, they could grow food instead of having to find it. They grew corn, squash, beans, and pumpkins.

People had to stay close by to care for and to protect their crops. In addition, agriculture required clearing the land. That involved much work. It made little sense to move to another place after one harvest.

As a result of agriculture, Native Americans began building **permanent**, or long-lasting, shelters and staying in one place. They formed villages.

Native Americans used boats to travel long distances to **barter**, or trade. They got items such as seashells and copper, which they used to make better tools and weapons.

READING CHECK **MAIN IDEA AND DETAILS**
What crops did Native Americans grow?

> **EARLY FARMING** Men used large sticks to break up the soil, and women used hoes to make grooves. Then, smaller sticks were used to make holes in which the seeds were planted.

Building Mounds

About 3,000 years ago, the **Woodland Indians** lived in Indiana. Woodland groups such as the **Adena** and the **Hopewell** are known for building mounds. These mounds had many purposes. Some were used for ceremonies and social gatherings. Others were burial places, home-building sites, and trading centers.

Angel Mounds

The **Mississippian** people, who lived about 1,000 years ago, built a village near where the city of **Evansville** is today. Now called **Angel Mounds**, the site includes 11 mounds located along the **Ohio River**. One mound is 44 feet high. This settlement was the largest known town of its time in Indiana.

READING CHECK **MAIN IDEA AND DETAILS**
What were some purposes of mounds?

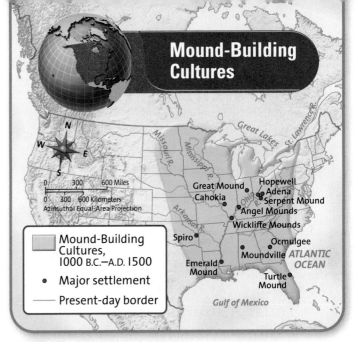

MAP SKILL **LOCATION** Where in Indiana is the Great Mound located?

Summary

The earliest people to live in North America may have crossed a land bridge from Asia. Early people hunted animals and gathered wild plants. Later, they planted crops. Eventually, Native Americans formed villages.

REVIEW

1. **WHAT TO KNOW** How did life change for the early people of Indiana?

2. **VOCABULARY** What is another word for **barter**?

3. **CULTURE** How did early Native Americans depend on animals?

4. **CRITICAL THINKING** Why did growing their own food encourage people to stay in one place longer?

5. **DRAW SCENES** Draw two scenes showing Native American life in Indiana at two different times. Write a caption for each scene.

6. **CAUSE AND EFFECT** On a separate sheet of paper, copy and complete this graphic organizer.

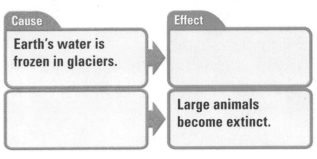

Cause	Effect
Earth's water is frozen in glaciers.	
	Large animals become extinct.

READ ABOUT

From 1100 to 1450, Angel Mounds was the site of a town where several thousand Mississippian people lived. They hunted and farmed on the rich lands near the Ohio River. Today, exhibits at Angel Mounds State Historic Site show Mississippian ways of life.

Visitors can see some of the original mounds built by early Native Americans. Interactive video programs describe how these people used natural resources and how they interacted with wildlife. Workshops show visitors how to make their own souvenir stone tools.

FIND

INDIANA

Angel Mounds State Historic Site

PARK ACTIVITIES Visitors can view exhibits that show scenes from daily life in the Mississippian culture.

SPADE AND HOE

NATIVE AMERICAN DAYS

LOOKING AT A MURAL

CLAY POT

STONE CARVING

ANGEL MOUNDS Mississippian groups built mounds for many different reasons. Some mounds were used to bury the dead. Temples were built on the tops of other mounds.

A VIRTUAL TOUR

GO ONLINE For more resources, go to www.harcourtschool.com/ss1

Time

1400   1850

Late 1600s
The Miami arrive in
what is now Indiana

Early 1700s
The Shawnee move to
southeastern Indiana

1770s
The Lenape settle in
what is now Indiana

WHAT TO KNOW
Who were some of the
early Native American
groups of Indiana, and
how did they live?

VOCABULARY
historic p. 83

tribe p. 83

specialize p. 84

longhouse p. 86

clan p. 87

artifact p. 88

legend p. 89

PEOPLE
Miami
Shawnee
Lenape
Potawatomi

PLACES
Maumee River
Kekionga
White River
Lake Michigan
St. Joseph River
Tippecanoe River
Wabash River

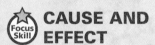

CAUSE AND EFFECT

Cause	Effect

Native Peoples of Indiana

YOU ARE THERE It's a busy day in your village. Your father
and your uncles are building a new
house. Your mother and the other women of the
village are working in the fields. Your mother
calls to you to weed the pumpkin patch. Your
tribe's survival depends on the contributions
of all.

A Miami Village

Animal skins

hoe

Tribes and Culture

By 1650, groups known as the Historic Indians lived in Indiana. They are called **historic** because they lived after written history began.

These groups of Native Americans did not have their own written languages. However, the Europeans who met them did. Written records from Europeans tell us much about these Native Americans.

Forming Tribes

After they settled in villages, Native Americans in Indiana developed different ways of life. Some formed groups called **tribes**. Each tribe had its own leaders and lands.

Tribe members spoke the same language, wore the same kind of clothing, and lived in similiar houses. Tribes had their own dances, beliefs, and ceremonies. All of these ways of living made up a tribe's culture.

Environment and Culture

Cultures were shaped in part by the environment. Depending on where they lived, tribes used different natural resources. For example, tribes who lived near rivers fished and hunted beavers. The fertile soil of river valleys made good farmland.

On the nearby prairies, Native Americans hunted buffalo. They made clothing and shelters from the animals' skins. They gathered fruits and nuts in the forests.

READING CHECK Ŏ**CAUSE AND EFFECT**
How were Native American groups affected by their environment?

MAP SKILL **PLACE** The Miami used poles and bark or grass mats to build dome-shaped houses. Where in Indiana did the Miami live?

Smoke hole

Wooden poles and bark

Indiana's Native American Tribes

POTAWATOMI

MIAMI

LENAPE

Wabash River

White River

East Fork White River

SHAWNEE

Ohio River

N S W E

----- Present-day border

Miami Children

Miami children grew up doing many of the same things children do today. They played and did chores. From an early age, they were taught to follow the laws and customs of their tribes. Fathers taught sons, and mothers taught daughters.

Boys played sports that involved running, swimming, and jumping. They learned how to use bows and arrows. These activities helped them grow strong and develop their skills as hunters and warriors. Girls played house by following what their mothers did. They had dolls made from cornhusks.

Make It Relevant **Think about some of the games you like to play. What skills do you learn by playing these games?**

The Miami

During the late 1600s, the **Miami** people moved into what is now northern and western Indiana. They settled along the **Maumee River**, where Fort Wayne is now located.

Village Life

The Miami built a settlement called **Kekionga** (kee•kee•OHN•guh). Over time, the Miami became the largest group of Native Americans in what is now Indiana.

The people in each village elected two chiefs. One chief led them in times of peace and the other in times of war. A council of older men and women helped chiefs make decisions. The Miami lived in dome-shaped houses called wigwams. An opening in the roof let out smoke from the fire.

Miami men hunted buffalo, deer, rabbits, and beavers. They also fished and carried on trade. The women cared for the children, prepared meals, and made clothing. They grew beans, squash, pumpkins, melons, and corn.

As farmers, the Miami did not have to spend as much time looking for food. Some people could specialize in other jobs, such as making pots or weaving. To **specialize** is to work at one kind of job and learn to do it well.

READING CHECK **MAIN IDEA AND DETAILS**
What were some sources of food for the Miami?

The Shawnee

The **Shawnee** first lived in the Ohio Valley. During the late 1600s, the Iroquois forced the Shawnee to move southward. In the early 1700s, the Shawnee moved back north to present-day southeastern Indiana. They settled near the **White River**.

Trading and Hunting

The waterways in Indiana provided the Shawnee with a good way to travel and trade. They used dugout canoes, which they made by hollowing out large tree trunks.

Shawnee men hunted deer, turkeys, and other small animals. They also fished. The women grew crops, gathered firewood, and cooked meals.

Community Life

In the summer, the Shawnee lived in large villages. Their homes were made from poles and covered with bark or animal skins. During the winter, family groups moved to hunting camps.

Each village had a council house for meetings and ceremonies. Shawnee festivals, such as the Green Corn Dance and the Fall Bread Dance, were often filled with music and dancing.

In Shawnee tribes, the oldest man in each family led the household. The title of chief was usually passed down from father to son. Shawnee families had different responsibilities. Some were warriors, others were healers, and still others were religious leaders.

READING CHECK ♻ **CAUSE AND EFFECT**
Why did the Shawnee move to Indiana?

▶ **A SHAWNEE VILLAGE** The Shawnee once lived in villages along the White River and depended on the natural resources there.

▶ **LENAPE INDIAN CAMP** Exhibits at the Conner Prairie Living History Museum show visitors how the Lenape lived in the 1700s. The Lenape made colorful deerskin bags (right).

The Lenape

The **Lenape** (len•AH•pay), also known as the Delaware, arrived in Indiana in the 1770s. They had been forced by European settlers from their lands in New Jersey, Pennsylvania, Delaware, and New York. The Miami invited the Lenape to settle along the White River in central Indiana.

Ways of Life

The Lenape built many villages in their new location. They lived in wigwams and longhouses. A **longhouse** is a large rectangular building made from wooden poles and covered with bark. As many as 60 people could live in one longhouse. Many villages also had sweat lodges.

Lenape women grew beans, squash, and corn. The men hunted and fished. They also made maple sugar from maple tree sap. The Lenape traded the sugar as well as furs and skins from deer, bears, and beavers. They traveled the rivers in dugout canoes.

The Lenape made clothes and moccasins from deerskin. They decorated the clothing with feathers, shells, and porcupine quills. From copper, they made arrowheads.

In Lenape tribes, the oldest woman in each family led the household. The oldest women in the village also held the power to choose the village chief.

READING CHECK **MAIN IDEA AND DETAILS**
What kinds of buildings were in a Lenape village?

The Potawatomi

In the late 1700s, the **Potawatomi** (paht•uh•WAHT•uh•mee) moved southward from their home near **Lake Michigan**. Some settled in what is now Indiana. They built settlements along the **St. Joseph River**, the **Tippecanoe River,** and the upper **Wabash River.**

Using Resources

During the summer, the Potawatomi lived in large villages near rivers or streams. Their houses were covered with bark or grass mats. During the winter, they lived in small hunting camps. Like other Native Americans, the Potawatomi used the resources around them to meet their needs.

The Potawatomi fished, hunted, and gathered nuts, berries, and roots. They also planted corn, beans, peas, and melons. During the spring, they made maple syrup from tree sap.

Living in Groups

Each Potawatomi village had its own leader and council. In times of war, one war chief was often in charge of several villages.

Every Potawatomi person belonged to a clan. A **clan** is a group of closely related people. Clans were based on one's male relatives. Married women lived with their husband's clan but were still members of their own clan.

READING CHECK **COMPARE AND CONTRAST**
How were the Potawatomi like the Miami?

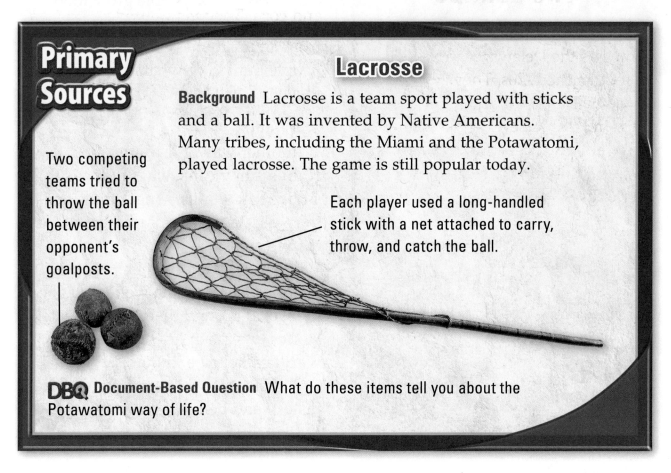

Primary Sources

Lacrosse

Background Lacrosse is a team sport played with sticks and a ball. It was invented by Native Americans. Many tribes, including the Miami and the Potawatomi, played lacrosse. The game is still popular today.

Two competing teams tried to throw the ball between their opponent's goalposts.

Each player used a long-handled stick with a net attached to carry, throw, and catch the ball.

DBQ **Document-Based Question** What do these items tell you about the Potawatomi way of life?

Indiana Artifacts

▶ **ARTIFACTS** made by early Native Americans have been found in Indiana.

▶ **SCIENTISTS** dig up a Native American site at Angel Mounds.

▶ **DIG** A university student searches a site along the White River near Noblesville.

Learning from the Past

Native Americans left no written record of their experiences. Even so, people who study the distant past have ways to learn about how Native Americans lived. They can learn about the customs, tools, foods, and beliefs of people who lived long ago.

Artifacts

Much of what we know about Native Americans in Indiana comes from the artifacts (AR•tih•fakts) they left behind. An **artifact** is an object made by people in the past.

From artifacts such as spear points and arrowheads, scientists can figure out how people hunted or fought. Hoes, needles, and other tools can give clues about how people grew food and made their clothes. Artifacts made from animal bones can show how people hunted or what kinds of meat they ate.

Storytelling

Another way of learning about Native Americans' ways of life is to study their stories, songs, and teachings that have been passed down for many years.

Like people everywhere, Native Americans in Indiana wondered about the world around them. They created stories to explain how things in the world came to be. Indiana's Native Americans also told stories about their history and beliefs.

Children listened carefully as their elders repeated these legends. **Legends** are stories that are handed down over time. In time, they learned the legends by heart and passed them on to their own children.

One Lenape legend tells of how the people learned to make syrup from the sap of maple trees. Other legends tell how animals came to be.

`READING CHECK` **MAIN IDEA AND DETAILS**
How can we learn about the lives of early Native American tribes?

Summary

The Miami, Shawnee, Lenape, and Potawatomi were Native American tribes that lived, farmed, and hunted in Indiana. Each group used natural resources. Most passed down their history and culture through stories.

▶**STORYTELLERS** pass Native American history and beliefs on to the next generation.

REVIEW

1. **WHAT TO KNOW** Who were some of the early Native American groups of Indiana, and how did they live?

2. **VOCABULARY** What is an example of an **artifact**, and what might it tell you about the past?

3. **CULTURE** How did the early Native Americans pass on their history and beliefs?

4. **CRITICAL THINKING** What effect did specialization have on the way Native Americans lived?

5. ✎ **WRITE A STORY** Write a legend that explains how a landform or body of water in Indiana came to be.

6. ⭐ *Focus Skill* **CAUSE AND EFFECT** On a separate sheet of paper, copy and complete this graphic organizer.

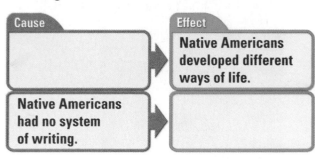

Cause		Effect
	▶	Native Americans developed different ways of life.
Native Americans had no system of writing.	▶	

Native Americans in Indiana

Background Native Americans have lived in what is today Indiana for thousands of years. Over time, Native Americans learned to use the natural resources around them to meet their needs for food, clothing, and shelter. They grew crops and hunted animals. They made tools, weapons, boats, and art. You can view some Native American art and artifacts at the Eiteljorg Museum of American Indians and Western Art in Indianapolis.

DBQ **Document-Based Question** Study these primary sources and answer the questions.

HEDDLE

Native Americans used looms to make thread into cloth by weaving the strands together. The heddle is the part of a loom that spaces the threads evenly apart.

DBQ **1** How do you think the use of looms changed the Native Americans' clothing?

CARVING

The Lenape used wood to make many objects, such as this carving used in a religious ceremony.

DBQ **2** What else do you think the Lenape used wood for?

PICTURE STONES

Lenape picture writing was scratched on stones or painted or cut on wood.

DBQ ❸ What do you think the Lenape recorded with these pictures?

LEGGINGS

Miami men and women wore leggings. Men wore longer leggings originally made from buckskin but later from cloth. Women's leggings were shorter and were worn under skirts.

DBQ ❺ Why do you think the Miami wore leggings?

DOLL

Shawnee girls often played with dolls. This doll's head is made from a walnut.

DBQ ❹ Where did Native American children's toys come from?

WRITE ABOUT IT

What do these primary sources tell you about Native American ways of life? Write a paragraph that describes the daily life of Native Americans in the past.

GO ONLINE For more resources, go to www.harcourtschool.com/ss1

Lesson 3

1492
Columbus sails
to the Americas

1679
La Salle explores
what is now Indiana

1754
The French and
Indian War begins

Exploration and Settlement

WHAT TO KNOW
Why did Europeans
explore and settle what is
now Indiana?

VOCABULARY
explorer p. 93
colony p. 94
expedition p. 94
missionary p. 95
scarce p. 95
voyageur p. 95
allies p. 96
treaty p. 96
proclamation p. 97

PEOPLE
Christopher Columbus
Sieur de La Salle
Chief Demoiselle
Pontiac
King George III

PLACES
Great Lakes
South Bend
Kankakee River
Fort Ouiatanon
Fort Miami
Vincennes

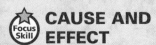

CAUSE AND EFFECT

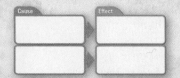

YOU ARE THERE

The year is 1720. You live in a French fort near the Wabash River with a few soldiers and other fur traders. You miss your family back in France. Each day, you trade with Native Americans from a nearby village. In exchange for cloth and tools from France, they give you beaver furs. As you begin your day by stacking furs, you wonder if you'll soon have enough to send back to France to sell.

▶ FRENCH FORTS—such as
Fort Ouiatanon, whose replica is
shown here—provided shelter and
protection for French soldiers
and fur traders.

▶ **CROSSING THE OCEAN SEA** Columbus sailed with three ships across the Ocean Sea, today called the Atlantic Ocean.

Exploring the Americas

For thousands of years, Native Americans were the only people living in the Americas. Then, in the late 1400s, Europeans sailed across the Atlantic Ocean.

Looking for a Route to Asia

People in Europe traded with people in Asia. The routes to Asia were mostly over land. The trip was long, difficult, and dangerous. In 1492, explorer **Christopher Columbus** left Spain to find a shorter sea route to Asia. An **explorer** is someone who travels to unfamiliar places. Columbus thought he could reach Asia by sailing west across the Atlantic Ocean.

Arriving in the Americas

Though he thought he had reached Asia, Columbus actually landed in the Americas. He claimed the land for Spain. Columbus returned home with gold and exciting stories. His adventures made other explorers want to sail there.

By the 1600s, explorers from Spain, France, England, and other European countries had claimed vast areas of land in North America and South America. Native Americans lived in many of these areas. Most could not defend their lands because, unlike the Europeans, they did not have horses or guns. Thousands died from the diseases the Europeans brought, such as smallpox and measles.

READING CHECK ⚙ **CAUSE AND EFFECT**
What was one effect of Columbus's stories?

Exploring Indiana

The French claimed lands in what is today Canada. In the early 1600s, they had founded a colony called New France. A **colony** is a settlement that is ruled by a faraway government. The English started colonies along the Atlantic coast of North America.

French Explorers

From New France, French explorers traveled around the **Great Lakes**. The first European to visit what is now Indiana was René-Robert Cavelier (ka•vuhl•YAY), known as **Sieur de La Salle**. La Salle wanted to find a water route across North America to the Pacific Ocean. He also wanted to expand the fur trade and to claim new lands for France.

In the fall of 1679, La Salle led an expedition around the eastern shore of Lake Michigan. An **expedition** is a journey into an area to learn more about it. Eventually, the explorers found the mouth of the St. Joseph River. La Salle and his crew paddled up the river. After two days, they reached the southern bend in the river, where the city of **South Bend**, Indiana, is today.

La Salle's Native American guide, White Beaver, led the explorers overland to the **Kankakee River**. From there, they paddled west to the Illinois River. La Salle built a fort near where Peoria, Illinois, is today. Then he went back to New France for supplies.

READING CHECK **MAIN IDEA AND DETAILS**
Why did La Salle come to the Indiana area?

The Fur Trade

La Salle's reports about fur-bearing animals in the region brought fur traders to Indiana. Missionaries also came to teach Native Americans about the Christian religion. A **missionary** is a person who teaches his or her religious beliefs to others.

Trade Grows

Native Americans trapped beavers and other animals for their fur. These furs sold for high prices in Europe, where they were **scarce**, or hard to find. The fur trade in North America grew quickly.

In return for the furs, European traders offered Native Americans goods such as tools, knives, guns, blankets, and beads. When the French traders had gathered a large number of furs, they gave them to **voyageurs** (voy•uh•ZHERZ). *Voyageur* is a French word meaning "traveler."

The voyageurs took the furs by canoe to Montreal. From there, the furs were shipped to Europe. Then the voyageurs brought back more goods to trade with Native Americans.

The arrival of the French changed the way Native Americans lived. They began to hunt with guns and wear clothing made of cloth instead of animal skins. Their religious beliefs were questioned by missionaries.

READING CHECK SUMMARIZE
How did the fur trade work?

TABLE Native Americans in Indiana traded goods with Europeans. Usually, the two groups traded along the riverbanks. How many beaver furs was a blanket worth?

Value of Some Trade Items

Trade Items	Beaver Furs
4 Knives	1
Blanket	8
2 Copper Kettles	3
4 Buttons	1
Pair of Shoes	3

= 1 Beaver Fur

War over Land

The French built trading posts protected by soldiers in what is now Indiana. They hoped to stop the British, as the English became known, from trading with Native Americans and from taking French land.

Forts and Trading Posts

The French built **Fort Ouiatanon** in 1717 near present-day Lafayette. In 1721, **Fort Miami** was built near the Native American village of Kekionga. In 1732, **Vincennes**, on the Wabash River, became the first permanent European settlement in Indiana.

The French and Indian War

British colonists wanted to settle and farm lands in the Ohio Valley that the French had already claimed.

Also, both the French and the British wanted to control the fur trade. Each had some tribes of Native Americans as their **allies**, or partners. Most tribes sided with the French, but a part of the Miami tribe led by **Chief Demoiselle** (duh•mwah•ZEL) signed a treaty with the British. A **treaty** is an agreement among nations or groups.

In 1754, the bad feelings between the French and the British turned to war, known as the French and Indian War. The French won most of the early battles. Then the British captured Fort Miami and Fort Ouiatanon, giving Britian control of the fur trade.

The war ended in 1763, when the French and the British signed the Treaty of Paris. Britain gained control of Canada and the French lands east of the Mississippi River.

> ❯ **THE FRENCH AND INDIAN WAR** was fought to settle land claims.

An Ottawa chief named **Pontiac** did not want the British to control Native American lands. Many Native American tribes agreed with him. His followers attacked many British forts.

To avoid further conflicts, **King George III** of Britain issued a **proclamation**, or public announcement. The Proclamation of 1763 said that no colonists could move to the lands west of the Appalachian Mountains. Only Native Americans could use those lands.

READING CHECK ☼ **CAUSE AND EFFECT**
What caused the French and Indian War?

Summary

The French explored what is now Indiana. After the French and Indian War, the British gained control of the land from the French.

❱ **THE PROCLAMATION OF 1763** met the demands of Chief Pontiac (below).

REVIEW

1. **WHAT TO KNOW** Why did Europeans explore and settle what is now Indiana?

2. **VOCABULARY** How are the words **expedition** and **colony** related?

3. **ECONOMICS** How was Indiana's fur trade connected to Europe?

4. **CRITICAL THINKING** How might the United States be different today if the French had won the French and Indian War?

5. ✎ **WRITE A PERSUASIVE LETTER** Write a letter from the point of view of a French or a British fur trader to persuade a Native American group to trade only with your country.

6. ⭐ (Focus Skill) **CAUSE AND EFFECT** On a separate sheet of paper, copy and complete this graphic organizer.

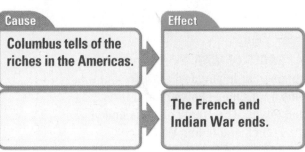

Cause		Effect
Columbus tells of the riches in the Americas.	→	
	→	The French and Indian War ends.

Compare Historical Maps

Why It Matters A **historical map** shows a place at a certain time in the past. By comparing historical maps of a place, you see how the place changed over time.

❯ LEARN

Follow these steps to compare the historical maps on page 99.

Step 1 Read the title of each map. The title tells the place and time the map shows.

Step 2 Study the map key for each map. The colors show the areas claimed by different countries.

Step 3 Notice that Map B has a pattern of stripes called hatch lines. **Hatch lines** show areas claimed by two or more countries. Hatch lines may also show land that has a special use.

❯ **TRACES OF WAR** Soldiers carried gunpowder in powderhorns (far right). This horn's map shows rivers, forts, and towns. The Treaty of Paris ended the French and Indian War.

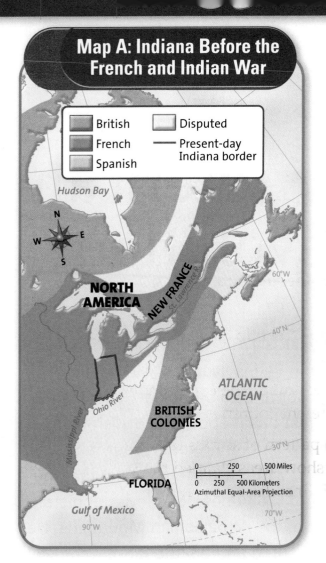

Map A: Indiana Before the French and Indian War

British
French
Spanish
Disputed
Present-day Indiana border

Hudson Bay

NORTH AMERICA
NEW FRANCE
St. Lawrence

60°W
40°N

ATLANTIC OCEAN

Mississippi River
Ohio River

BRITISH COLONIES

0   250   500 Miles
0   250   500 Kilometers
Azimuthal Equal-Area Projection

FLORIDA

Gulf of Mexico
90°W
70°W
30°N

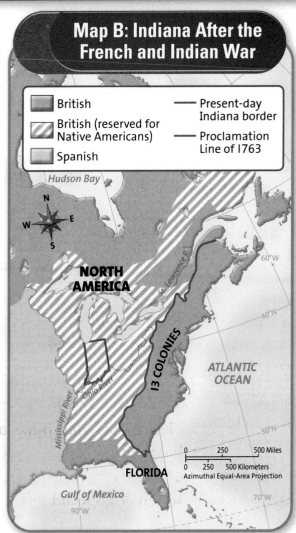

Map B: Indiana After the French and Indian War

British
British (reserved for Native Americans)
Spanish
Present-day Indiana border
Proclamation Line of 1763

Hudson Bay

NORTH AMERICA
St. Lawrence R.

60°W
40°N

13 COLONIES

ATLANTIC OCEAN

Mississippi River
Ohio River

0   250   500 Miles
0   250   500 Kilometers
Azimuthal Equal-Area Projection

FLORIDA

Gulf of Mexico
90°W
70°W
30°N

❯ PRACTICE

Compare Map A and Map B to answer these questions.

1 Which country or countries controlled land that is now Indiana before the French and Indian War?

2 Which country or countries controlled land that is now Indiana after the French and Indian War? What special use did that land have?

❯ APPLY

Write a paragraph that describes what these historical maps show. Explain why historical maps are useful. Share your work with a classmate.

Map and Globe Skills

1776
The colonies declare their independence from Britain

1779
George Rogers Clark recaptures Fort Sackville

1781
George Washington defeats Lord Cornwallis at Yorktown

WHAT TO KNOW
How did the American Revolution affect Indiana?

VOCABULARY
tax p. 101
independence p. 101
revolution p. 101
militia p. 102
surrender p. 102

PEOPLE
Henry Hamilton
George Rogers Clark
Patrick Henry
Father Gibault

PLACES
Kaskaskia
Cahokia
Fort Sackville

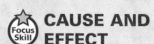

CAUSE AND EFFECT

The American Revolution

YOU ARE THERE
The year is 1765. You and your family are living in Pennsylvania. One evening, your father comes home with a booklet. It was written by a colonist upset about the British taxes on sugar, paper, and other items. Your father agrees with the writer. He is also upset that the Proclamation of 1763 does not allow colonists to settle west of the Appalachian Mountains. He had wanted to settle and build a farm in the Ohio River valley.

▶ **THE BOSTON TEA PARTY**

A War for Freedom

Britain had spent a lot of money fighting the French and Indian War. The British government wanted American colonists to help pay for the costs of the war.

Anger over Taxes

In 1765, the British government passed the Stamp Act. This law placed a tax on paper goods in the colonies. A **tax** is money that a government collects to pay for the services it provides. Over time, items such as glass, paint, and tea were also taxed.

Many colonists did not want to pay these taxes. They felt that they should not have to follow these laws because they did not have representation in the British government. Some wrote angry letters to the British government. The government responded by sending soldiers to Boston.

The Revolution Begins

Some colonists began to call for **independence**, or the freedom to govern themselves. In 1775, anger turned to war. Battles broke out between colonists and British soldiers. Britain fought to keep the colonies under its rule. The colonists' war for independence is called the American Revolution. A **revolution** is a sudden, complete change of government.

READING CHECK ⟳ **CAUSE AND EFFECT**
What caused the American Revolution?

⚡ FAST FACT

In December 1773, about 150 colonists dressed as Native Americans boarded British tea ships in Boston Harbor. They dumped all the tea into the harbor.

The War in Indiana

The main battles of the American Revolution took place in the 13 colonies. Few British soldiers were in what is now Indiana, so the British wanted to join forces with Native Americans to fight settlers in the West.

Native Americans Join the Fight

Britain's main base in the West was Fort Detroit, in what is today Michigan. Lieutenant Governor **Henry Hamilton** was in command. In June 1777, he met with Native American tribes, including the Miami and the Potawatomi.

Hamilton told them that the Americans would take their lands if they won the war. He offered them food, guns, and knives in exchange for their help. Hoping to stay in their homelands, Native Americans joined the British and began fighting the settlers.

The Settlers Fight Back

George Rogers Clark of Kentucky had a plan to stop attacks by Native Americans and to weaken British influence in the West. Clark led the Kentucky **militia**, or volunteer army.

At this time, Kentucky was a county of Virginia. Clark asked Virginia's governor, **Patrick Henry**, for help in carrying out his plan. The governor gave Clark money and permission to raise an army.

> ▶ **SOLDIER GEAR**

Clark's Army

In the spring of 1778, Clark and about 175 soldiers set off down the Ohio River. On July 4, 1778, they captured a fort at **Kaskaskia** with no fighting. Villagers in the nearby French settlement promised loyalty to Clark. Then Clark led his army to **Cahokia**, about 60 miles north. They took that fort without firing a shot.

Father Gibault, a Jesuit priest, convinced the French citizens of Vincennes to support the American cause. With their help, Clark occupied **Fort Sackville**, an abandoned British fort near the city.

Fort Sackville

When news of Clark's successes reached Fort Detroit, Hamilton decided to recapture the forts. Hamilton's soldiers set out for Vincennes, and several hundred Native Americans joined them. In mid-December, Hamilton's forces defeated the soldiers protecting Fort Sackville.

Clark knew that his only chance to recapture the fort would be a surprise mid-winter attack. On February 6, 1779, he left Kaskaskia with 170 soldiers. They marched through water and mud for more than two weeks.

Clark's soldiers fired on the fort at night. Hamilton and his soldiers were surprised to see Clark's army. Hamilton decided to **surrender**, or give up, the fort.

THE AMERICAN REVOLUTION IN INDIANA

Clark led his troops over many miles of rough ground.

Fort Detroit

Fort Pitt

Kekionga

Redstone Old Fort

Battle of Fort Sackville

Cahokia

Vincennes

Ohio River

Kaskaskia

Fort Massac

Hamilton surrendered to Clark at Fort Sackville.

Francis Vigo provided Clark with supplies and information that helped the American cause.

Key

🔥 Battle

•••••► Hamilton's route, 1778

•••••► Clark's route, 1778–1779

– – – Present-day border

► THE YORKTOWN VICTORY MONUMENT in Virginia

The War Ends

The fighting between Britain and the colonies continued for several more years. General George Washington led the colonists' Continental Army. In 1781, with the help of the French navy, he defeated Britain's Lord Cornwallis at Yorktown, Virginia. The Americans had won the war.

READING CHECK **MAIN IDEA AND DETAILS**
Why did George Rogers Clark plan a surprise attack on Fort Sackville?

Summary

Tensions between the colonists and the British led to the American Revolution in 1775. The British needed help from Native Americans to win the war in the West. George Rogers Clark fought the British in the West. The American Revolution ended in 1781.

REVIEW

1. **WHAT TO KNOW** How did the American Revolution affect Indiana?

2. **VOCABULARY** Use **independence** to help explain what a **revolution** is.

3. **HISTORY** What were some of the causes of the American Revolution?

4. **CRITICAL THINKING** Why do you think the British wanted Native Americans to fight settlers in the West?

5. **DRAW A CARTOON** Imagine that you are a colonist who is against British tax laws. Draw a cartoon that encourages other colonists not to buy British goods.

6. **CAUSE AND EFFECT** (Focus Skill) On a separate sheet of paper, copy and complete this graphic organizer.

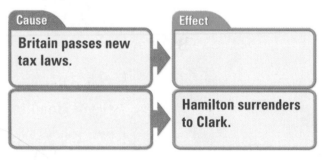

Cause	Effect
Britain passes new tax laws.	
	Hamilton surrenders to Clark.

George Rogers Clark

"Our cause is just... our country will be grateful."

George Rogers Clark was born in Virginia. At age 18, he became a surveyor, or a person who measures and maps land. In 1772, Clark worked as a surveyor in Kentucky. He helped protect Kentucky's settlers from Native American conflicts.

Clark became a leader in the Kentucky militia, a part of the Virginia army. During the American Revolution, Clark organized attacks against British-held forts in what are now Illinois and Indiana. He captured the forts with only a small armed force, often without fighting. Following these victories, Clark continued working for the American cause.

After the war, Clark lived for a time in southern Indiana. He died near Louisville, Kentucky, in 1818. More than 100 years later, a memorial was built in his honor in Vincennes.

Why Character Counts

How did George Rogers Clark show patriotism?

Time

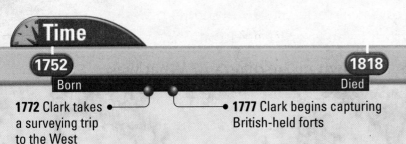

1752		1818
Born		Died

1772 Clark takes a surveying trip to the West

1777 Clark begins capturing British-held forts

Identify Multiple Causes and Effects

Why It Matters Identifying the causes and effects of events can help you understand why things happen.

❯ LEARN

Sometimes events have more than one cause and more than one effect. A **cause** is an action or event that makes something else happen. An **effect** is what happens as a result of that action or event. Use the following steps to help you identify causes and their effects.

Step 1 Look for the effects. Decide whether there is more than one effect.

Step 2 Look for the causes of those effects.

Step 3 Think about the connections between the causes and their effects. An effect of one event can become the cause of another event.

❯ A TRICORNERED HAT AND BUTTON

❯ PRACTICE

The diagram on page 107 shows some events from the American Revolution that took place in what is now Indiana. Use the diagram to answer these questions.

1 What is the last cause shown in the diagram? What was the effect of that cause?

2 Identify one event that was both a cause and an effect.

❯ APPLY

Turn to pages 96–97 in your textbook. With a partner, make a diagram showing the causes and effects of the French and Indian War.

The American Revolution in Indiana

CAUSES

The American colonists did not want to pay more taxes to Britain.

The colonists wanted representation in the British government.

↓

EFFECTS

The Americans began a fight for independence called the American Revolution.

↓

The British persuaded local Native American tribes to fight with American settlers in what is now Indiana.

↓

George Rogers Clark captured British forts at Kaskaskia, Cahokia, and Fort Sackville in what is now Indiana.

↓

Clark's victories helped the Americans win the war and gain their independence.

Critical Thinking Skills

Time

1400 — 1850

1787
The Northwest
Ordinance is passed

1800
The Indiana Territory
is formed

1811
Native Americans
are defeated in the
Battle of Tippecanoe

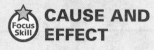

WHAT TO KNOW
How did the Northwest
Ordinance affect settlers
and Native Americans?

VOCABULARY
debt p. 109
territory p. 109
ordinance p. 110
township p. 110
right p. 110

PEOPLE
Arthur St. Clair
Michikinikwa
Anthony Wayne
Blue Jacket
William Henry Harrison
Tecumseh
Tenskwatawa

PLACES
Northwest Territory
Clarksville
Indiana Territory
Prophetstown

CAUSE AND EFFECT

The Northwest Territory

YOU ARE THERE

"We deserve to be paid!" a soldier next
to you shouts. "We fought the British, but
now we can't even feed our families!" You and
other soldiers who fought under George Rogers
Clark are meeting with a member of Congress.
He says, "It's true—there is not enough money to
pay you." Then he asks, "Would any of you want
land near the Ohio River?" The soldiers cheer.
They want to hear more.

▶ **THE GEORGE ROGERS CLARK MEMORIAL** was built in 1933 in
Vincennes, Indiana. It stands on what was then believed to be the
site of Fort Sackville.

Frances Slocum

Frances Slocum was kidnapped by Native Americans from her home in Pennsylvania in 1778. She was just five years old. Slocum grew up among the Lenape. She later moved to a Miami village in what is now Indiana. There, she married a Miami chief. She took the Miami name Maconaquah (muh•KAHN•uh•kwah).

In 1835, she was recognized by a trader near where the town of Peru, Indiana, is located today. Her brothers and sister visited two years later. Maconaquah would not return with them. She said she was an old woman and happy with her Native American family.

Make It Relevant How was Frances Slocum's life different from your life today?

Expanding West

In 1783, the British and the Americans signed a second Treaty of Paris. It recognized the United States of America as a new country. The treaty gave most British lands south of the Great Lakes and east of the Mississippi River to the United States. The British still held some forts in North America, and Spain claimed lands west of the Mississippi River.

A New Territory

Because of the high cost of fighting the American Revolution, the United States had many debts. A **debt** is something owed, often money. Many American soldiers had not been paid. France was also owed money.

Congress decided to use lands west of the Appalachians to help pay debts. At first, several states claimed these lands. In time, the states turned them over to the United States government.

The area north of the Ohio River became known as the **Northwest Territory**. A **territory** is an area owned and governed by a country. It included lands that are now the states of Michigan, Ohio, Indiana, Illinois, Wisconsin, and part of Minnesota.

Congress planned to sell lands in the territory to raise money. Some soldiers would also be paid with land. George Rogers Clark and his soldiers received land on the Ohio River. There they founded the town of **Clarksville**.

READING CHECK ☼**CAUSE AND EFFECT**
How did the Revolutionary War cause debt?

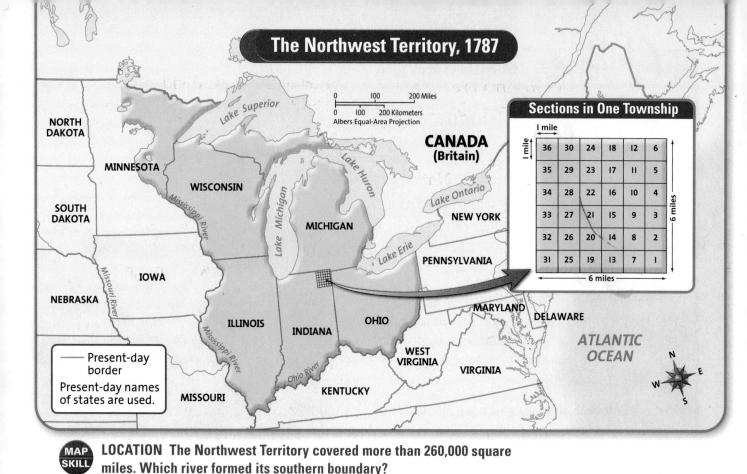

The Northwest Territory, 1787

Sections in One Township

36	30	24	18	12	6
35	29	23	17	11	5
34	28	22	16	10	4
33	27	21	15	9	3
32	26	20	14	8	2
31	25	19	13	7	1

1 mile
6 miles

MAP SKILL   **LOCATION** The Northwest Territory covered more than 260,000 square miles. Which river formed its southern boundary?

Settling the Northwest Territory

A plan was needed for the settlement of the Northwest Territory. Congress passed the Land Ordinance of 1785. An **ordinance** is a law. The ordinance told how land in the territory would be divided and sold.

Land was first divided into squares called **townships**. Each township was divided into 36 smaller sections. One section was set aside for a school. Some land was set aside to be sold.

The Northwest Ordinance

In 1787, Congress passed the Northwest Ordinance. This law set up a plan for governing the Northwest Territory. It also told how new states would be formed. When any region of the territory had more than 60,000 people, it could become a state.

The Northwest Ordinance promised settlers freedom of religion and various legal and property rights. A **right** is a freedom that belongs to a person. Congress appointed former general **Arthur St. Clair**, who fought in the American Revolution, governor of the Northwest Territory.

Conflicts over Land

Native Americans were unhappy about the increasing number of settlers moving to the West. To stop this movement, Native Americans in the Northwest Territory decided to unite. One of their leaders was Miami chief **Michikinikwa**, or Little Turtle.

In the early 1790s, Native Americans won several battles in what are now Indiana and Ohio. President George Washington chose **Anthony Wayne** to lead the Americans in the fight.

In 1794, Michikinikwa urged Native American leaders to seek peace. They did not listen to him. Instead, they ordered Shawnee chief **Blue Jacket** to lead the Native Americans into battle.

On August 20, 1794, Blue Jacket's warriors and General Wayne's forces met at the Battle of Fallen Timbers. The Native Americans were defeated.

After the Battle of Fallen Timbers, the Native Americans signed the Treaty of Greenville. By this treaty, they gave up most of their land in the Northwest Territory. In the early 1800s, Native Americans signed more treaties. In these treaties, they gave up even more of their lands.

The Indiana Territory

In 1800, Congress divided the Northwest Territory. Part of it became the **Indiana Territory**. Its first governor was **William Henry Harrison**, and Vincennes became its capital.

Harrison wanted to take more land from the Native Americans. Two Shawnee leaders, **Tecumseh** and his brother **Tenskwatawa**, thought this was unfair.

The brothers urged the tribes to unite against the settlers. In 1808, they built a village called **Prophetstown**. In 1811, the Battle of Tippecanoe took place near Prophetstown. One of Harrison's soldiers said of the battle,

> **"Ours was a bloody victory, theirs [the Native Americans'] a bloody defeat."**

▶ **THE TREATY OF GREENVILLE** Michikinikwa and the leaders of other tribes agreed to sign the Treaty of Greenville. During the battle of Tippecanoe, William Henry Harrison carried a chest with supplies (right).

▶ **THE TREATY OF GHENT** was signed in Ghent in what is today Belgium. It officially ended the War of 1812.

The War of 1812

Many people thought that the British had armed Native Americans to fight the settlers. Also during this time, the British navy was attacking American trading ships. For these and other reasons, the United States declared war on Britain in 1812.

In 1813, Harrison led American soldiers to victory in the Battle of the Thames. Tecumseh was among those killed in the battle. His death caused the Native Americans' union to fall apart. The war ended in 1814.

READING CHECK **SUMMARIZE**
What began the War of 1812?

Summary

Congress created the Northwest Territory. Then in 1800, the Indiana Territory was created. Conflicts with Native Americans continued until after the War of 1812.

REVIEW

1. **WHAT TO KNOW** How did the Northwest Ordinance affect settlers and Native Americans?

2. **VOCABULARY** Use the word **township** to explain how the Northwest Territory was divided.

3. **HISTORY** How did the Battle of Tippecanoe affect people in Indiana?

4. **CRITICAL THINKING** Why did Tecumseh want to unite Native Americans?

5. ✏️ **WRITE A NEWSPAPER EDITORIAL** Write a newspaper editorial about the conflicts over land.

6. ⭐ (Focus Skill) **CAUSE AND EFFECT** On a separate sheet of paper, copy and complete this graphic organizer.

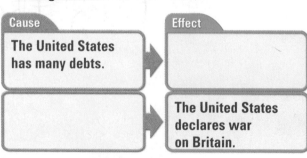

Cause		Effect
The United States has many debts.	→	
	→	The United States declares war on Britain.

Tecumseh

Biography

Trustworthiness
Respect
Responsibility
Fairness
Caring
Patriotism

"*Let us form one body, one heart, and defend to the last warrior our country, our homes, our liberty, and the graves of our fathers.*"

Tecumseh was a Shawnee leader. He wanted to unite Native American tribes to prevent the government from taking more of their lands. His brother, Tenskwatawa, also called the Prophet, was a religious leader. Tenskwatawa urged Native Americans to return to their own traditions. The brothers started a settlement called Prophetstown in what is now Indiana.

In 1809, William Henry Harrison arranged the Treaty of Fort Wayne. This treaty turned over a large amount of Native American land to the United States. Tecumseh believed the treaty was unfair. In 1811, Harrison's troops defeated the Native Americans in the Battle of Tippecanoe. Prophetstown was destroyed.

Tecumseh later joined the British to fight against the Americans during the War of 1812. He was killed in the Battle of the Thames, in Canada.

Why Character Counts

How did Tecumseh show fairness?

Time

1768
Born?

1813
Died

1808 Tecumseh and his brother start a settlement called Prophetstown

1813 Tecumseh is killed in the Battle of the Thames

GO ONLINE
For more resources, go to
www.harcourtschool.com/ss1

Critical Thinking Skills

Compare Primary and Secondary Sources

Why It Matters To know what happened in the past, people study and compare sources of information.

❯ LEARN

A **primary source** is any record made by people who took part in an event or saw it happen. A primary source might be a letter, a diary, a book, an interview, a drawing, or a photograph.

A **secondary source** is any record made by people who did not take part in an event or did not see it take place. An encyclopedia is a secondary source. Written articles, paintings, and drawings made by people who did not see the event are also secondary sources.

❯ **TRACING HISTORY** This ❶ compass, ❷ survey chain, and ❸ 1801 map of the Indiana Territory are all sources related to the Land Ordinance of 1785.

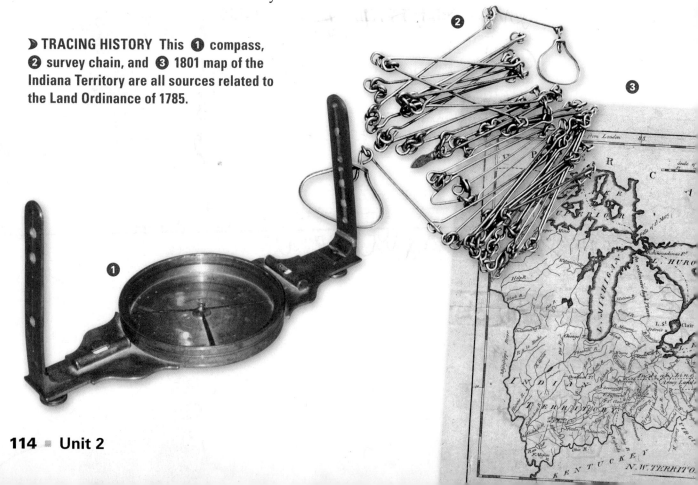

❯ PRACTICE

Examine the images on these two pages. Then answer the following questions.

1 Which images show primary sources? Which images show secondary sources?

2 When is a book a primary source? When is a book a secondary source?

3 Why might the map on page 114 be considered both a primary and a secondary source?

❯ APPLY

Your textbook is a secondary source. It has some primary sources in it. Working with a partner, find examples of primary and secondary sources in your textbook. Discuss what makes each source primary or secondary.

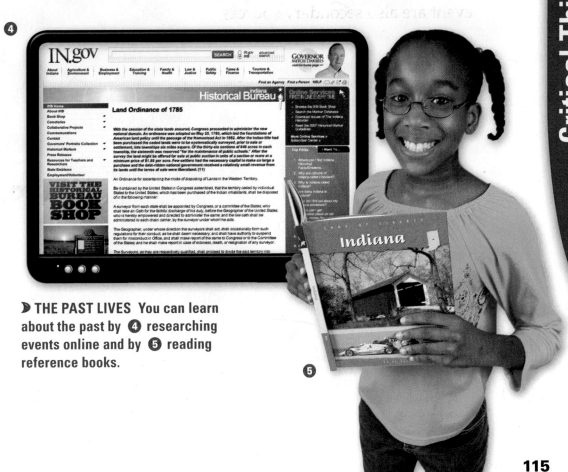

❯ **THE PAST LIVES** You can learn about the past by **4** researching events online and by **5** reading reference books.

Land Treaties

Following the Battle of Fallen Timbers in 1795, the United States and Native American leaders signed the Treaty of Greenville. This and other treaties were supposed to keep peace between settlers and Native Americans. However, settlers continued to push west, ignoring the boundaries set by the treaties. Some Native Americans worked for peace, while others fought against the settlers.

1

CHIEF RED JACKET

Chief Red Jacket, a chief of the Seneca, was originally against selling Native American lands but later gave up his opposition.

“There was a time when our fore-fathers owned this great island. . . . our seats were once large and yours were small. You have now become a great people, and we have scarcely a place left to spread our blankets.”

2

CHIEF LITTLE TURTLE

Chief Little Turtle, or Michikinikwa, was a chief of the Miami. He urged cooperation with the Americans.

“The Americans are now led by a chief who never sleeps. . . . And during all the time that he has been marching upon our villages . . . we have never been able to suprise him. Think well of it. . . . it would be prudent to listen to his offers of peace.”

3

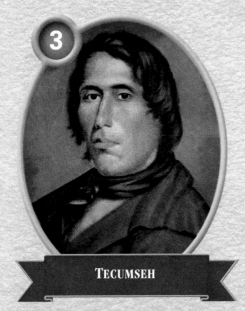

TECUMSEH

Tecumseh was a leader of the Shawnee. He wanted to unite all Native Americans in stopping the settlers from moving west.

❝Brothers—The white men are not friends to the Indians: at first, they only asked for land sufficient for a wigwam; now, nothing will satisfy them but the whole of our hunting grounds, from the rising to the setting sun.❞

4

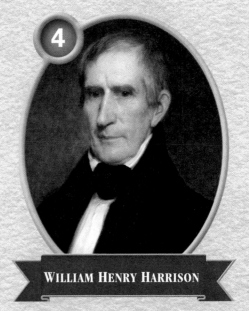

WILLIAM HENRY HARRISON

William Henry Harrison was governor of the Indiana Territory. He signed many treaties with Native American leaders. Often, as part of these treaties, Native Americans agreed to sell their lands to the United States government.

❝. . . for without such a further purchase [of Native American lands] Indiana cannot for many years become a member of the Union and I am heartily tired of living in a Territory.❞

It's Your Turn

Compare Points of View
Summarize each person's point of view. Then answer the questions.

1. Who seemed to have the strongest feelings against settlers moving west?

2. How does the point of view of Tecumseh differ from that of Chief Little Turtle?

3. What might influence the opinions of these people?

Make It Relevant What do *you* think? Explain why one argument is more persuasive to you than the others.

1813
Indiana Territory capital is moved from Vincennes to Corydon

1816
Indiana becomes the nineteenth state

1851
Indiana's leaders write a new constitution

WHAT TO KNOW
How did the people of Indiana work to set up their new state?

VOCABULARY
census p. 119
enabling act p. 119
delegate p. 119
constitution p. 119
slavery p. 120
illegal p. 120

PEOPLE
Jonathan Jennings
James Madison

PLACES
Corydon

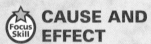

CAUSE AND EFFECT

Cause	Effect

A New State

YOU ARE THERE

It is the summer of 1816. You and your mother are walking down High Street in **Corydon**, Indiana. You see a group of men sitting under a large elm tree. They had been working inside the limestone courthouse, but the heat has driven them outdoors to the shade of the tree. Your mother tells you, "They are writing the plan for Indiana's government." You wonder what kind of plan they will make.

THE CONSTITUTION ELM served as the setting for the writing of Indiana's constitution.

▶ **THE HARRISON COUNTY COURTHOUSE** in Corydon was used as Indiana's state capitol from 1816 to 1825.

Statehood for Indiana

The Indiana Territory grew quickly. In 1813, the government moved the capital from Vincennes to Corydon. The 1815 census showed Indiana's population to be more than 63,000 free adults—enough to apply for statehood. A **census** is an official government count of people.

Steps Toward Statehood

Jonathan Jennings represented the Indiana Territory in Congress. Early in 1816, he asked Congress to pass an **enabling act**. This law would enable, or allow, Indiana to become a state. In April, President **James Madison** signed the enabling act into law.

The enabling act set Indiana's state boundaries. It also called for voters to elect **delegates**, or representatives, to attend a convention. Forty-three delegates met for this special meeting in Corydon in the summer of 1816.

Thirty-four of the delegates voted to form a state. The other nine delegates thought that Indiana needed more money, more people, and stronger leaders before it could become a state.

Because a majority voted to apply for statehood, the plan went forward. The delegates wrote a constitution for the future state. A **constitution** is a written plan for government.

READING CHECK ☝CAUSE AND EFFECT
What were the effects of the enabling act?

The Nineteenth State

The delegates signed Indiana's new constitution on June 29, 1816. Then they sent it to Washington, D.C. On December 11, 1816, President Madison signed the act that made Indiana the nineteenth state.

A Plan for Government

The Indiana Constitution of 1816 established the first state government. Like today's government, it was made up of the governor, General Assembly, and state supreme court.

The Indiana Constitution of 1816 promised to protect the basic rights of the people. These rights included freedom of religion and freedom of speech. However, the constitution did not give women, African Americans, or Native Americans the right to vote.

The delegates disagreed about the issue of slavery. **Slavery** is the practice of treating people as property. Some delegates wanted to allow it, but others believed it was wrong. Finally, the delegates voted to make slavery **illegal**, or against the law, in Indiana. They also wrote a section in the constitution that promised a state public school system.

Indiana Leaders

In August 1816, voters made their choices for leaders of the new government in elections. They chose Jonathan Jennings to be Indiana's first governor. They also chose the first representatives to the General Assembly.

The Indiana Constitution named Corydon as the state capital. Corydon remained the center of the state government until 1825.

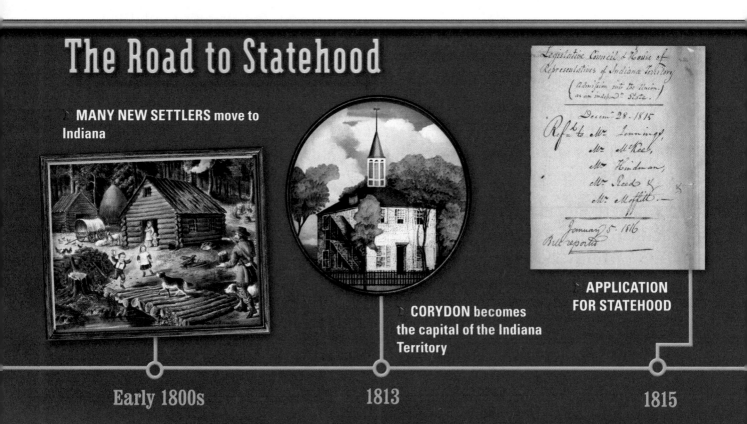

The Road to Statehood

▶ **MANY NEW SETTLERS** move to Indiana

▶ **CORYDON** becomes the capital of the Indiana Territory

▶ **APPLICATION FOR STATEHOOD**

Early 1800s   1813   1815

A New Constitution

The Constitution of 1816 served for 35 years. Then voters decided that the constitution needed to be revised. They elected 150 delegates to a second constitutional convention.

The Indiana Constitution of 1851 is still in use today. However, over the years, it has been amended, or changed, many times.

READING CHECK **SEQUENCE**
When did Indiana become a state?

Summary

Indiana became a state in 1816. Jonathan Jennings became the first governor. Corydon was named as the state capital. In 1851, a new constitution was written that is still in use today.

REVIEW

1. **WHAT TO KNOW** How did the people of Indiana work to set up their new state?

2. **VOCABULARY** Use the words **delegate** and **constitution** in a sentence about Indiana statehood.

3. **CIVICS AND GOVERNMENT** What did the Indiana Constitution of 1816 say about slavery?

4. **CRITICAL THINKING** What might have happened if most of the delegates at the convention in 1816 had voted against forming a new state?

5. **MAKE A FLOWCHART** Make a flowchart showing the steps that led to Indiana becoming a state.

6. **CAUSE AND EFFECT** On a separate sheet of paper, copy and complete this graphic organizer.

Cause		Effect
	→	The Indiana Territory applies for statehood.
Congress passes an enabling act.	→	

> **JONATHAN JENNINGS** and 42 other delegates sign Indiana's first constitution.

> **INDIANA** becomes the nineteenth state.

June 1816

December 1816

INDIANA'S CONSTITUTION

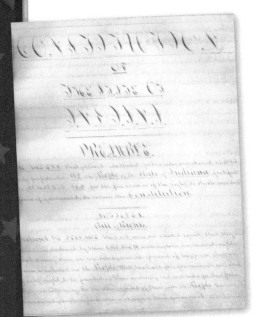

Indiana leaders approved its first constitution on June 29, 1816. The people of Indiana voted for a new constitution in 1851. The Constitution of 1851 set up the form of government that Indiana has today. Indiana's constitution describes the duties of the government. It also lists the rights and responsibilities of citizens.

The constitution's purpose is stated in the preamble, or introduction. The constitution provides justice, order, and freedom to the people of Indiana. The preamble states that the people have the right to freely choose their own form of government.

> ❯ **THE CONSTITUTION** Lawmakers in Indiana today (below) follow the laws set out in the Indiana Constitution of 1851 (above).

The Indiana Bill of Rights is the First Article of the Indiana Constitution. It lists the rights and freedoms promised to Indiana citizens. For example, people have the right to speak out and the right to worship as they please. Citizens also have the right to a fair trial in court if they are accused of a crime. The constitution protects these and other rights.

The Indiana Constitution also describes the responsibilities that citizens have. They have responsibilities to vote, to pay taxes, and to obey the law. By meeting these responsibilities, treating each other with respect, and working together for the common good, Hoosiers show how to be good citizens.

Make It Relevant What are some of the rights and responsibilities of citizens of Indiana?

VOTING Indiana voters have to show identification to recieve a ballot.

FREEDOM OF SPEECH Indiana University students exercise their right to free speech by protesting the closing of a library on campus.

Fun with Social Studies

Indiana Film FESTIVAL

SHOWING TONIGHT

MIAMI NICE
A year in the life of the Miami people!

The Kankakee River Runs Through It
Adventures of the La Salle expedition!

BEAUTY AND THE EAST
A journey along the Atlantic Coast

PATRIOT NAMES
Stories of George Rogers Clark and Francis Vigo

TICKETS

Odd Movie Out

Which movie doesn't belong in the Indiana Film Festival?

Museum Mix-up

Which two items do not belong in the *Early Native Americans of Indiana* exhibit?

Lenape longhouse

Potawatomi lacrosse stick

Comanche arrow

Legend written by Paleo-Indians

Shawnee warrior's bow

Miami wigwam

What's Behind There?

Write the letters that belong in the yellow squares in number order, and you'll know.

☐ ③ ⑦ ⑧ ☐
Someone who moves from place to place

☐ ☐ ☐ ⑨ ☐ ☐ ☐ ⑫
Long-lasting

☐ ④ ☐ ☐
A group of closely-related people

☐ ② ☐ ☐ ⑥
A settlement ruled by a faraway government

⑩ ☐ ⑤ ☐ ☐ ☐
Volunteer army

☐ ⑪ ① ☐ ☐ ⑬ ☐ ☐
A square of land made up of 36 sections

Online Adventures

GO ONLINE

This is the first clue I brought to find out about my ancestors. It is from my great-grandfather.

▶ GO ON!

HARCOURT

ECO

Eco has started a detective agency, but the first case looks tricky. Eco's client wants to find out who her great-grandparents were. To solve her case, you need to know the early history of Indiana. Log on to join the Eco Detective Agency, and solve the case of the lost ancestors. Play now at **www.harcourtschool.com/ss1**

Visual Summary

1679
La Salle explores
what is now Indiana

1770s
The Lenape arrive
in what is now Indiana

Summarize the Unit

Focus Skill **Cause and Effect** Complete this graphic organizer to show that you understand the causes and effects of the settlement of the Northwest Territory.

Cause

The United States has trouble paying Revolutionary War soldiers.

Effect

Cause

Effect

Conflict erupts between settlers and Native Americans in the Northwest Territory.

TEST PREP Vocabulary

Write a term from the word bank to complete each sentence.

1. A _____ is an area owned and governed by a country.

2. The practice of treating people as property is called _____.

3. The colonists fought a war to gain _____, or the freedom to govern themselves.

4. A _____ is an agreement among nations or groups.

5. An _____ is a journey to an area to learn more about it.

6. An early family member is an _____.

7. To _____ is to work at one kind of job and learn to do it well.

8. An object made by people in the past is an _____.

Word Bank

ancestor p. 77	**treaty** p. 96
specialize p. 84	**independence** p. 101
artifact p. 88	**territory** p. 109
expedition p. 94	**slavery** p. 120

1700   1800

1779
George Rogers Clark recaptures Fort Sackville

1795
The Treaty of Greenville is signed

Time Line

Use the unit summary time line above to answer these questions.

9. When did George Rogers Clark recapture Fort Sackville?

10. How many years after La Salle explored Indiana was the Treaty of Greenville signed?

Facts and Main Ideas

Answer these questions.

11. What caused Native Americans to stay in one place for longer periods of time?

12. Why did the French build trading posts in what is now Indiana?

13. How did the enabling act help Indiana become a state?

Write the letter of the best choice.

14. What was the name of the first group to settle in what is now Indiana?
    A Paleo-Indians
    B Adena
    C Woodland Indians
    D Archaic Indians

15. Which chief led the Native Americans in the Battle of Fallen Timbers?
    A Tecumseh
    B Michikinikwa
    C Tenskwatawa
    D Blue Jacket

Critical Thinking

Answer these questions.

16. How were Native American cultures dependent on their environment?

17. Why did many Native Americans in Indiana support the British during the American Revolution?

Skills

Compare Historical Maps

Look at the maps on page 99.

18. Which country controlled land north of the Ohio River before the French and Indian War?

19. Which country controlled Florida after the French and Indian War?

20. Which country controlled land west of the Mississippi River after the French and Indian War?

writing

Write a Narrative Imagine you are a Shawnee Indian in Indiana long ago. Write a short story that describes how you interact with the environment in your daily life.

Write a Summary Write a summary about the role of George Rogers Clark in the American Revolution.

Show What You Know

 ### Unit Writing Activity

Write a Narrative Imagine that your family is moving to Indiana shortly after the American Revolution.

■ Write a narrative about your travels. Describe the land you see and the people you meet.

■ Include details such as sights and sounds to illustrate time and place.

Unit Project

Publish a Newspaper Put together a newspaper that tells about life in Indiana before it became a state.

■ Create articles, advertisements, and cartoons for your newspaper.

■ Describe what people in your community do for a living and how they are affected by events.

Read More

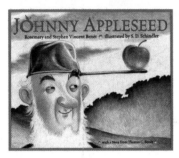

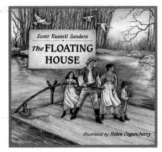

■ *Johnny Appleseed* by Rosemary and Stephen Vincent Benét. Margaret K. McElderry Books.

■ *The Floating House* by Scott Russell Sanders. Aladdin.

■ *The School at Crooked Creek* by Laurie Lawlor. Holiday House.

 For more resources, go to www.harcourtschool.com/ss1

Indiana's Later History

 Start with the Standards

INDIANA'S ACADEMIC STANDARDS FOR SOCIAL STUDIES

History 4.1.5, 4.1.6, 4.1.7, 4.1.8, 4.1.9, 4.1.10, 4.1.11, 4.1.12, 4.1.13, 4.1.14, 4.1.15, 4.1.16, 4.1.17

Civics and Government 4.2.6

Geography 4.3.9

Economics 4.4.1, 4.4.2

The Big Idea

Growth and Change

Historical events have caused Indiana to grow and change over time. People have also changed Indiana.

What to Know

- ✓ How did new communities start in Indiana?
- ✓ What role did Indiana play in the Civil War?
- ✓ How did Indiana grow and change in the nineteenth century?
- ✓ What events affected Indiana in the first part of the twentieth century?
- ✓ How did challenging times affect Indiana?
- ✓ How did Indiana change after World War II?
- ✓ How has Indiana changed in recent times?

Indiana Historic Sites

▶ A field in Historic Prophetstown

In honor of Indiana's past, places around the state have been named as historic sites. Visitors to these sites learn about events that happened there. They also learn about Hoosiers who lived long ago.

The city of Vincennes has many historic sites. When the Indiana Territory was formed, Vincennes became its capital. Visitors can see where the early government met. This place is a two-story building called the Red House.

Also in Vincennes is the Stout Print Shop. Indiana's first newspaper was printed in this shop. In addition, visitors can see Native American burial grounds at Sugar Loaf Mound. They can also visit a memorial to Revolutionary War hero George Rogers Clark.

▶ The Indianapolis home of the Hoosier poet James Whitcomb Riley is open to visitors.

▶ Abraham Lincoln's childhood home has become a living history museum.

Historic Prophetstown shows much of the history of Indiana's Wabash River valley. The town has a restored Shawnee Native American community. It also has a farm built to look like farms of the 1920s. Visitors can see how the state's farming industry has grown. Reenactors plow the fields, raise horses, and plant crops. Visitors can see a farmhouse, a barn, and animals.

Indiana keeps up the homes of some famous Hoosiers. The early home of painter T. C. Steele is in Nashville. Visitors can see the subjects of his works. The homes of writers James Whitcomb Riley and Gene Stratton-Porter are also preserved.

▶ Elihu Stout published the *Indiana Gazette* in this shop.

▪ INDIANA ✓TEST PREP

① **What was the capital of the Indiana Territory?**
A Terre Haute
B Indianapolis
C Vincennes
D Corydon

② **Which industry is shown in Historic Prophetstown?**
A manufacturing
B farming
C mining
D shipping

③ **In which city can visitors see the home of T. C. Steele?**
A Nashville
B Vincennes
C Historic Prophetstown
D Clarksville

④ **Writing** Why should historic sites in Indiana be preserved?

Time

Indiana's Later History

1800

1870

Indiana's Later History

Around 1910 The Great Migration begins, p. 168

1920 The Nineteenth Amendment is passed, p. 169

1964 The Civil Rights Act of 1964 is passed, p. 184

2001 Terrorists attack the United States, p. 189

1940

Present

1914 World War I begins

1945 World War II ends

Robert Owen

1771–1858
- Social reformer from Wales
- Started a model community in Indiana called New Harmony

Levi and Catharine Coffin

1798–1877, 1803–1881
- Quakers whose home in Fountain City, Indiana, was a safe house for people escaping slavery
- Helped more than 2,000 people reach freedom

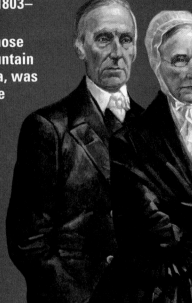

People

1750		1800		1850

1771 • Robert Owen   1858

1798 • Levi Coffin

1803 • Catharine Coffin

1814 • Sarah T. Bolton

1823 • Oliver P. Morton

1844 • May Wright Sewall

1857 •

May Wright Sewall

1844–1920
- Founded the Girls' Classical School of Indianapolis and served as principal
- Helped start the Indianapolis Equal Suffrage Society

Elwood Haynes

1857–1925
- Designed one of the first successful gasoline-powered automobiles
- Invented a material called stellite and helped develop stainless steel

Sarah T. Bolton

1814–1893
- Had her work published in newspapers from the age of 13
- Wrote many famous poems about Indiana, such as "Madison" and "Indiana"

Oliver P. Morton

1823–1877
- Governor of Indiana during the Civil War
- United States senator from 1867 to 1877

1900   **1950**   **Present**

7
881
1893
7
1920
ood Haynes   1925
1933 • Richard G. Hatcher
1956 • Janice Voss

Richard G. Hatcher

1933–
- Mayor of Gary, Indiana, for five terms
- Worked as a professor of African American studies at Indiana University Northwest

Janice Voss

1956–
- Earned a bachelor's degree in engineering science from Purdue University
- Took part in five spaceflights and has traveled almost 19 million miles in space

Unit 3

Place

Indiana in the United States, 1886

CANADA
Seattle
WASHINGTON TERRITORY
Portland
Columbia River
ROCKY MOUNTAINS
Missouri River
MONTANA TERRITORY
NORTH DAKOTA
Bismarck
Northern Pacific Railroad
OREGON
IDAHO TERRITORY
GREAT PLAINS
SOUTH DAKOTA
Snake River
WYOMING TERRITORY
Union Pacific Railroad
Platte River
NEBRASKA
Central Pacific Railroad
Great Salt Lake
Salt Lake City
Sacramento
Lake Tahoe
NEVADA
Omaha
San Francisco
UTAH TERRITORY
Denver
CALIFORNIA
COLORADO
KANSAS
Topeka
Colorado River
Arkansas River
Atlantic & Pacific Railroad
Los Angeles
Southern Pacific Railroad
Santa Fe
ARIZONA TERRITORY
INDIAN TERRITORY
NEW MEXICO TERRITORY
PACIFIC OCEAN
Dallas
El Paso
TEXAS
Southern Pacific Railroad
Houston
San Antonio
Rio Grande
MEXICO
At the Same Time
Transcontinental Railroad in operation

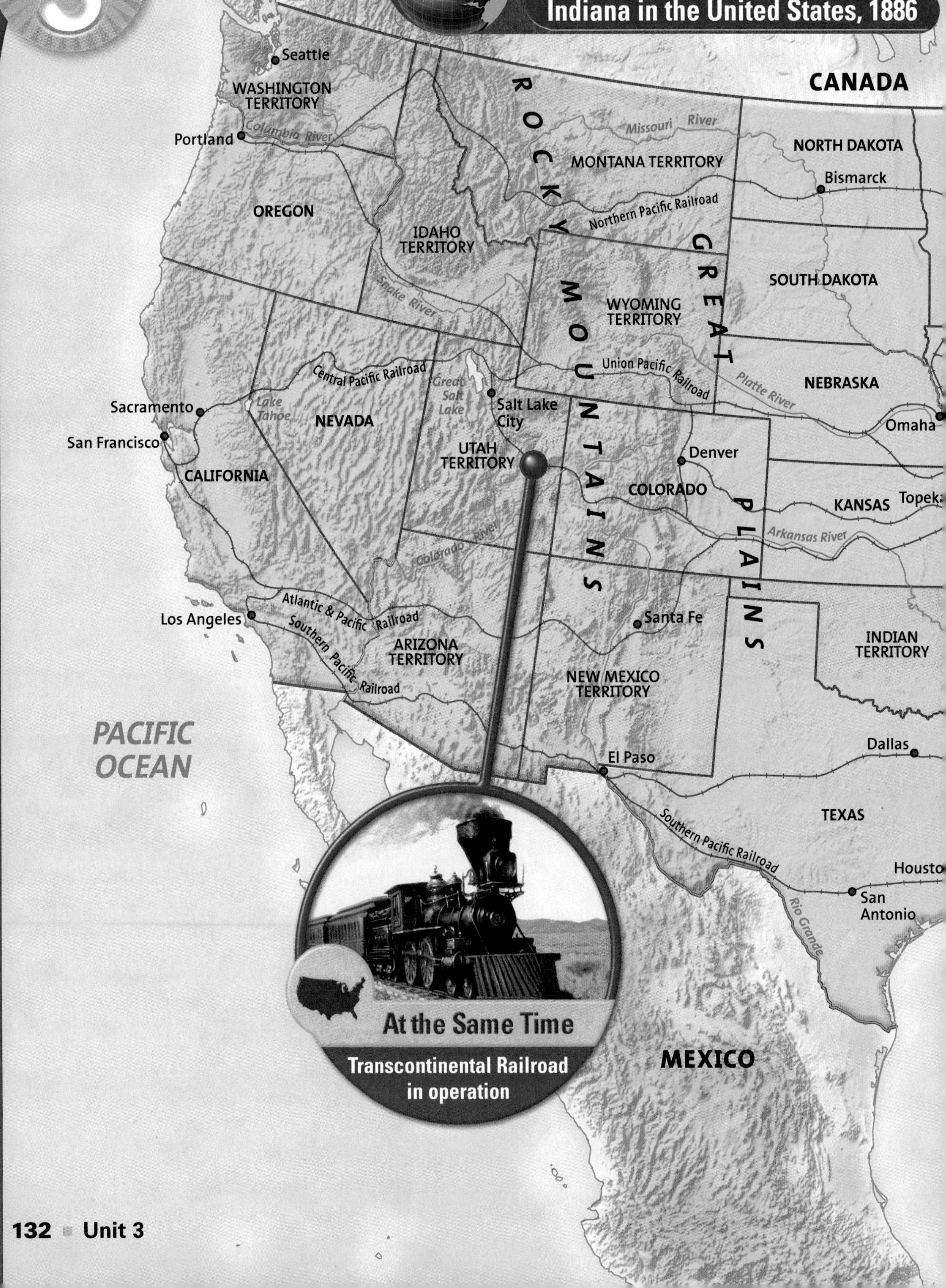

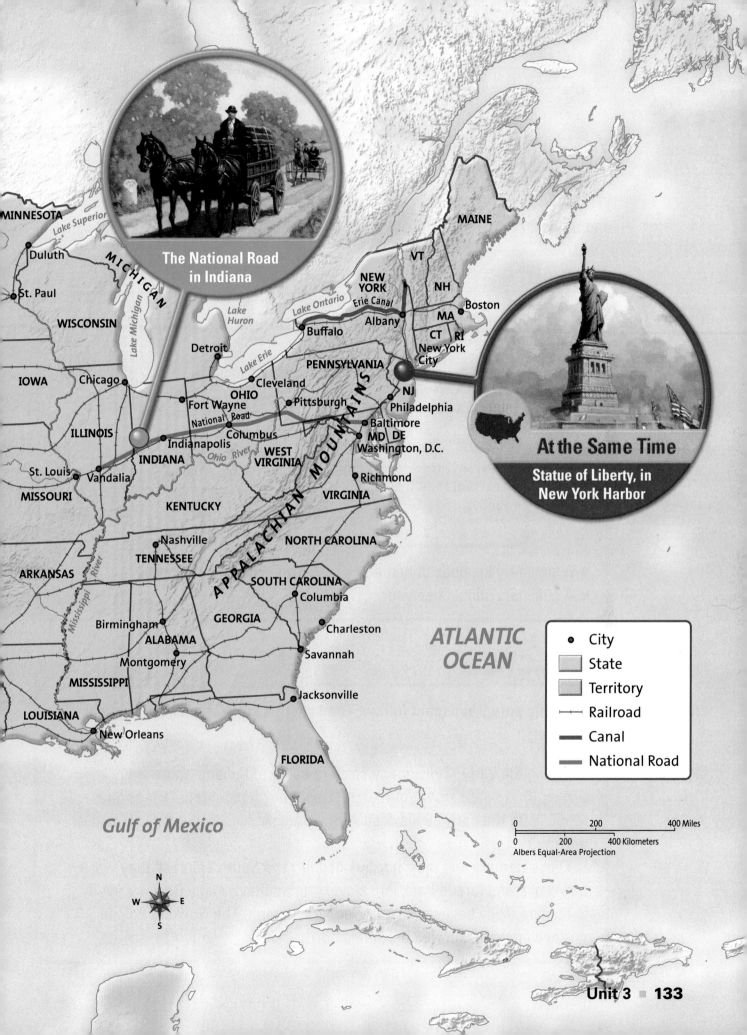

The National Road in Indiana

At the Same Time

Statue of Liberty, in New York Harbor

MINNESOTA
Lake Superior
Duluth
St. Paul
WISCONSIN

MICHIGAN
Lake Michigan
Lake Huron

MAINE
VT
NEW YORK
NH
Boston
Lake Ontario
Erie Canal
Albany
MA
Buffalo
CT RI
New York City

IOWA
Chicago
Detroit
Lake Erie
PENNSYLVANIA
Cleveland
OHIO
Pittsburgh
NJ
Fort Wayne
Philadelphia
National Road
Baltimore
ILLINOIS
Columbus
MD DE
Indianapolis
Washington, D.C.
Ohio River
INDIANA
St. Louis
WEST VIRGINIA
Vandalia
Richmond
MISSOURI

APPALACHIAN MOUNTAINS

VIRGINIA
KENTUCKY

Nashville
NORTH CAROLINA
TENNESSEE
ARKANSAS
Mississippi River
SOUTH CAROLINA
Columbia
GEORGIA
Charleston
Birmingham
ALABAMA
Savannah
Montgomery
MISSISSIPPI
Jacksonville
LOUISIANA
New Orleans
FLORIDA

ATLANTIC OCEAN

Gulf of Mexico

N
W E
S

Legend:
- City
- State
- Territory
- Railroad
- Canal
- National Road

0   200   400 Miles
0   200   400 Kilometers
Albers Equal-Area Projection

Reading Social Studies

Focus Skill Summarize

Why It Matters Summarizing a passage can help you understand and remember the most important information.

❯ LEARN

When you **summarize**, you state in your own words a shortened version of what you read.

Key Facts		Summary
Important idea from the reading	➤	Important information you read, shortened and written in your own words
Important idea from the reading	➤	

- A summary includes only the key facts from what you have read.
- A summary should use your own words.

❯ PRACTICE

Read the paragraphs that follow. Then write a summary for the second paragraph.

During the early 1800s, many settlers came to Indiana. **Some were free African Americans from Southern states. They bought land and began farming. (In the early 1800s, free African Americans settled and farmed in Indiana.)**

[Key Facts / Summary]

These farmers and their families had left the South because they were afraid of being forced back into slavery. In addition, many Quakers lived in Indiana. They believed that slavery was wrong. The Quakers helped enslaved people and free blacks go north.

Read the paragraphs, and answer the questions.

African American Settlements in Indiana

In about 1800, African Americans began settling in Indiana and in other parts of the Northwest Territory. By 1850, there were about 11,000 free blacks living in Indiana. Like most other settlers, African Americans were farmers and small-business owners. They often lived in small rural settlements. Two such settlements were the Huggart Settlement in St. Joseph County and the Roberts Settlement in Hamilton County.

Although Indiana was a free state, African Americans still faced many hardships. They were not allowed to vote or serve on juries. They often had to work the lowest-paid jobs. African American children could not attend public schools. Despite these hardships, African Americans created their own schools, often run by black churches. They also published their own newspapers. African Americans formed societies to work for equal rights.

Summarize

1. **What are the key facts in the passage?**
2. **How would you summarize the passage in your own words?**

ABE LINCOLN
THE BOY WHO LOVED BOOKS

WRITTEN BY KAY WINTERS

ILLUSTRATED BY NANCY CARPENTER

Abe Lincoln was born in 1809 in Kentucky. In 1816, his family moved to Perry County, Indiana. Life as a settler was a lot of hard work. Hard work helped Abe grow up to be our country's sixteenth President. Read now to find out what life was like for Abe Lincoln growing up.

They walked and rode
a hundred miles to Indiana.

They crossed the Ohio River
on a makeshift ferry.
Abe helped his father
hack a trail
through forests thick
    with trees
and tangled vines.
Until at last they came
to land they claimed.

No cabin waited
at Little Pigeon Creek.
Instead a half-faced camp
of branches, twigs, and logs
was where they had to stay.
One side opened wide
to wilderness.

The family kept the woodpile
    stacked.
The blazing fire
scared off wild animals
that roamed the woods.

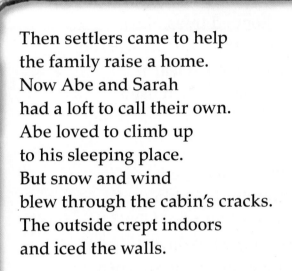

Then settlers came to help
the family raise a home.
Now Abe and Sarah
had a loft to call their own.
Abe loved to climb up
to his sleeping place.
But snow and wind
blew through the cabin's cracks.
The outside crept indoors
and iced the walls.

Just once
Abe shot a turkey in the woods.
But not again.
He vowed he would not
take the breath from living things.

When Abe was eight,
he helped his father
clear their land.
He learned to swing an ax
and fell the trees,
but he longed to learn from
books,
go back to school.

When Abe turned nine,
dark days fell upon him.
Milk sickness took his mother
to her grave.
Abe whittled pegs
to put in her pine coffin,
his grief so deep,
he could not speak her name.

A year limped by.
His father went to find a wife.
He brought back a widow
with three children.
Her heart so wide,
she took in Abe and Sarah
as her kin.

And she owned books!
She let Abe read when chores were
    done.
Once more their house of logs
became a home.

She sent the children
back to school.
Abe wore too-short buckskins
and a raccoon cap.
He drew his letters with
a turkey-buzzard quill.
"Abraham Lincoln
his hand and pen
he will be good but
God knows when."

He learned to add,
subtract on planks of wood.
But most of all he loved to read,
win spelling bees,
spin yarns, tell tales.

When school was shut,
Abe hired out to farmers.
His father kept the earnings
for the family.
Abe split rails, dug wells,
    chopped trees.
But all the while he worked,
he yearned to learn.
To anyone who'd listen
he liked to say, "The things
I want to know are in books."

Once rain leaked
through the cabin roof
and soaked a book he'd borrowed.
For three hot days
Abe pulled stalks of corn
in his friend's field
to pay him back.

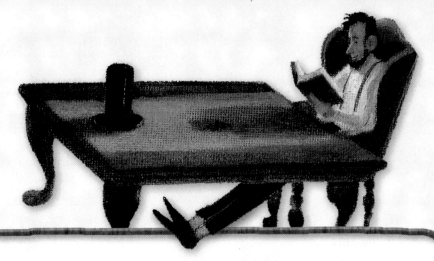

When Abe plowed,
a book sat in his back pocket.
At each row's end
he'd take it out and read.
His horse would wait
for him to turn the page.
The neighbors shook their heads
and called him lazy.

They did not understand this
   bookish boy.
Abe knew he must move on,
out of the wilderness.

Splitting rails and plowing land
was not his dream.

***

Abraham Lincoln—
born in a log cabin,
child of the frontier,
head in a book—
elected our sixteenth president!
From the wilderness
to the White House.
He learned the power of words
and used them well.

Response Corner

1. **Focus Skill** **Summarize** Why did Abe Lincoln love books?

2. **Make It Relevant** How was Abe Lincoln's childhood different from yours?

Lesson

Time

1800   **Present**

1825
The state capital is
moved from Corydon
to Indianapolis

1838
The Potawatomi are
forced to march the
Trail of Death

1855
Seven railroad lines
connect Indianapolis
to other cities

WHAT TO KNOW
**How did new
communities start in
Indiana?**

VOCABULARY
migration p. 141

flatboat p. 144

steamboat p. 144

navigable p. 144

stagecoach p. 145

PEOPLE
Abraham Lincoln
George Rapp
Robert Owen
John Tipton
Alexander Ralston
Sarah T. Bolton
Robert Fulton
Andrew Jackson

PLACES
Harmonie
New Harmony
Knox County
Indianapolis

SUMMARIZE

New Communities

YOU ARE THERE
The year is 1818. Your family has decided
to leave its farm in Kentucky and move
to southern Indiana. Indiana has cheap land and
rich soil for farming. You pack your wagon and
cross the Ohio River. You will have a lot of work
to do when you get to your new home. Your family and other settlers will have to clear the forest
and build homes. Indiana has few good roads,
so trade is difficult. You will have to make everything you need.

▶ **SETTLERS ON THE MOVE** Many early settlers to Indiana crossed
the Ohio River from Kentucky.

Young Abraham Lincoln

Everyone on the frontier had to work to survive—including children. In 1816, Abraham Lincoln and his parents settled in what is now Indiana. "It was a wild region, with many bears and other wild animals still in the woods," Lincoln later remembered.

Even though he was only seven years old, Abe did a lot of work. He cleared trees and bushes and split logs for firewood. He helped his father build the family's log cabin and helped plant and harvest crops. Many people today think Lincoln's frontier experiences helped him become a great President.

Make It Relevant How might hard work help make a good leader?

A Thriving State

During the early 1800s, thousands of Americans migrated to Indiana and other lands west of the Appalachian Mountains. **Migration** is the movement of people from one place to live in another place. One traveler wrote in 1817 that it seemed as if the United States were "breaking up and moving westward."

Population Growth

At this time, Indiana had a great deal of land available for sale. Settlers who moved to the new state were looking for the chance to build a better life. People bought land, and the population grew quickly. It rose from about 24,000 people in 1810 to about 343,000 people in 1830.

Pioneers Come to Indiana

Most early settlers to Indiana came from southern states. Later settlers came from New England and Mid-Atlantic states.

The Quakers moved to Indiana in the early 1800s. They came from North Carolina, South Carolina, and Virginia. They were drawn to Indiana by the state's fertile farmland and opposition to slavery. European immigrants, especially the Germans and the Irish, came to Indiana in the 1830s.

Pioneers came to Indiana by horse and wagon or traveled in rafts down the Ohio River. Some pioneers, such as **Abraham Lincoln** and his family, crossed the Ohio River from Kentucky.

READING CHECK ⏻SUMMARIZE
Where did Indiana's pioneers come from?

Indiana Grows

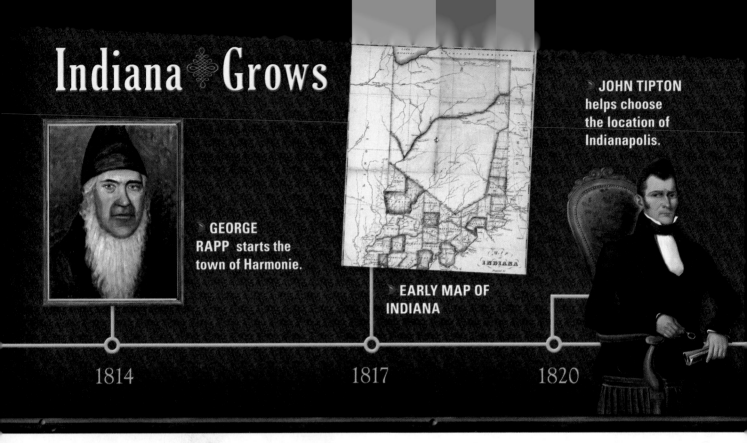

GEORGE RAPP starts the town of Harmonie.

EARLY MAP OF INDIANA

JOHN TIPTON helps choose the location of Indianapolis.

1814   1817   1820

Growing Communities

At first, most pioneer families lived far from their neighbors. Trade was difficult, so families had to be self-sufficient. Pioneers hunted and grew their own food. They also made their own clothes, furniture, and medicine.

Pioneers got together to help one another clear land, plant and harvest crops, and build houses and barns. They also gathered for religious and social meetings. Eventually, they began forming communities.

New Harmony

A few towns in Indiana started as planned communities. **George Rapp** was a preacher who did not have the freedom to preach about his beliefs when he was in his German homeland. He and his followers, called Harmonists, moved to the United States. In 1814, Rapp built the town of **Harmonie** (HAR•muh•nee) in Indiana. In 1825, the Harmonists sold their land to **Robert Owen** and moved away.

Owen renamed the settlement **New Harmony**. He wanted to make the community a center for education and social equality. Owen invited more than 1,000 world-famous scientists, writers, and teachers from the United States and Europe to move to New Harmony. Although the town was not a success, many of its talented residents stayed in Indiana.

The Formation of Counties

As settlers continued to move into Indiana, they needed to organize local governments. To help them do this, the Indiana General Assembly

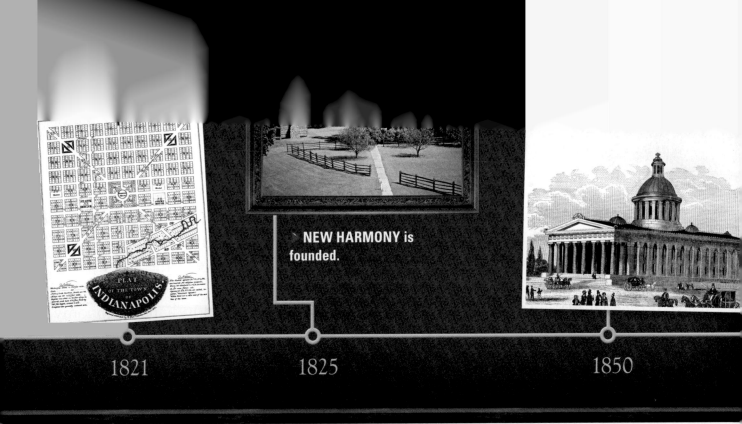

> **NEW HARMONY is founded.**

1821   1825   1850

created new counties. Each county had its own government, which was responsible for collecting taxes, protecting citizens, and making laws. In 1816, **Knox County** took up most of Indiana. Over time, many other counties were formed from it.

Indianapolis

Most early Indiana pioneers settled in the southern part of the state. In time, people began settling in central and northern Indiana. State leaders began to think that Corydon, Indiana's first capital, was located too far south to remain the capital.

In 1820, the General Assembly set up a commission to select a new location for the state capital. **John Tipton** and the other members of the commission chose an area in the center of the state. The General Assembly accepted the site in 1821 and named the new capital **Indianapolis**, or "city of Indiana."

The General Assembly hired **Alexander Ralston** to develop a plan for the city. He had earlier worked on the plan for Washington, D.C. In 1824, wagons carried the state's records to the new capital. By 1825, government business was taking place in Indianapolis.

Two years later, about 1,000 people lived in the city. In 1832, Nathaniel Bolton and **Sarah T. Bolton** came to Indianapolis. Nathaniel was the editor of a newspaper called the *Indiana Democrat*. Sarah became famous for writing poems and songs about her home state of Indiana.

READING CHECK **MAIN IDEA AND DETAILS**
Why did lawmakers move the state capital?

Transportation

Transportation was a challenge for Indiana's pioneers. However, new ways of travel introduced in the 1800s helped the state grow and change.

Steamboats

Early pioneers used flatboats to take goods to market and to carry people. A **flatboat** was a large, flat-bottomed boat that could only float downstream.

A better way of going up and down rivers came when **Robert Fulton** invented a steam-powered boat in the early 1800s. A **steamboat** has a large paddle wheel and is powered by steam. Steamboats traveled up and down **navigable** rivers, or rivers that were wide and deep enough for ships.

Canals

Indiana's only navigable rivers were the Ohio River and the Wabash River. Many farmers lived far from these two rivers. Canals gave them a way to get to the rivers more easily.

The Wabash and Erie Canal was the longest canal built in Indiana. It was begun in 1832. Eventually, the canal connected Lake Erie to the Wabash and Ohio Rivers.

Canals improved Indiana's economy by giving farmers a better way to get their goods to market. Many workers, mostly immigrants, came to build the canals. Some settled in Indiana. However, canals caused the state to take on debt to pay for them. By the 1840s, canal construction in Indiana had stopped.

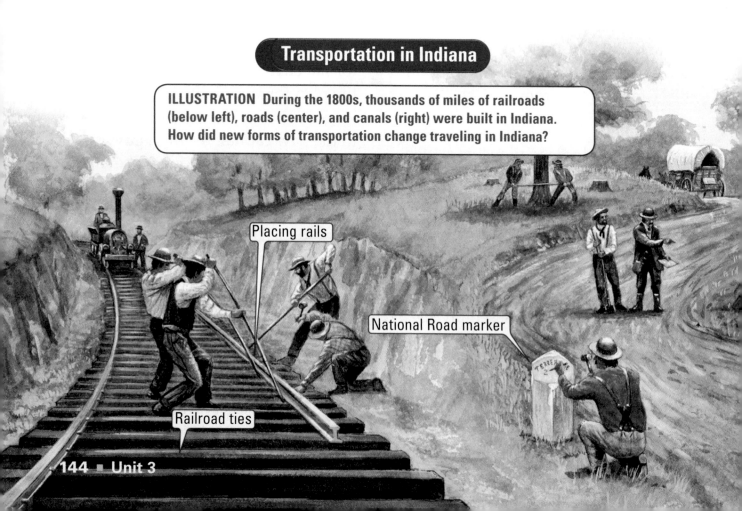

Transportation in Indiana

ILLUSTRATION During the 1800s, thousands of miles of railroads (below left), roads (center), and canals (right) were built in Indiana. How did new forms of transportation change traveling in Indiana?

Placing rails

National Road marker

Railroad ties

Roads

The United States government began work on the National Road in 1811. The road started in Cumberland, Maryland, and was built across Indiana in the 1830s. By 1839, it ran through Richmond, Terre Haute, and Indianapolis and connected Indiana to states in the East and West.

Indiana's leaders wanted to connect the state's towns with one another and with places outside the state. To do this, they began building the Michigan Road in the 1820s. The road linked Madison, on the Ohio River, to Michigan City in the north.

Wagons and stagecoaches carried people and goods along these roads. A **stagecoach** was a wagon with a closed carriage, pulled by horses.

Railroads

A new form of transportation was also becoming popular. Railroads were being built across the United States and Indiana.

Indiana's first railroad line, a single railroad car pulled by horses, linked Madison and Indianapolis. By 1855, seven lines ran into Indianapolis, nicknamed "Railroad City."

Travel on railroads was faster and more dependable than on canals. Trains could carry more passengers than wagons or stagecoaches. They could also carry more goods than flatboats or steamboats. Cities located along railroad lines grew quickly.

READING CHECK ☼SUMMARIZE

What changes in transportation occurred in Indiana during the 1800s?

Stone for canal edge

Canal boat

▶ **GIVING UP LANDS** Artist George Winter painted the Potawatomi signing a land treaty.

Indian Removal

President **Andrew Jackson** wanted to make more land available for settlers. On May 28, 1830, he signed the Indian Removal Act. Under this law, Native Americans living east of the Mississippi River would have to move west to what are now Kansas, Oklahoma, and Texas.

In 1838, more than 800 Potawatomi were forced to leave Indiana. Under armed guard, they marched to Kansas. This march became known as the Trail of Death because 42 Native Americans died along the way. The Miami were also forced to leave Indiana and resettle in Kansas.

READING CHECK **MAIN IDEA AND DETAILS**
What was the Trail of Death?

Summary

Indiana's population increased during its early years as a state. Many communities were formed. During this time, new developments in transportation helped Indiana grow and change. Native Americans were forced to leave Indiana and settle in western lands.

REVIEW

1. **WHAT TO KNOW** How did new communities start in Indiana?

2. **VOCABULARY** Use the words **steamboat** and **navigable** in a sentence about river travel.

3. **HISTORY** How did new forms of transportation improve life in Indiana?

4. **CRITICAL THINKING** How might Indiana be different today if President Jackson had not signed the Indian Removal Act?

5. **MAKE AN ADVERTISEMENT** Make an advertisement to persuade people to come live in New Harmony.

6. **SUMMARIZE** (Focus Skill) On a separate sheet of paper, copy and complete this graphic organizer.

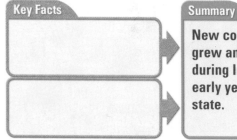

Key Facts		Summary
	→	New communities grew and changed during Indiana's early years as a state.
	→	

Robert Owen

Trustworthiness
Respect
Responsibility
Fairness
Caring
Patriotism

"*I know that society may be formed so as to exist without crime, without poverty, with health greatly improved.*"

Robert Owen was born in Newtown, in Wales. At the age of ten, he became an apprentice in a drapery business in London. Owen later became part-owner of the New Lanark cotton mills in Scotland. There, he started a nursery school where children were cared for while their mothers worked at the mills.

Owen believed that businesses should take care of workers' needs. In 1825, he took his ideas to the United States. Owen started the town of New Harmony in Indiana. He wanted it to be a utopia, or perfect society.

New Harmony had the country's first kindergarten. It also had the first school system that offered equal education to boys and girls. However, economic problems and disagreements between the residents led to the town's failure in 1827. Owen returned to Britain, where he continued to write about social reform.

Why Character Counts

How did Robert Owen's actions show caring?

Time

1771	1858
Born	Died

1800 Owen becomes the head of the New Lanark mills

1825 Owen starts the town of New Harmony, Indiana

GO ONLINE
For more resources, go to
www.harcourtschool.com/ss1

FIELD TRIP

READ ABOUT

In 1823, trader and community leader William Conner built a home for his family on the prairie. Today, his house is part of the Conner Prairie Living History Museum in Fishers, Indiana. This museum covers 1,400 acres and re-creates the life of early settlers in Indiana.

Among the museum's exhibits, you can observe people cooking or see a one-room schoolhouse. You can see the restored Conner house and farm.

At the 1816 Lenape Indian Camp, visitors can learn about the culture of the Lenape. There, you can help make a wigwam and grind corn.

FIND

INDIANA

Fishers

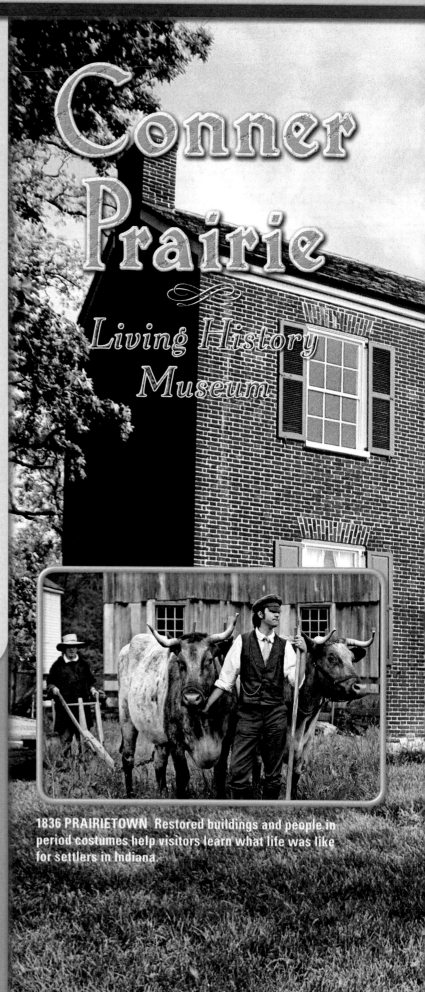

Conner Prairie
Living History Museum

1836 PRAIRIETOWN Restored buildings and people in period costumes help visitors learn what life was like for settlers in Indiana.

PIONEER VILLAGE

MAKING POTTERY

GENERAL STORE

MEALS LONG AGO

LENAPE CAMP

CONNER HOMESTEAD The Conner house is thought to be the first brick home built in central Indiana. Visitors can explore the house and surrounding buildings, such as the barn and the Loom House.

A VIRTUAL TOUR

GO ONLINE For more resources, go to www.harcourtschool.com/ss1

Time

1800   **Present**

1826
Levi and Catharine
Coffin begin helping
enslaved people
escape slavery

1861
The Civil War begins

1865
The Civil War ends

The Civil War

WHAT TO KNOW
What role did Indiana play in the Civil War?

VOCABULARY
plantation p. 151
slave state p. 151
free state p. 151
abolitionist p. 151
Underground Railroad
 p. 152
secede p. 154
civil war p. 154

PEOPLE
Chapman Harris
George DeBaptiste
Levi and Catharine Coffin
Oliver P. Morton
James Lanier
Lew Wallace
John Hunt Morgan

PLACES
Fountain City
Republic of Liberia
Camp Morton

SUMMARIZE

Key Facts	Summary

YOU ARE THERE The year is 1845. Your family is running away from slavery in the South. You have been traveling north for months. You've gotten little help, and you're afraid of being caught. However, a Kentucky farmer has promised to take you in his wagon across the Ohio River tomorrow. Then some people in Indiana will help you move even farther north to freedom.

▶ **ESCAPING SLAVERY** About 100,000 people escaped slavery between 1810 and 1850.

Free States and Slave States

Free state
Slave state
Territory

MAP SKILL **REGIONS** This map shows the United States in about 1860. How many free states were there? How many slave states?

North and South

Since colonial times, enslaved Africans had been forced to work in North America on **plantations**, huge farms that grew crops such as cotton, rice, and tobacco.

By 1840, there were almost 2.5 million enslaved Africans in the United States. Most lived in Southern states, where slavery was legal. These state were known as **slave states**.

Slavery was against the law in the Northern states, including Indiana. These states were known as **free states**. As new states were added, Congress tried to keep a balance between free states and slave states.

The Issue of Slavery

Arguments about slavery were dividing the nation. Some people wanted the government to abolish, or end, slavery. They were known as **abolitionists**. Other people wanted to limit the spread of slavery. Still others felt that states should decide for themselves whether to allow slavery.

Although Indiana was a free state, not all Hoosiers were abolitionists. Some felt that slavery should be allowed to continue in states where it already existed.

READING CHECK **☼SUMMARIZE**

How did the issue of slavery divide the United States during the mid-1800s?

Indiana Abolitionists

Many Hoosiers fought slavery. Two Indiana politicians, Stephen S. Harding and George W. Julian, were well-known abolitionists. They gave speeches and wrote newspaper articles against slavery.

The Underground Railroad

Some abolitionists helped enslaved people escape on a system of secret routes known as the **Underground Railroad**. The routes led to places, such as Canada, where slavery was against the law. Along the routes, runaways were fed and given shelter by people who opposed slavery.

The homes where runaways hid were called stations. The people who helped move runaways from one station to another were known as conductors. Most Underground Railroad conductors were free African Americans or white Northerners.

Two well-known African American conductors in Indiana were **Chapman Harris** and **George DeBaptiste**. They lived in Jefferson County along the Ohio River. Both faced many dangers to help enslaved people reach safety.

Some religious organizations, such as African American churches and the Quakers, were involved in helping enslaved people escape. In 1826, Quakers **Levi** and **Catharine Coffin** opened their home in **Fountain City**, Indiana, to runaways. The Coffins helped more than 2,000 enslaved people reach freedom.

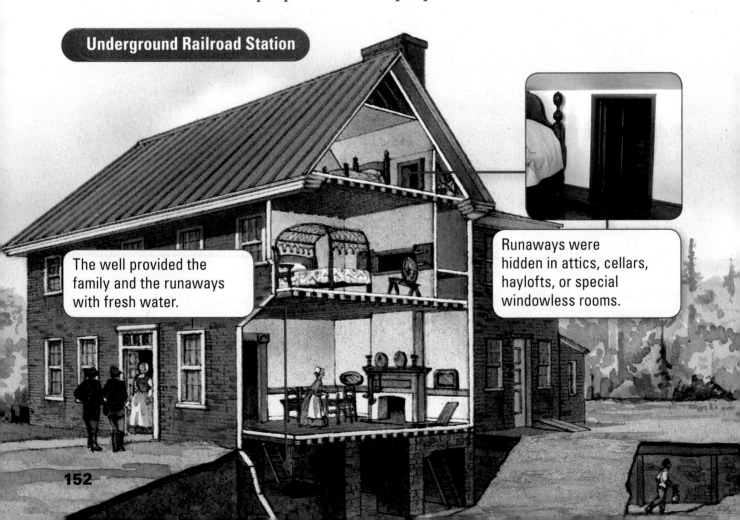

Underground Railroad Station

The well provided the family and the runaways with fresh water.

Runaways were hidden in attics, cellars, haylofts, or special windowless rooms.

Levi Coffin said of his work,

> **"I was willing to receive and aid as many fugitives [runaways] as were disposed [wanted] to come to my house."**

Anti-Slavery Groups

In the 1830s, many people in Indiana formed groups to oppose slavery. These groups were called anti-slavery societies, and they were often supported by churches.

Lyman Hoyt was a founding member of the Neil's Creek Anti-Slavery Society. He was also a conductor on the Underground Railroad.

The Henry County Female Anti-Slavery Society asked Congress to abolish slavery. Although the women themselves could not vote, they encouraged their male relatives to vote against slavery.

Colonization Movement

Some people in Indiana and elsewhere believed that free African Americans should leave their homes in the United States to settle in the **Republic of Liberia**, in West Africa.

In 1829, the Indiana Colonization Society formed. Its members provided money for resettlement. Between 1840 and 1862, as many as 83 free African Americans from Indiana went to live in Liberia. Very few African Americans supported colonization. Most did not want to leave their homes in Indiana.

READING CHECK **MAIN IDEA AND DETAILS**
How did Indiana's abolitionists help runaway enslaved people?

ILLUSTRATION Many stations on the Underground Railroad had special places for hiding runaways. Why do you think many runaways traveled at night?

Wagons with false bottoms were used to hide runaways.

Tunnels were used to travel underground.

Indiana Soldiers

▶ **FIGHTING FOR THE UNION** Many Indiana soldiers trained at Camp Morton (above). African American Hoosiers fought on the side of the Union during the Civil War (left). This flag belonged to the Twenty-Eighth Regiment of the United States Colored Troops.

The Civil War in Indiana

In 1861, Abraham Lincoln became President of the United States. Many Southerners believed that President Lincoln would abolish slavery. For this reason, 11 Southern states **seceded**, or withdrew, from the United States. They formed their own government called the Confederate States of America, or the Confederacy.

Hoosiers in the Civil War

President Lincoln wanted to keep together the United States, known as the Union. In 1861, however, Confederate soldiers fired on Union troops at Fort Sumter in South Carolina. This battle marked the start of the American Civil War. A **civil war** is a war between people in the same country.

Oliver P. Morton served as governor of Indiana during the Civil War. To aid the Union, Morton helped raise twice the number of volunteers requested by President Lincoln.

About 200,000 Hoosiers served in the Union army. **James Lanier**, a banker from Madison, lent money to the state of Indiana. This money was used to provide supplies to the Union army.

Some Hoosiers enlisted in the Twenty-Eighth Regiment of the United States Colored Troops. This all–African American regiment included many formerly enslaved people.

Governor Morton appointed General **Lew Wallace** to raise an army of volunteers. Many new recruits trained at

Camp Morton, near Indianapolis. The camp was later a prison for captured Confederate soldiers.

Some Hoosiers, called Peace Democrats, wanted to save the Union without using military action. A few Hoosiers wanted the Confederacy to win. They were called copperheads, after the name of a poisonous snake.

Morgan's Raid

Only one Civil War battle took place in Indiana. In 1863, Confederate general **John Hunt Morgan** led about 2,000 soldiers from Kentucky across the Ohio River into southern Indiana.

Union forces tried to stop Morgan in what became known as the Battle of Corydon. However, the Confederates won the battle. Morgan's Raiders then continued north, burning bridges, stores, and farms. Along the way, they stole food, money, and horses.

Governor Morton asked General Wallace to organize troops to protect Indianapolis. When Morgan heard this, his Raiders moved into Ohio. A few weeks later, Union forces captured Morgan and his soldiers.

The Home Front

More than 25,000 Hoosiers died in the Civil War. Those who did not fight were also affected by the war. Many women took over businesses and farms while men were away fighting. Others worked as nurses at military hospitals. Some women even worked at the state arsenal, or a place where weapons are stored, in Indianapolis.

> **MORGAN'S RAIDERS** fought Union troops in Indiana before they entered Montgomery, Ohio, on July 14, 1863.

> **EMANCIPATION PROCLAMATION** President Lincoln reads the Emancipation Proclamation to his cabinet.

An End to Slavery

In 1863, President Lincoln issued the Emancipation Proclamation. It gave freedom to enslaved people in the Confederate states. On April 9, 1865, Confederate general Robert E. Lee met with Union general Ulysses S. Grant at Appomattox Court House in Virginia. There, Grant wrote out the terms of surrender for Lee to sign. The Union had won the Civil War.

READING CHECK ☼SUMMARIZE
How did Hoosiers help the Union during the Civil War?

Summary

The issue of slavery divided the United States. Many Hoosiers helped enslaved people find freedom. Disagreements between the North and the South led to a civil war. Hoosiers fought on the side of the Union. The Union won the war in 1865.

REVIEW

1. **WHAT TO KNOW** What role did Indiana play in the Civil War?

2. **VOCABULARY** What is the difference between a **free state** and a **slave state?**

3. **HISTORY** How did women help the war effort in Indiana?

4. **CRITICAL THINKING** What effects do you think the Civil War had on Indiana?

5. ✎ **WRITE A REPORT** Using a variety of information sources, write a report about the Underground Railroad in Indiana.

6. ⭐(Focus Skill) **SUMMARIZE** On a separate sheet of paper, copy and complete this graphic organizer.

Key Facts	Summary
Enslaved Africans worked on plantations in the South.	
Many Northerners were abolitionists.	

Levi and Catharine Coffin

Biography

Trustworthiness
Respect
Responsibility
Fairness
Caring
Patriotism

"We knew not what night or hour of the night we would be roused . . . by a gentle rap at the door."

Levi and Catharine Coffin were Quakers who opposed slavery. They became conductors on the Underground Railroad in 1826. Their house in Fountain City, Indiana, became a station on the Underground Railroad.

The Coffins kept a team of horses and a wagon ready to help fugitives who had come across the Ohio River to Indiana from Kentucky. The Coffins helped more than 2,000 enslaved people reach safety. After the Civil War, Levi Coffin became a leader in the Western Freedmen's Aid Society. He helped raise money for freedmen, or formerly enslaved people.

Today, the Coffins' house is open to the public. Visitors can see the hidden upstairs room and the wagon with a false bottom that Levi Coffin used to transport runaways.

Why Character Counts

How did Levi and Catharine Coffin show trustworthiness?

Time

1790 — 1885

1824 Levi Coffin marries Catharine White

1826 The Coffins move to Fountain City, Indiana

GO ONLINE For more resources, go to www.harcourtschool.com/ss1

Distinguish Facts

Why It Matters Knowing whether a statement is a fact, an opinion, or fiction helps you understand what you read.

❯ LEARN

Facts are statements that can be proved or supported by evidence. Facts often give names, places, and dates that you can check. You can look up these facts in reference books, such as encyclopedias.

Opinions are statements that cannot be proved. They tell what a person thinks or believes. An opinion may include words such as *I think*, *I believe*, or *in my opinion*.

Fiction is made up. Fiction may be about people and events that seem real but are imaginary. Examples of fiction include legends, novels, cartoons, and many television shows and movies.

THE UNDERGROUND RAILROAD

The Underground Railroad was a system of routes that helped enslaved people from the South escape to Northern states during the mid-1800s. The Underground Railroad was neither underground nor a railroad. It was called the Underground Railroad because its activities were carried out in secret, in darkness, or in disguise. The runaways and the people who helped them used code words to communicate.

❯ Harriet Tubman (far left), an African American who had escaped from slavery herself, guided more than 300 people to safety along the Underground Railroad.

▶ PRACTICE

Read the three selections below. Then answer these questions.

1 Which selection is mainly fiction? How do you know?

2 Which selection is mainly opinion? What clues tell you this?

3 Which selection contains the most facts? What sources can you use to check those facts?

▶ APPLY

Make It Relevant Look through a local newspaper. Find a story that contains facts and opinions. Circle the facts. Underline the opinions. What part of the newspaper has examples of fiction?

B

Adam and his mother hid in the forest. They huddled together, wrapped in a quilt. Adam was scared they would be caught. He noticed a pattern of bears' paws on the quilt. His grandmother had told him that the quilt contained a secret message that would help them find a way to freedom. Was this a clue that would help him?

C

Dear Sister Sally,

Last week, two more runaways stayed with us. They came to us in a pitiful condition, hungry and tired. We let them rest for a night in our attic room and sent them on their way with some clothing, food, and a little money. I hope they reach Canada safely.

I know that what we are doing is dangerous, but I believe it is our duty to aid people trying to escape slavery. I think slavery goes against the values of our Constitution and should be illegal.

Your affectionate brother,
William

Time

1800   Present

• **1865**   • **1876**   • **1906**
The Thirteenth   Eli Lilly invents a way   U.S. Steel builds
Amendment   to coat pills with gelatin   the town of Gary
is ratified   for its workers

WHAT TO KNOW
How did Indiana grow and change in the nineteenth century?

VOCABULARY
Reconstruction p. 161
sharecropping p. 161
automobile p. 162
manufacturing p. 163
refinery p. 163
labor union p. 164

PEOPLE
James Oliver
Eli Lilly
Elwood Haynes
Ball brothers
Elbert H. Gary
Benjamin Harrison
Eugene V. Debs

PLACES
Kokomo
Muncie
Calumet region
Gary
Fort Wayne

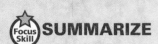

SUMMARIZE

Changes in Indiana

YOU ARE THERE It's a very cold morning in Cannelton in 1850. You're on your way to your job in a cotton mill. Children as young as ten years old also work there. A rush of warm air hits you when you open the door. Bits of fine cotton fiber float in the air and make you cough. You hear the machinery clank. You take your place at your workstation. Your boss signals everyone to start working. Another long day of work begins.

CHILD LABOR Children, such as this girl at an Evansville cotton mill, worked at factories in Indiana.

Time of Reconstruction

After the Civil War ended in 1865, the hard feelings between the North and the South continued. Thousands of soldiers on both sides had been killed. Many buildings, railroads, and bridges were destroyed during the war. The South's economy was in ruins. Both sides faced the challenge of bringing the nation back together. This period of rebuilding is called **Reconstruction**.

Constitutional Amendments

In December 1865, the Thirteenth Amendment to the Constitution was ratified. It ended slavery in the United States. The Fifteenth Amendment, passed in 1870, says that no citizen can be denied the right to vote because of race.

African Americans

Many formerly enslaved people did not have land or money. To survive, many began **sharecropping**, or farming a landowner's property for a share of the crop. Others moved to cities in Indiana and other Northern states to look for jobs in factories.

The Freedmen's Bureau was created to help formerly enslaved people. It provided people with food and money and built schools where African Americans could learn new skills. However, African Americans still faced threats. In many Southern states, African Americans were denied rights.

READING CHECK ⏱SUMMARIZE
What happened during Reconstruction?

> SHARECROPPING Under this system, the landowner took a share of all the crop raised. Most workers' shares were very little, if anything at all.

> FREEDMEN'S BUREAU SCHOOL

> THE FIFTEENTH AMENDMENT (left) g African American men the right to vote.

Industries Grow

The late nineteenth century and early twentieth century brought many changes to Indiana. Industries in the state grew rapidly.

Changes in Agriculture

In the late 1800s, most Hoosiers still made their living by farming. New technologies made farm work easier and faster. Horse-drawn reapers cut and bundled grain. Steam-powered threshers quickly separated wheat grains from stalks. **James Oliver** invented a new kind of plow that did not break in the thick prairie soil.

Farmers found out about new farming methods from state fairs and agricultural societies. New methods led to the creation of new industries. For example, milling grain into flour grew into an industry. Raising hogs also became a big industry in Indiana.

New Businesses

Some new businesses used natural resources to make products. In 1852, the H & C Studebaker blacksmith shop in South Bend began making wagons from Indiana timber.

Inventors started other new businesses. In 1876, Indianapolis pharmacist **Eli Lilly** invented a way to coat pills with gelatin. He started Eli Lilly and Company, now one of the world's largest drug companies.

Elwood Haynes invented one of the first gasoline-powered **automobiles**, or cars, in 1894. He formed a company in **Kokomo**, Indiana, that sold some of the first cars in the United States.

INDIANA INDUSTRIALISTS

Agriculture ✝ Business ✝ Manufacturing

➤ **JAMES OLIVER invented the chilled iron plow.**

➤ **THE BALL BROTHERS FACTORY produced jars and other glass products.**

Manufacturing

Indiana's natural resources and its transportation systems helped manufacturing grow in the state. **Manufacturing** is the making of finished products from raw materials.

In 1886, natural gas was discovered in northern Indiana, near Portland. Natural gas was an important source of fuel for factories. Government leaders offered free natural gas to businesses from other states that built factories in Indiana.

In 1888, the **Ball brothers** were offered free land and natural gas in **Muncie**, Indiana. They moved their glass factory from New York. It soon became the largest producer of glass jars in the United States. The glass industry grew quickly. By 1905, there were 71 glass factories in Indiana.

Some manufacturers moved to the **Calumet region** of Indiana, near Lake Michigan. This region had inexpensive land, supplies of oil, and access to transportation by rail and water. In 1889, the Standard Oil Company built one of the world's largest oil refineries near Whiting. A **refinery** is a factory where resources such as oil are made into products that people can use.

In 1906, the United States Steel Corporation built a steel mill on the shore of Lake Michigan. The company started a new town for its workers on the Grand Calumet River. The town was named **Gary** after **Elbert H. Gary**, the chairman of the board of United States Steel at the time.

READING CHECK **CAUSE AND EFFECT**
Why did many businesses from other states move to Indiana in the late 1800s?

▶ **ELWOOD HAYNES** test-drove his new invention at a speed of 7 miles an hour.

▶ **GAS CITY** This mural shows a boom time in Gas City, Indiana, after natural gas was found in the area.

Changes in Society

During the late 1800s, the United States continued to grow. During **Benjamin Harrison's** presidency, six new states were added to the union. Life for Hoosiers changed as people left farms to work in factories.

Labor Unions

Industries in Indiana continued to grow. To improve working conditions, workers formed labor unions. A **labor union** is an organization of workers who do the same kinds of jobs.

Eugene V. Debs helped start a railway union. Labor leaders helped pass laws, such as making it illegal to hire children under 14. The Mine Workers Union won an eight-hour workday.

Urban Centers

During the late 1800s, cities in Indiana began to grow. People looking for work in factories were moving to cities from rural Indiana, southern states, and countries in Europe.

Railroads contributed to the growth of Indiana's cities by linking them to each other and to cities in other states. Railroads transported raw materials to factories and goods to markets. Railroad towns in Indiana included Evansville, **Fort Wayne**, and South Bend. Indianapolis became an important national rail center.

As cities grew, city governments faced new challenges. They formed fire companies and police forces to protect citizens. They also created water and sewer facilities, paved the streets, and installed street lamps.

❯ HOOSIERS ON THE MOVE An Indianapolis police officer directs traffic (above). Many miles of railroad tracks were built in Indiana during the late 1800s (below).

FAST FACT

Benjamin Harrison was the first United States President to cross the country by train.

Education

The Indiana Constitution of 1851 called for the state to provide free elementary school public education. After the Civil War, many schools were built. As time went on, more children were able to go to school. In 1897, the General Assembly passed a law that required children between the ages of 8 and 14 to attend school. The age was raised to 16 in 1913.

Changes also occurred in higher education. Indiana University in Bloomington, founded in 1820, grew during the late 1800s. A teacher's training college called a normal school was opened in Terre Haute in 1870.

Several private colleges were also established in the nineteenth century, including Hanover College in 1827, the University of Notre Dame in 1842, and Purdue University in 1869.

READING CHECK **MAIN IDEA AND DETAILS**
How did labor unions help workers?

> **INDIANA SCHOOLCHILDREN**

Summary

The United States went through a period of rebuilding after the Civil War. In Indiana, new industries grew, and people moved to cities. Labor unions were formed. Hoosiers had many more educational opportunities.

REVIEW

1. **WHAT TO KNOW** How did Indiana grow and change in the nineteenth century?

2. **VOCABULARY** Use the term **labor union** in a sentence about manufacturing in Indiana.

3. **HISTORY** In what ways did railroads help cities develop?

4. **CRITICAL THINKING** How do you think a system of education changed Indiana?

5. **MAKE A CHART** Make a chart of industries that developed in Indiana in the late nineteenth century and early twentieth century.

6. **SUMMARIZE**
   (Focus Skill) On a separate sheet of paper, copy and complete this graphic organizer.

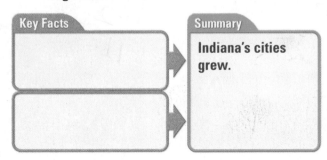

Key Facts		Summary
	→	Indiana's cities grew.
	→	

Time

1800 | Present

About 1910
The Great Migration begins

1917
The U.S. enters World War I

1920
The Ninteenth Amendment is passed

A New Century

WHAT TO KNOW
What events affected Indiana in the first part of the twentieth century?

VOCABULARY
bond p. 167
suffrage p. 169
interurban rail p. 170
consumer goods p. 171

PEOPLE
Woodrow Wilson
May Wright Sewall
Ida Husted Harper
Julia D. Nelson
Studebaker brothers
Fred and August
 Duesenberg

PLACES
Terre Haute

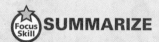
SUMMARIZE

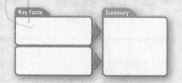

You Are There
It's 1917. The world is at war. You've often seen "doughboys," or United States soldiers, at Union Station in Indianapolis. They are on their way to ships bound for Europe. The war seems far away. However, today you are at a parade. Trucks and floats decorated with American flags roll down the street. Most of Indianapolis has turned out to support the war effort. Maybe the war isn't so far away after all.

▶ **WORLD WAR I** soldiers are sent off to war with a farewell parade in Indianapolis.

World War I

In 1914, a war broke out in Europe. The Allied Powers, led by Britain, France, and Russia, fought the Central Powers, led by Germany and Austria-Hungary. At first, the United States sent supplies to support the Allies. Then, in 1917, German submarines attacked United States ships in the Atlantic Ocean. President **Woodrow Wilson** asked the United States Congress to declare war on Germany.

Hoosiers Go to War

The United States sent about 2 million soldiers to fight in Europe. About 130,000 of these soldiers were from Indiana. By the end of the war, in 1918, more than 3,000 Hoosiers had lost their lives in the fighting.

On the Home Front

All Hoosiers helped with the war effort. Indiana farmers planted millions of acres of wheat and corn. They sold the crops to countries in Europe that were not able to grow enough food.

Indiana's factories started making war supplies. Women went to work in the factories. They also volunteered with the Red Cross and served in the military as nurses.

Many Hoosiers bought war bonds. The **bonds** allowed the government to use people's money for a certain amount of time and pay it back later.

World War I ended in November of 1918 when Germany surrendered. Many people hoped for lasting peace.

READING CHECK ŏSUMMARIZE
How did Hoosiers help the war effort?

▶ **AFRICAN AMERICANS GO NORTH** Between 1900 and 1920, the number of African Americans in Indianapolis increased from 16,000 to about 35,000.

The Great Migration

Between 1910 and 1930, thousands of African Americans moved from the South to cities in the North. They moved because farms in the South were going through hard times while the North needed factory workers. This movement of people became known as the Great Migration.

Facing Challenges

Many African Americans moved to Indiana to build a better life. Between 1900 and 1920, Indianapolis's African American population doubled.

However, African Americans were often treated unfairly because of their race. Most were hired only for low-paying jobs. In 1927, Indianapolis and Gary opened separate schools for African American children and white children.

Overcoming Challenges

African Americans did not let these challenges stop them. They started their own businesses and published newspapers, such as the *Indianapolis Recorder*. They took charge of their schools. One such school, Crispus Attucks High School in Indianapolis, was famous for its excellent teachers.

READING CHECK ⚙SUMMARIZE
What challenges did African Americans in Indiana face?

Women Gain the Vote

For many years, women had not enjoyed the same rights as men. Most were not able to own their own land or businesses until the early 1900s. After that, they were still not allowed to hold public office or vote.

Banding Together

As early as 1850, women in Indiana worked for **suffrage**, or the right to vote. **May Wright Sewall** played an important part in the women's movement in Indiana. In 1878, she founded the Indianapolis Equal Suffrage Society. By 1890, about 100,000 women in Indiana had joined groups that worked for woman's suffrage and other rights.

The Nineteenth Amendment

Many Hoosiers worked to help pass the Nineteenth Amendment, which would give women the right to vote. Writer **Ida Husted Harper** of **Terre Haute** wrote magazine and newspaper articles persuading citizens and lawmakers to support the amendment.

On August 26, 1920, the Nineteenth Amendment to the Constitution was ratified. Women finally had the right to vote in national elections. That same year, **Julia D. Nelson** became the first woman elected to Indiana's state government. She won the election even without the votes of women. A year later, women in Indiana were given the right to vote in state elections.

READING CHECK **CAUSE AND EFFECT**
What helped women win suffrage?

❯ **WINNING THE VOTE** Suffragists in Indiana rallied for the passage of the Nineteenth Amendment.

Developments in Indiana

The 1920s were good times for many Americans. People looked forward to new opportunities and wanted to enjoy themselves. This period is often called the Roaring Twenties.

Many developments also took place in Indiana during this time. Improvements in transportation and industry helped the state grow and change.

Transportation

Elwood Haynes had started the first automobile factory in Indiana in 1895. Soon, many other automobile factories opened for business. The largest of these was owned by the **Studebaker brothers**. In 1902, they started making automobiles instead of wagons. German-born brothers **Fred** and **August Duesenberg** started a company in Iowa that made sports cars used in the Indianapolis 500.

The automobile industry brought growth to Indiana's cities and towns. In time, companies were able to sell automobiles for lower prices. Travel was made easier as dirt roads were paved. New businesses, such as gas stations and garages, were opened.

Another invention that made travel easier was the electric railroad. This **interurban rail** was a network of rail lines that connected rural areas with nearby cities and towns. People could now get to jobs in the city quickly.

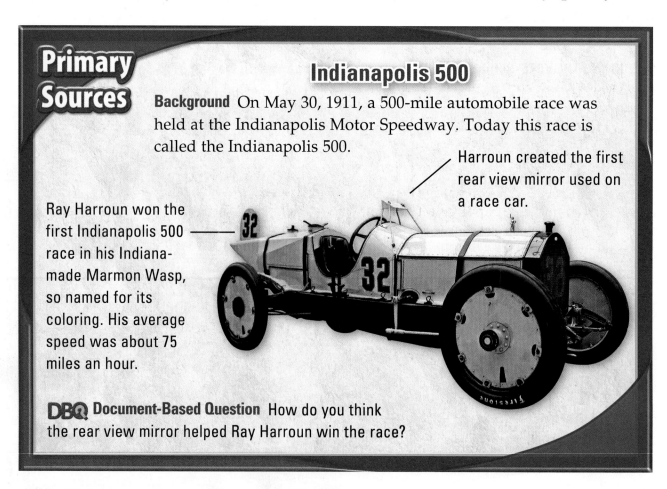

Primary Sources

Indianapolis 500

Background On May 30, 1911, a 500-mile automobile race was held at the Indianapolis Motor Speedway. Today this race is called the Indianapolis 500.

Harroun created the first rear view mirror used on a race car.

Ray Harroun won the first Indianapolis 500 race in his Indiana-made Marmon Wasp, so named for its coloring. His average speed was about 75 miles an hour.

DBQ Document-Based Question How do you think the rear view mirror helped Ray Harroun win the race?

▶ **MECHANIZATION** Many farmers in Indiana began to use tractors in the 1920s.

Industry

When World War I ended, factories no longer needed to make war supplies. They switched to making **consumer goods**, or products made for personal use. These goods included vacuum cleaners, washing machines, refrigerators, and radios.

During the 1920s, changes also took place in agriculture. The ways in which farmers planted and harvested crops became mechanized, or powered by machines. For example, gasoline-powered tractors reduced the time it took to plow fields. Mechanization allowed farms to produce more crops with fewer workers.

READING CHECK **MAIN IDEA AND DETAILS** How did automobile manufacturing begin in Indiana?

Summary

In the early 1900s, the United States took part in World War I. During this time, many African Americans moved to northern cities. The Nineteenth Amendment gave women the right to vote. Indiana continued to grow because of developments in transportation and industry.

REVIEW

1. WHAT TO KNOW What events affected Indiana in the first part of the twentieth century?

2. VOCABULARY Use the word **suffrage** in a sentence about the Nineteenth Amendment.

3. HISTORY What was produced in Indiana's factories during World War I?

4. CRITICAL THINKING How did the automobile change life for people in Indiana?

5. ✏️ **WRITE A DIARY ENTRY** Write a diary entry about the passing of the Nineteenth Amendment in Indiana.

6. ⭐ (Focus Skill) **SUMMARIZE** On a separate sheet of paper, copy and complete this graphic organizer.

Key Facts	Summary
Farmers grew corn and wheat. →	
Hoosiers bought war bonds. →	

Read a Time Line

Why It Matters A **time line** shows the order in which events happened. It also shows the length of time between events. Seeing events in the order in which they took place can help you understand how events are connected.

▶ LEARN

The time line below shows when some important events in Indiana history took place. The earliest date is on the left. The latest date is on the right. The marks on the time line show units of time. The red dates show every 50 years. The black dates show when events on the time line happened.

A time line can show events that took place during one day, one month, one year, one decade, one century, or longer. A **decade** is a period of ten years. A **century** is a period of 100 years.

Indiana History

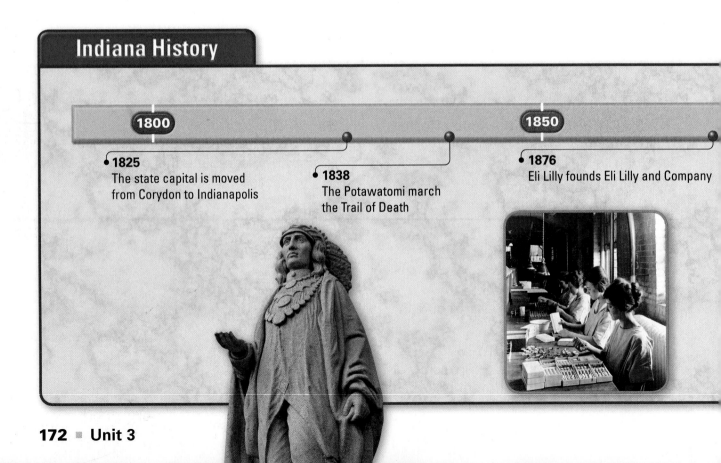

1800

1850

1825
The state capital is moved from Corydon to Indianapolis

1838
The Potawatomi march the Trail of Death

1876
Eli Lilly founds Eli Lilly and Company

> PRACTICE

Use the time line to answer these questions.

1 What are the earliest and latest events on this time line?

2 What event happened in 1929?

3 How many years after Indianapolis became the capital of Indiana did Eli Lilly start his company?

> APPLY

Make It Relevant Make a time line that shows 1990 to 2040. Label each decade. Show the year in which you were born. Mark the year in which you will graduate from high school. Add other dates in the past and future that are important to you. Share your time line with classmates or family members.

Chart and Graph Skills

1900

1950

1906
U.S. Steel builds
the town of Gary

1929
The Great Depression begins

1945
World War II ends

Time

1800   Present

1929
The stock
market crashes

1941
Japan attacks
Pearl Harbor

1945
The Allies win
World War II

WHAT TO KNOW
How did challenging
times affect Indiana?

VOCABULARY
stock p. 175
depression p. 175
unemployed p. 176
shortage p. 178
rationing p. 178
recycle p. 178

PEOPLE
Franklin D. Roosevelt
Paul V. McNutt

PLACES
Pearl Harbor

SUMMARIZE

Key Facts   Summary

Challenging Times

YOU ARE THERE
The year is 1932. You and your family
live on a farm in southern Indiana. Lately,
times have been tough. Your family and other
farmers cannot get good prices for your crops.
Your parents worry that the bank will take away
the farm. Many of your neighbors have already
left. They are hoping to find jobs somewhere
else. You hope that your family can keep your
farm and that times will get better soon.

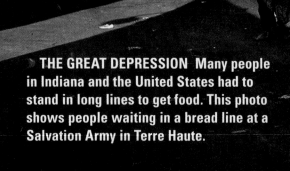

THE GREAT DEPRESSION Many people
in Indiana and the United States had to
stand in long lines to get food. This photo
shows people waiting in a bread line at a
Salvation Army in Terre Haute.

The Great Depression

Many people thought that the good times of the 1920s would never end. Businesses in Indiana and all over the United States grew during this time. Factories in Indiana produced cars, glass, and steel. This fast growth made stocks go up in value. A **stock** is a share of ownership in a company.

Because times were so good, many people borrowed money from banks. Many people used this money to buy stocks. However, businesses began to make more things than people could buy. There was also an extra amount of farm products because European countries no longer needed to buy American crops. Crop prices dropped. Many farmers lost their farms.

The Stock Market Crash

In October 1929, stock prices began to fall. People rushed to sell their stocks before prices fell more. So many stocks were sold that stock prices crashed, or fell very low. Most stocks became worthless.

The stock market crash of 1929 helped lead to a severe depression. A **depression** is a time when there are few jobs and people have little money. The depression of the 1930s was so bad that it became known as the Great Depression.

People could not repay the money they had borrowed from banks. Most banks were forced to close, and many people lost all their savings.

READING CHECK ♻ **SUMMARIZE**
What caused the stock market to crash?

FAST FACT

The United States government hired some of the best photographers in the country to record the state of the country during the Great Depression. Many of the photographs they took show the hardships Americans faced.

· THE NEW DEAL ·

▶ President Roosevelt announced his New Deal programs in a radio broadcast (right). In Indiana, WPA workers built roads (left). Artists were hired to paint murals, such as this one in a post office in Liberty (below).

The Government Helps

The Great Depression affected the whole nation. Because people had less money, they bought fewer goods and services. Most of Indiana's steel mills, mines, and factories cut back production or closed. People who worked there became **unemployed**, or lost their jobs. By 1933, one out of four Hoosiers was unemployed.

A Plan for the Nation

In 1932, **Franklin D. Roosevelt** was elected President. He came up with a plan to help the country. The plan was called the New Deal.

Under this plan, the government set up programs to give people jobs. One program was run by the Works Progress Administration, or WPA. In Indiana, the WPA hired workers to build roads, public buildings, and swimming pools.

Other workers provided services such as school lunch programs. The WPA also hired writers and artists. Indiana artists painted murals in the state's post offices.

In 1933, **Paul V. McNutt** became governor of Indiana. He started state programs to feed the hungry and help the unemployed.

The Great Depression lasted until 1940. By that time, countries in Europe and Asia were at war again.

READING CHECK ☼SUMMARIZE
How did the Great Depression change life in Indiana?

World War II

World War II began in 1939. In this conflict, the Allied Powers—Britain, France, and the Soviet Union—fought against Germany, Italy, and Japan. As in World War I, the United States at first did not fight in this war.

On December 7, 1941, Japanese warplanes attacked United States Navy ships at **Pearl Harbor**, in Hawaii. More than 2,400 Americans were killed. The next day, the United States entered the war.

Indiana Lends a Hand

About 300,000 men and women from Indiana served in the United States armed forces. They fought in Europe, Africa, and the South Pacific. More than 10,000 Hoosiers died.

To help with the war effort, Indiana's factories were changed to produce war equipment. Mills in East Chicago and Gary provided millions of tons of steel used to make war materials. Other factories made airplane engines and propellers, army trucks, and weapons.

Indiana farmers planted millions of acres of corn, wheat, and soybeans. New varieties of corn helped increase how much the farms grew. These crops helped feed American soldiers and people in Europe.

Women took many of the jobs left behind by the men who became soldiers. They ran machines in factories, drove tractors on farms, and worked for the Red Cross. Some African Americans were also able to find new job opportunities in factories.

▶ **THE EVANSVILLE SHIPYARD** made warships during World War II. Evelyn Cox was the first female welder to work at the shipyard.

▶ **RATIONING** A clerk in Terre Haute looks at a customer's ration coupon book.

Hoosiers at Home

The armed forces needed large amounts of food and fuel. Their needs created shortages of meat, sugar, and gasoline. When there is a **shortage** of something, there is not enough of it. To make sure that soldiers had enough, the government called for **rationing**, or limiting what people could buy.

Many people planted vegetable gardens, called victory gardens, to lessen food shortages. They collected scrap metal, old tires, and paper to be **recycled**, or used again, by factories.

In 1945, the United States and its allies won the war. Life for Hoosiers began to return to normal.

READING CHECK **MAIN IDEA AND DETAILS**
How did rationing help the war effort?

Summary

The United States went through the Great Depression in the 1930s. Government programs helped people by providing jobs. Indiana's citizens fought in World War II. Hoosiers worked hard at home to support the war effort.

REVIEW

1. **WHAT TO KNOW** How did challenging times affect Indiana?

2. **VOCABULARY** How are **rationing** and **recycling** related?

3. **HISTORY** In what year did the United States enter World War II?

4. **CRITICAL THINKING** Why were Indiana's factories and farms important during World War II?

5. 🖌 **MAKE AN ILLUSTRATED TIME LINE** Make an illustrated time line that shows the major events in this lesson.

6. ⭐ **SUMMARIZE**
   On a separate sheet of paper, copy and complete this graphic organizer.

Key Facts		Summary
	▶	The years between 1930 and 1950 were a challenging time for the United States.
	▶	

Ernie Pyle

Biography

Trustworthiness
Respect
Responsibility
Fairness
Caring
Patriotism

"I'd quit [reporting on the war] and come home for good except I don't suppose I could live with myself if I did. . ."

Ernest Taylor "Ernie" Pyle was born near Dana, Indiana, in 1900. After high school, Pyle studied news reporting at Indiana University. By the 1930s, he had become a popular newspaper columnist.

During World War II, Pyle went to Europe and Asia to report on the war. However, he did not write about battles. Instead, Pyle wrote about ordinary soldiers. He told about how they missed their families or how they coped with the death of a friend. Pyle also wrote that soldiers deserved more pay. Congress agreed. It passed the "Ernie Pyle bill," which gave soldiers a raise for combat service.

Pyle stayed close to the soldiers at the front. He often worried that he might be killed. Still, he felt it was his duty to tell the stories of the soldiers who were fighting for their country. On April 18, 1945, Pyle was killed by Japanese machine-gun fire on the island of Ie Shima. His death saddened people across the United States.

Why Character Counts

How did Ernie Pyle show patriotism?

Time

1900
Born

1923 Pyle begins his career as a journalist at the *La Porte Herald*

1944 Pyle wins the Pulitzer Prize for reporting

1945
Died

GO ONLINE
For more resources, go to
www.harcourtschool.com/ss1

1950
The Korean War begins

1964
The Civil Rights Act
of 1964 is passed

1968
500,000 United States
soldiers are serving
in Vietnam

WHAT TO KNOW
How did Indiana change
after World War II?

VOCABULARY
communism p. 182
cold war p. 182
cease-fire p. 182
civil rights p. 184
discrimination p. 184
segregation p. 184

PEOPLE
Richard G. Hatcher
Dr. Martin Luther King, Jr.
Robert F. Kennedy

PLACES
Soviet Union
North Korea
South Korea
North Vietnam
South Vietnam

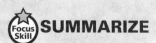

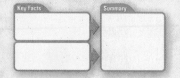

SUMMARIZE

Key Facts	Summary

Into Modern Times

YOU ARE THERE
Your mom and dad pull into the driveway with huge grins on their faces. Dad has been making good money since the end of the war. Now your parents have just bought a brand-new 1960 Studebaker Lark. The sleek new car was made in South Bend, Indiana. You can't wait to have your parents take you for a spin in it with the radio on and the top down!

▶ **AFTER THE WAR** many families were able to afford cars. The Studebaker Lark was a popular car at the time.

▶ **CONSUMER GOODS** People shop at stores along Main Street in Evansville in 1946.

Growth After World War II

Indiana's returning soldiers were eager to get on with their lives. For many, this meant going to college, getting married, buying a home, and starting a family.

A Changing State

In the years right after the war, many babies were born across the nation. In Indiana, this "baby boom" helped the population grow. More than 1 million babies were born in Indiana between 1950 and 1959.

Babies were not the only new Hoosiers. Thousands of people from neighboring states moved to Indiana. Many took jobs in Indiana's factories.

Times were good for many Hoosiers during the 1950s. They had good jobs, and they had money to spend. People bought cars, televisions, and houses. Highways made it easier for people to live farther from their jobs. During the 1950s, many highways, such as the Indiana Toll Road, were built. New houses were built in suburbs.

Ports were built to link Indiana to the rest of the world. The Port of Indiana on Lake Michigan opened in 1970. It has access to the Atlantic Ocean through the St. Lawrence Seaway. Two other major ports, Southwind Maritime Center and Clark Maritime Center, are located on the Ohio River.

READING CHECK ○**SUMMARIZE**
How did Indiana grow after World War II?

The Korean War

After World War II, the United States and 11 other nations started the North Atlantic Treaty Organization, or NATO. Its purpose was to stop the **Soviet Union** from setting up more communist governments in Europe. **Communism** is a system in which the government controls all the industries, land, and businesses in a country.

A war was never fought with the Soviet Union, but the threat was always present. The conflict became known as the Cold War. A **cold war** is a war that is fought mostly with ideas and money instead of soldiers.

North and South Korea

Korea was divided after World War II. Soviet troops occupied **North Korea**. United States troops occupied **South Korea**. North Korea set up a communist government.

On June 25, 1950, North Korean soldiers invaded South Korea. The United States and its allies sent more troops to help restore the peace.

Many soldiers from Indiana fought in the Korean War. Camp Atterbury and the Atterbury Army Air Force Base in Indiana were used as training centers. Hoosiers sent food and clothing to the South Koreans.

The fighting continued until 1953. Both sides agreed to a **cease-fire**, or a temporary end to the fighting, and the war ended. North Korea and South Korea remain separate countries.

READING CHECK **CAUSE AND EFFECT**
What caused the Korean War?

MAP SKILL **LOCATION** The Korean War Memorial in Evansville (below) honors soldiers who fought in the war. Where was the Soviet Union in relation to North Korea?

A Divided Korea

CHINA

SOVIET UNION

Turmen R.

Yalu River

NORTH KOREA

Pyongyang ⊛

Cease-fire line, 1953

⊛ National capital

Yellow Sea

⊛ Seoul

Sea of Japan (East Sea)

SOUTH KOREA

Korea Strait

JAPAN

0   100   200 Miles
0   100   200 Kilometers
Azimuthal Equal-Area Projection

N W E S

1950   KOREA   1953

A Divided Vietnam

CHINA

Hanoi
NORTH VIETNAM

BURMA

LAOS
Vientiane

Gulf of Tonkin

Hainan

THAILAND

Mekong River

South China Sea

Bangkok

CAMBODIA

SOUTH VIETNAM

Phnom Penh

Saigon

Gulf of Thailand

Mekong Delta

⊛ National capital

0   100   200 Miles
0   100   200 Kilometers
Azimuthal Equal-Area Projection

MAP SKILL LOCATION American soldiers board a helicopter to take part in the Battle of Khe Sanh in South Vietnam. What was the capital of South Vietnam?

The Vietnam War

During the 1950s, the spread of communism worried many people. Several United States citizens were tried for and found guilty of being communist spies. Others were falsely accused. Cold War relations grew more tense.

The United States Sends Soldiers

In the late 1950s, war broke out between **North Vietnam** and South Vietnam in Southeast Asia. North Vietnam had a communist government. **South Vietnam** was a republic. The United States sent American soldiers to help the South Vietnamese fight. By 1968, more than 500,000 American soldiers were in Vietnam.

Divided Support

Soldiers, doctors, and nurses from Indiana were among the Americans who fought in the Vietnam War. Many Hoosiers supported the war. Others were upset by the loss of life it caused. They took to the streets to protest.

In 1973, the United States agreed to a cease-fire, and its troops came home. Two years later, however, North Vietnam took over South Vietnam. In 1976, the two countries were unified.

Hoosiers have not forgotten the Vietnam War. The Vietnam War Memorial in Indianapolis honors the 1,525 Hoosiers who died in the war.

READING CHECK ☼SUMMARIZE

Why did the Vietnam War divide Indiana and the United States?

Civil Rights

In the 1950s and 1960s, many African Americans and white people in the United States joined the Civil Rights movement. **Civil rights** are the rights of citizens to equal treatment.

Working for Equality

African Americans often faced **discrimination**, or unfair treatment, because of their race. Many African American children went to segregated schools. **Segregation** is the act of keeping people of one race or culture separate from other people. In 1949, the Indiana General Assembly made segregation in schools illegal.

Civil rights workers in Indiana wanted equal housing, education, and jobs for all. In 1963, civil rights supporters called for these rights as they marched through Indianapolis.

The national Civil Rights Act of 1964 made segregation in public places against the law. Over time, African Americans in Indiana gained more power in government. For example, **Richard G. Hatcher** became mayor of Gary in 1967.

Dr. Martin Luther King, Jr., was one of the leaders of the Civil Rights movement. On April 4, 1968, King was assassinated. On the same night, Presidential candidate **Robert F. Kennedy** told voters in Indianapolis,

> **"What we need . . . is not division . . . but . . . a feeling of justice for those who still suffer within our country, whether they be white or whether they be black."**

READING CHECK **MAIN IDEA AND DETAILS**
When was the Civil Rights Act passed?

▶ CIVIL RIGHTS supporters march in Indianapolis on August 10, 1963.

Immigration

Indiana's population has grown and changed in recent years. Between 1970 and today, immigrants from all over the world settled in Indiana. Many were from Hispanic or Asian countries such as Mexico, China, and India. These cultural groups became an important part of Indiana's growing population.

Immigrants have helped Indiana's businesses grow. They have worked as bankers, teachers, doctors, and farm-workers. Immigrants have also started businesses, such as real estate offices, restaurants, and hair salons.

By the end of the twentieth century, Hispanics and Asians owned more than 9,000 Indiana businesses. They have also contributed to the state's culture with their music, food, and festivals.

READING CHECK ☼**SUMMARIZE**

How have immigrants changed Indiana?

▶ **A BUSINESS OWNER** Many immigrants have started their own businesses.

Summary

After World War II, Indiana's population grew. Hoosiers took part in the Korean War and the Vietnam War. They joined the Civil Rights movement. New immigrants helped Indiana grow.

REVIEW

1. **WHAT TO KNOW** How did Indiana change after World War II?

2. **VOCABULARY** How are the words **discrimination** and **civil rights** related?

3. **HISTORY** What was Indiana's role in the Korean War?

4. **CRITICAL THINKING** Why did the Vietnam War divide people in the United States and Indiana?

5. ✎ **WRITE NEWSPAPER HEADLINES** Write a newspaper headline that tells how the Korean War began and another that tells how the United States responded.

6. ⭐ (Focus Skill) **SUMMARIZE** On a separate sheet of paper, copy and complete this graphic organizer.

Key Facts	Summary
New roads and ports were built after World War II. ▶	
Immigrants have helped Indiana grow. ▶	

Read a Line Graph

Why It Matters A **line graph** shows patterns in information over time.

❯ LEARN

The line graph on page 187 shows how Indiana's population changed from 1950 to 2000. The left side of the graph shows the number of people living in Indiana. The bottom shows the years. Each point on the graph shows the population for a given year. The line connecting the points shows how the population changed over time. Use these steps to find Indiana's population for a given year.

Step 1 Find a year, such as 1980, at the bottom of the graph.

Step 2 Move your finger straight up from that date until you reach the purple point.

Step 3 Move your finger left to the number of people. That is the population for that year. Your finger might not end up exactly at a marked number. If this happens, make an estimate, or close guess.

❯ **A GROWING STATE** Indiana's population has grown since the 1950s. Many of the state's new residents live in Indianapolis.

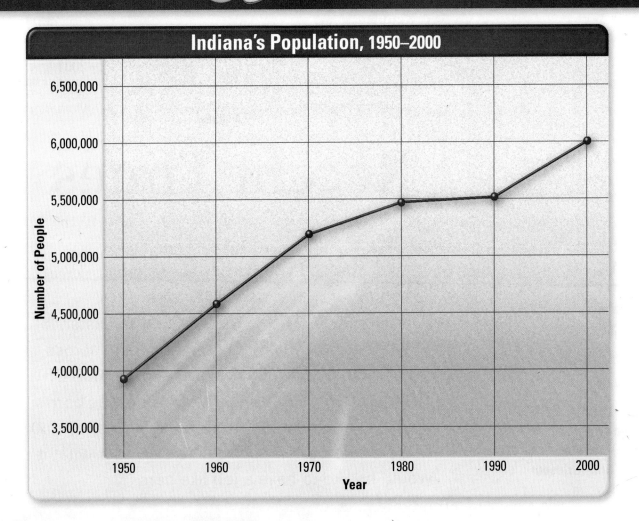

Indiana's Population, 1950–2000

Number of People

6,500,000
6,000,000
5,500,000
5,000,000
4,500,000
4,000,000
3,500,000

1950 1960 1970 1980 1990 2000

Year

▶ PRACTICE

Use the line graph to answer these questions.

1 Did Indiana's population increase or decrease between 1950 and 2000? How do you know?

2 About how many people lived in Indiana in 1950? in 1970?

3 In which ten-year period did Indiana's population change the least? How do you know?

▶ APPLY

Create a line graph that shows changes in the population of Marion County, Indiana's largest county, during the same period of time as that in the graph above. Use these figures: 550,000 in 1950; 700,000 in 1960; 800,000 in 1970; 750,000 in 1980; 800,000 in 1990; 850,000 in 2000.

Chart and Graph Skills

Time

1800 · Present

• **1963**
The Studebaker
automobile factory
in South Bend closes

• **1965**
Indiana astronaut
Virgil "Gus" Grissom
orbits Earth in *Gemini 3*

• **2001**
Terrorists attack
sites in the
United States

Recent Times

WHAT TO KNOW
How has Indiana
changed in recent times?

VOCABULARY

terrorism p. 189
efficient p. 191
service industry p. 191
high-tech p. 192
aerospace p. 192

PEOPLE

Janice Voss
George W. Bush
Frank O'Bannon
Virgil "Gus" Grissom
Frank Borman

PLACES

New York City
Washington, D.C.
Pennsylvania
Afghanistan
Princeton
Warsaw
West Lafayette

SUMMARIZE

Key Facts	Summary

YOU ARE THERE

You and your family are watching TV in your home on a chilly evening in February 2000. "There it is!" cries your sister. She points to a small dot of light gliding across the screen. It's the space shuttle *Endeavour*. On board is astronaut **Janice Voss**. She was born in your hometown of South Bend. Now she's 240 miles above Earth's surface! You wonder what it would be like to have a job like hers.

▶ **SPACE SHUTTLE ENDEAVOUR** lifts off from Cape Canaveral, Florida.

▶ **THE WORLD TRADE CENTER** in New York City was attacked on September 11, 2001. Government leaders look at a model plan for rebuilding the site.

Facing New Dangers

The Cold War was over in the early 1990s. All 15 Soviet republics declared independence. The United States set up friendly relations with the nations.

A New Threat

At home, the United States faced a new danger—terrorism. **Terrorism** is the use of violence to promote a cause. On September 11, 2001, terrorists took control of four airplanes. They flew two of the planes into the World Trade Center in **New York City**. A third plane hit the Pentagon in **Washington, D.C.** The fourth crashed into an empty field in **Pennsylvania**. In total, about 3,000 people were killed in the attacks.

President **George W. Bush** called for a War on Terrorism. In October 2001, the United States overthrew the government of **Afghanistan** because it had supported the terrorists. In 2003, the United States declared Iraq's leader a threat and removed him from power.

In 2002, President Bush set up the Department of Homeland Security to help prevent terrorist attacks. Indiana governor **Frank O'Bannon** created the Counter-Terrorism and Security Council. It helps communities and emergency workers learn how to plan for and respond to a terrorist attack.

READING CHECK ⚙**SUMMARIZE**
How did Indiana's leaders respond to the terrorist attacks of September 11, 2001?

> FARM AID is a benefit concert held since 1985 to help raise money for family farms in the United States. Indiana singer John Mellencamp is one of the concert's organizers.

Businesses Change

Starting in the 1960s, changes began taking place in Indiana's economy. These changes affected Indiana's farms and industries.

Farmers Struggle

Farmers with small family farms in Indiana were finding it hard to make money. Many farmers sold their farms. Farming companies bought their land and built large farms. The companies could afford new and updated farming equipment.

The new equipment helped farmers in Indiana raise more crops using fewer workers. Important Indiana farm products included corn, soybeans, wheat, hogs, and cattle.

Industries Struggle

Some of Indiana's coal mines and limestone quarries shut down during the 1960s. In 1963, the Studebaker automobile factory in South Bend closed its doors forever.

Many steel mills closed, too. They could not make steel as cheaply as factories in other countries could.

Some Indiana steel mills, such as U.S. Steel in Gary, bought updated equipment. The new machines helped the mills stay in business and keep production high. In fact, they were able to make more steel than before.

The new machines also helped cut costs because fewer workers were needed to run them. Many Indiana steelworkers lost their jobs.

Hoosiers Adapt to Change

Even though some of Indiana's factories closed, manufacturing remained key to Indiana's economy. One of Indiana's most important industries today is the manufacturing of trucks, cars, and auto parts.

New technology has helped these and other Indiana factories succeed. For example, at a truck plant in **Princeton**, robots do the painting and the welding. This helps the plant be **efficient**, or able to produce products with little waste of time or money.

Factory owners in Indiana provide their workers with education and training so they can use complex equipment correctly. This training helps them do their jobs better.

Indiana's service industries began to grow rapidly in the 1980s and 1990s. **Service industries** are industries that provide services to people.

Most service jobs are in or near Indiana's largest cities. In Indianapolis, for example, many service workers have jobs with the state government.

In recent years, Indianapolis has become an important meeting place for businesspeople from all over the country. Service workers help run hotels and restaurants for visitors. Service workers may also be doctors, lawyers, or teachers. They may repair cars, cut hair, or drive buses.

READING CHECK **CAUSE AND EFFECT**
What effect did improved equipment and technology have on Indiana's businesses?

▶ **INDIANA WORKERS** assemble truck engines in Columbus, Indiana (below). Service workers help a tourist at the Indiana Welcome Center in Lake County (right).

High Technology in Indiana

High-technology industries have helped Indiana do business with other parts of the world. High-technology, or **high-tech**, industries are those that invent, build, or use computers and other kinds of electronic equipment.

High-Tech Industries

Several high-tech companies make medical products in Indiana. The products are sold around the world. Eli Lilly and Company researches and develops pharmaceuticals (far•muh•SOO•tih•kulz), or medicines. They help people who have diseases such as diabetes and cancer.

Biomet and Zimmer are two medical manufacturers in **Warsaw**, Indiana. They make replacement hips, knees, and other body parts. Scientists test special metals and plastics used to make the parts. High-tech machines make sure the parts are the correct size and shape.

The Sony Corporation of America opened a factory in Terre Haute in 1983. This factory makes CDs, DVDs, and video game disks.

Indiana and Aerospace

About 100 aerospace companies are located in Indiana. **Aerospace** companies design and build aircraft and spacecraft parts.

Purdue University, in **West Lafayette**, has one of the nation's best aerospace programs. More than 20 astronauts were educated at Purdue.

Several astronauts were born in Indiana. **Virgil "Gus" Grissom** of Mitchell became one of the first American astronauts to travel into

▶ **HIGH-TECH** A packaging technician watches as medicine is placed into bottles at Eli Lilly and Company.

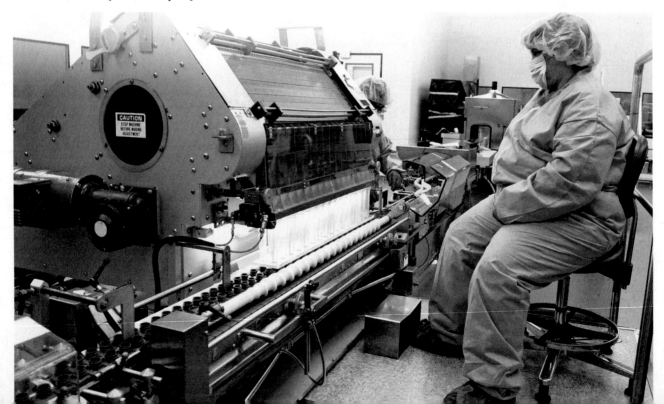

▶ **HOOSIER ASTRONAUT** Virgil "Gus" Grissom prepares for a mission.

space. In 1965, he successfully piloted the *Gemini 3* spacecraft around Earth three times. **Frank Borman** of Gary was the pilot of *Apollo 8*. In 1968, *Apollo 8* became the first spacecraft with a crew to orbit the moon.

READING CHECK 🖐 **SUMMARIZE**

What goods do Indiana's high-tech industries produce?

Summary

Today, Hoosiers are prepared to deal with the threat of terrorism. Indiana's farms and factories have begun using improved technology. Indiana's high-tech industries sell products to nations all over the world. Many astronauts are educated in Indiana.

REVIEW

1. **WHAT TO KNOW** How has Indiana changed in recent times?

2. **VOCABULARY** What are some examples of **high-tech** industries in Indiana?

3. **ECONOMICS** How have Indiana's farms changed in recent years?

4. **CRITICAL THINKING** How can training factory workers help a factory be more efficient?

5. ✏️ **WRITE AN ESSAY** Write a brief essay explaining how industries in Indiana have changed in recent years.

6. ⭐(Focus Skill) **SUMMARIZE** On a separate sheet of paper, copy and complete this graphic organizer.

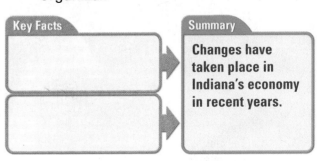

Key Facts

Summary

Changes have taken place in Indiana's economy in recent years.

Solve a Problem

Why It Matters People everywhere have problems at some time. Learning how to solve problems is an important skill. You can use this skill now and in the future.

▶ LEARN

Here are some steps you can use to help solve a problem.

Step 1 Identify the problem and its possible causes.

Step 2 Think about several solutions to the problem. Think about the advantages and disadvantages of each solution.

Step 3 Choose the best solution, and make a plan to carry out the solution.

Step 4 Follow the plan. Then think about whether your solution worked. Try other solutions if needed.

▶ **STEEL IN THE 1950s** A Gary Steel Works employee pours molten iron on scrap metal to make steel in 1952.

▶ **STEEL TODAY** A worker at Worthington Steel in Porter, Indiana, uses the latest equipment.

▶ PRACTICE

In the lesson, you read about a problem that Indiana's steel mills faced starting in the 1960s. They were not able to make steel as cheaply as factories in other countries. A solution for some steel mills was to buy updated equipment. Answer these questions.

1 What was an advantage of the solution?

2 What was a disadvantage of the solution?

3 Do you think the solution was a good one? Explain.

▶ APPLY

Make It Relevant Identify an important problem in your own community. Then use the steps to solve this problem. Write a plan, and share your ideas with your classmates.

Fun with Social Studies

Confusion in Cyberspace

These e-mails landed in the wrong mailboxes. Who should have received each one?

From: guest@harmony.com
To: ???
Subject: Nice town!

I am a scientist from London. Thank you for inviting me to your new town! I think I will make Indiana my permanent home.

May Wright Sewall

From: citizen@Indiana.com
To: ???
Subject: In support!

I have just joined the Equal Suffrage Society. Your work will one day pay off, and women everywhere will have the right to vote!

Richard G. Hatcher

From: citizen@Gary.com
To: ???
Subject: Represent me!

You are doing a great job as our new mayor. I hope you will continue to listen to the citizens of Gary.

Robert Owen

Crack the Code . . . and answer the riddle

Fill in the correct words, and unscramble the letters to answer the riddle.

VOCABULARY

When states withdraw from a country, they <u>1</u> _ <u>2</u> _ _ _ .

_ _ _ <u>3</u> - _ _ _ _ industries use computers and other electronic equipment.

Keeping people of one race or culture separate from other people is _ _ _ _ _ _ <u>4</u> _ _ _ .

Limiting what people can buy is _ _ _ _ <u>5</u> _ _ _ _ .

The period of rebuilding after the Civil War was called _ _ _ _ _ _ <u>6</u> _ _ _ _ _ _ .

_ _ _ _ _ _ <u>7</u> <u>8</u> is the right to vote.

What did the untalented actor need to help him in the play?

A _ _ _ _ _ _   _ _ _ _ _
   1 6 4 7 8 2 5 4 2 3

Where Are You?

Name the city you are in.

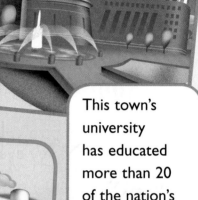

You're in the town that was Indiana's first capital. Where are you?

This town's university has educated more than 20 of the nation's astronauts. Where are you?

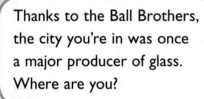

Thanks to the Ball Brothers, the city you're in was once a major producer of glass. Where are you?

Online Adventures

GO ONLINE

Which Apollo mission was the first to circle the moon?

Apollo 8

Apollo 1

Life as a newspaper reporter can be hard! Eco is being sent out to cover important events in Indiana's history, but nobody knows where Eco should go. You must use your knowledge of Indiana after 1850 to get the scoop. Can you get these stories done before the paper goes to press? Play now at **www.harcourtschool.com/ss1**

HARCOURT

ECO

Visual Summary

1825
The state capital is moved from Corydon to Indianapolis

1861
The Civil War begins

Late 1800s
Urban centers begin to grow as people move to cities to work in factories

Summarize the Unit

Summarize Use the graphic organizer below to help you summarize key events in the unit.

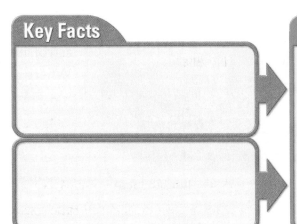

Key Facts

Summary
Indiana's statehood began as a time of much growth and change, which continues today.

Vocabulary

Identify the term from the word bank that correctly matches each definition.

1. a time when there are few jobs and people have little money
2. the use of violence to promote a cause
3. the rights of citizens to equal treatment
4. an organization of workers who do the same kinds of jobs
5. a person who wanted to end slavery
6. the making of finished products from raw materials
7. the right to vote
8. a war between people in the same country

Word Bank

abolitionist p. 151
civil war p. 154
manufacturing p. 163
labor union p. 164
suffrage p. 169
depression p. 175
civil rights p. 184
terrorism p. 189

1940

1945
The Allies win
World War II

1965
Indiana astronaut
Virgil "Gus" Grissom
orbits Earth in *Gemini 3*

Present

 Time Line

Use the unit summary time line above to answer these questions.

9. In what year was the state capital moved to Indianapolis?

10. How many years after the Allies won World War II did Gus Grissom orbit Earth in *Gemini 3*?

 Facts and Main Ideas

Answer these questions.

11. Who developed the plan for Indianapolis?

12. Why were Native Americans forced to leave Indiana?

13. What new industries developed in Indiana after World War II?

Write the letter of the best choice.

14. What was the only Civil War battle fought in Indiana?
  A Battle of Corydon
  B Battle of Indianapolis
  C Battle of Gettysburg
  D Battle of Vicksburg

15. Who was Eli Lilly?
  A a labor union leader
  B the first African American elected in Indiana
  C a pharmacist
  D the inventor of the steel plow

 Critical Thinking

Answer these questions.

16. Why do you think some Hoosiers worked to end slavery?

17. **Make It Relevant** How do you think the Civil Rights movement changed life in Indiana?

 Skills

Read a Time Line

Look at the time line on pages 172–173.

18. In what year did the Potawatomi march the Trail of Death?

19. What happened in 1906?

20. How many years after the start of the Great Depression did World War II end?

writing

Write a Letter Imagine that you are living in Indiana in the early 1800s. Write a letter to a friend who lives somewhere else, explaining the changes you see happening.

Write a Report Using Indiana government websites and other online sources, research Indiana's modern growth. Write a report that focuses on manufacturing, new technologies, and transportation.

Unit 3 ■ **199**

Show What You Know

Unit Writing Activity

Write an Explanation Write a paragraph that explains how Indiana has grown and changed from 1800 to today.

- Tell how inventions and new forms of transportation helped Indiana grow.
- Describe the changes in Indiana's population.

Unit Project

Make an Indiana Time Line Use long posterboard to make an illustrated time line.

- Make a time line from 1800 to present.
- Include important Indiana and United States events on the time line.
- Make illustrations for the events.

Read More

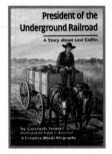

- *Boxes for Katje* by Candace Fleming. Berryville Graphics.

- *Log Cabin in the Woods: A True Story about a Pioneer Boy* by Joanne Landers Henry. Emmis Books.

- *President of the Underground Railroad: A Story About Levi Coffin* by Gwenyth Swain. Carolrhoda Books.

GO ONLINE For more resources, go to
www.harcourtschool.com/ss1

Indiana Today

Unit 4

Start with the Standards

INDIANA'S ACADEMIC STANDARDS FOR SOCIAL STUDIES

History 4.1.4, 4.1.12, 4.1.13, 4.1.14, 4.1.15

Civics and Government 4.2.1, 4.2.2, 4.2.3, 4.2.4, 4.2.5, 4.2.6, 4.2.7

Geography 4.3.2

Economics 4.4.1, 4.4.2, 4.4.3, 4.4.4, 4.4.5, 4.4.6, 4.4.7, 4.4.8, 4.4.9, 4.4.10

The Big Idea

Economy and Government

Indiana's citizens make economic choices. They also vote to choose their leaders.

What to Know

- ✓ What industries are important to Indiana's economy?
- ✓ In what ways have entrepreneurs changed life in Indiana?
- ✓ How does Indiana trade?
- ✓ What are the three branches of Indiana's state government?
- ✓ What are the different local governments of Indiana?
- ✓ What are the responsibilities of Indiana's citizens?

The Indiana Statehouse

When Indiana became a state in 1816, Corydon was the state capital. As more people settled in Indiana, Hoosiers wanted to move the capital to the center of the state. In 1821, the state government chose Indianapolis as the new capital. Architects made the new capitol building look like buildings that the ancient Greeks had made.

About 30 years later, part of the capitol ceiling fell. In 1877, the Indiana General Assembly held a contest for a new capitol design. The winner of the contest was Indianapolis architect Edwin May. He modeled the outside of the building after the United States Capitol.

▶ Indiana General Assembly in session

Indiana state capitol, today

▶ Stained-glass dome in rotunda

▶ Statue of Abraham Lincoln

The state capitol is called the Indiana Statehouse. It was built with materials from Indiana. The inside was made to look like Italian buildings from the 1600s. At its center is a rotunda, or a round hall. At the top of the rotunda is a stained-glass dome. Eight marble statues surround the hall. One of them stands for justice. It is modeled after May Wilson, the wife of an Indiana judge.

Near the Statehouse are several Government Center buildings. In one of these is a mosaic, or a picture made from pieces of glass. It shows the life of Abraham Lincoln.

The Indiana Statehouse is one of the few capitols that hold the meeting places of all three branches of state government. The House of Representatives and the Senate have their own chambers. The governor's office is also in the Statehouse. In addition, the state supreme court meets there.

INDIANA TEST PREP

1 Where was Indiana's first state capital?
A Lafayette
B Indianapolis
C Corydon
D Fort Wayne

2 Who won the contest to design Indiana's new capitol?
A William Henry Harrison
B Abraham Lincoln
C Edwin May
D May Wilson

3 What surrounds the rotunda?
A eight marble statues
B a mosaic of Abraham Lincoln's life
C the governor's office
D the Government Center buildings

4 Writing How is the Indiana state capitol like the United States Capitol?

Indiana's economy is based mostly on manufacturing and services.

Businesses in Indiana trade with businesses within the state, in other states, and around the world.

Indiana Today

The state and local governments provide services to Hoosiers.

The citizens of Indiana have many rights and responsibilities.

Clement and John Studebaker

1831–1901, 1833–1917
- Two of five brothers who ran a wagon-building company in South Bend
  - Their company later built automobiles

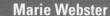

Marie Webster

1859–1956
- Designed quilts displayed in museums around the world
  - Wrote the first American book about quilting in 1915

 People

1800	1840	1880

1831 • Clement Studebaker

1833 • John Studebaker

1859 • Marie Webster

1867 • Madame C. J. Walker

1888

Richard Lugar

1932–
- United States senator representing Indiana since 1977
  - Ran for President in 1996
    - Is the longest-serving United States senator in Indiana history

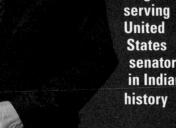

 Julia Carson

1938–2007
- Represented Indianapolis in the United States Congress 1997–2007
  - Received *The Indianapolis Star*'s Woman of the Year Award in 1984 and 1992

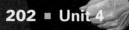

Madame C. J. Walker

1867–1919

- One of the first and most successful businesswomen in the United States
- Opened a factory in Indianapolis that made beauty products for African American women

Clessie Lyle Cummins

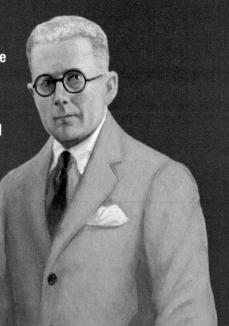

1888–1968

- Founder of Cummins Engine Company in Columbus
- Improved the design of diesel engines
- Was awarded 33 United States patents for his inventions

1920   **1960**   **Present**

01

1917

1956

1919

Clessie Lyle Cummins   1968

1932 • Richard Lugar

1938 • Julia Carson   2007

1955 • Evan Bayh

1955 • John Roberts

Evan Bayh

1955–

- Governor of Indiana from 1989 to 1997
- United States senator representing Indiana since 1999

John Roberts

1955–

- Grew up in Long Beach, Indiana
- Was appointed Chief Justice of the United States Supreme Court in 2005

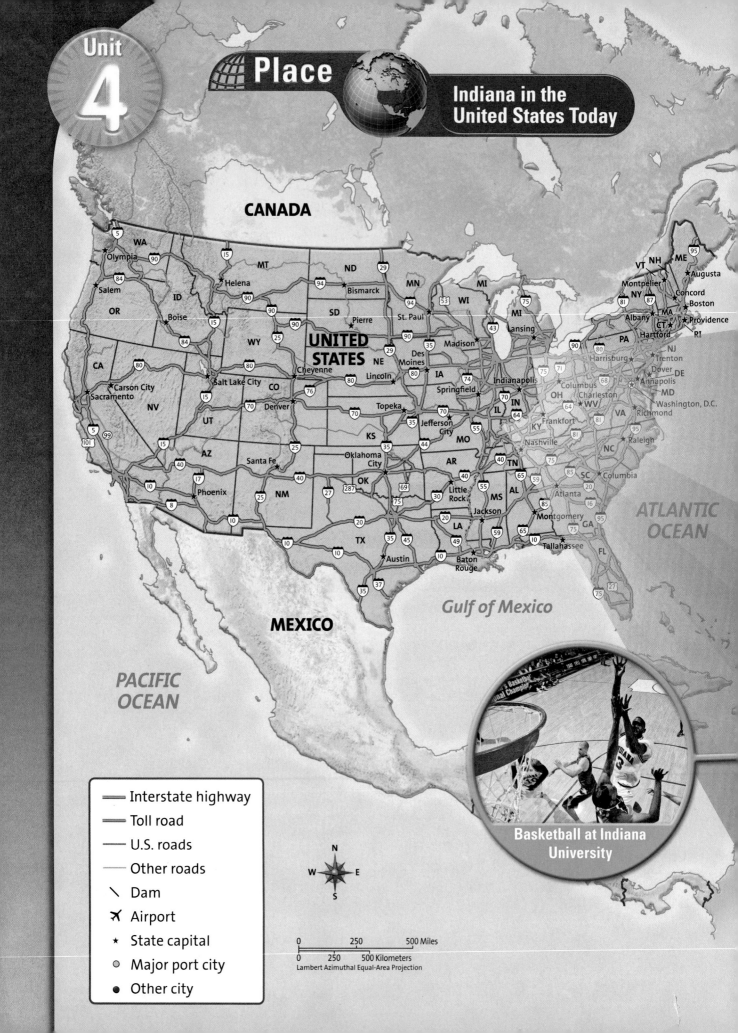

CANADA

WA
Olympia

MT

ND

MN

MI

VT NH ME
Augusta

Helena

Bismarck

WI

MI

Montpelier
NY
Concord
Boston

Salem

ID

SD

Pierre

St. Paul

Lansing

Albany

Providence

OR

Boise

Madison

PA

Hartford

RI

WY

Des Moines

NE

Cheyenne

UNITED
STATES

NJ
Harrisburg
Trenton
Dover DE

CA

Salt Lake City

CO

Lincoln

IA

Indianapolis

Columbus
OH

Annapolis
MD
Washington, D.C.

Carson City
Sacramento

NV

Denver

Springfield

IN

WV
Charleston

VA
Richmond

UT

Topeka

IL

Frankfort

KY

Raleigh

AZ

Santa Fe

KS

Jefferson
City

MO

Nashville

NC

Phoenix

NM

Oklahoma
City

AR

Little
Rock

TN

SC
Columbia

OK

AL

MS

Atlanta

GA

TX

Austin

Jackson

Montgomery

FL

Baton
Rouge

Tallahassee

MEXICO

PACIFIC
OCEAN

Gulf of Mexico

ATLANTIC
OCEAN

Basketball at Indiana
University

Legend:
— Interstate highway
— Toll road
— U.S. roads
— Other roads
\ Dam
✈ Airport
★ State capital
○ Major port city
● Other city

N W E S

0   250   500 Miles
0   250   500 Kilometers
Lambert Azimuthal Equal-Area Projection

Steelmaking in Gary

Fort Wayne at Maumee River

Indiana Statehouse

Ohio River at Evansville

East Chicago
Gary
Portage
Hammond
La Porte
South Bend Regional Airport
South Bend
Goshen
Angola
Kankakee River
Plymouth
Bourbon
La Crosse
Warsaw
Fort Wayne
Fort Wayne Intl. Airport
Decatur
Maumee R.
Rensselaer
Rochester
Huntington
Monticello
Peru
Wabash
Wabash R.
Mississinewa Lake
Lafayette
Kokomo
Marion
Portland
Frankfort
Muncie
Wabash R.
Crawfordsville
Anderson
Richmond
St. Bernice
Indianapolis
Indianapolis International Airport
Fontanet
Rushville
Terre Haute
Shelbyville
Brookville Lake
Columbus
Lawrenceburg
Bloomington
Versailles
Monroe Lake
Bedford
Washington
Madison
White River
Vincennes
Scottsburg
Paoli
Jeffersonville
Patoka River
Jasper
Patoka Lake
New Albany
Princeton
Evansville Regional Airport
Evansville
Ohio River

Unit 4

Reading Social Studies

Focus Skill Compare and Contrast

Why It Matters Knowing how to compare and contrast can help you figure out how things are alike and how they are different.

▶ LEARN

When you **compare**, you think about how two or more things are alike. When you **contrast**, you think about how they are different.

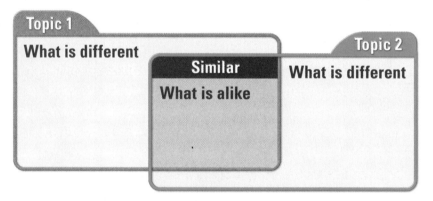

- *Like, alike, both, also*, and *same* are words that compare.
- *But, instead, however*, and *different* are words that contrast.

▶ PRACTICE

Read the paragraphs that follow. Compare and contrast the information in the second paragraph.

Same
Different

Both Indiana Constitutions set up its government and laws. Indiana was a territory applying for statehood when the first constitution was written in 1816, but it was a state when the second consitution was written in 1851.

Delegates at special conventions approved both constitutions. The first convention was held in Indiana's earlier capital, Corydon, and was attended by 43 delegates. The second convention, however, was held in the state's later capital, Indianapolis, and was attended by 150 delegates.

Read the paragraphs, and then answer the questions.

Farming in the Past and Today

When Indiana became a state, most Indiana farmers raised corn and hogs on small farms. At that time, farms needed many workers to plant and harvest crops. To plant corn, farmers used wooden plows pulled by animals. To harvest the corn, they picked each ear by hand.

Farming today is both like and different from farming in the past. Like Indiana's early farmers, many of its farmers today raise corn and hogs. However, some farmers now raise soybeans and cattle.

Modern machines have brought about many changes. Today, farmers do not use wooden plows pulled by animals, nor do they pick most crops by hand. Instead, they use large tractors equipped to plow and harvest. This allows farmers to produce more. As a result, most farms today are not small with many workers but large with few workers.

Compare and Contrast

1. How is Indiana's farming today like its early farming?
2. How is Indiana's farming today different from its early farming?

Start with a Song

Songs for Indiana

There are many songs that show the pride Hoosiers feel for the state of Indiana. These three songs share a common theme—the authors all wish to be home in Indiana. The first song, "On the Banks of the Wabash, Far Away," was chosen as the official state song of Indiana in 1913. Read these songs to learn more about the feelings Hoosiers have for our state.

On the Banks of the Wabash, Far Away

lyrics and music by Paul Dresser

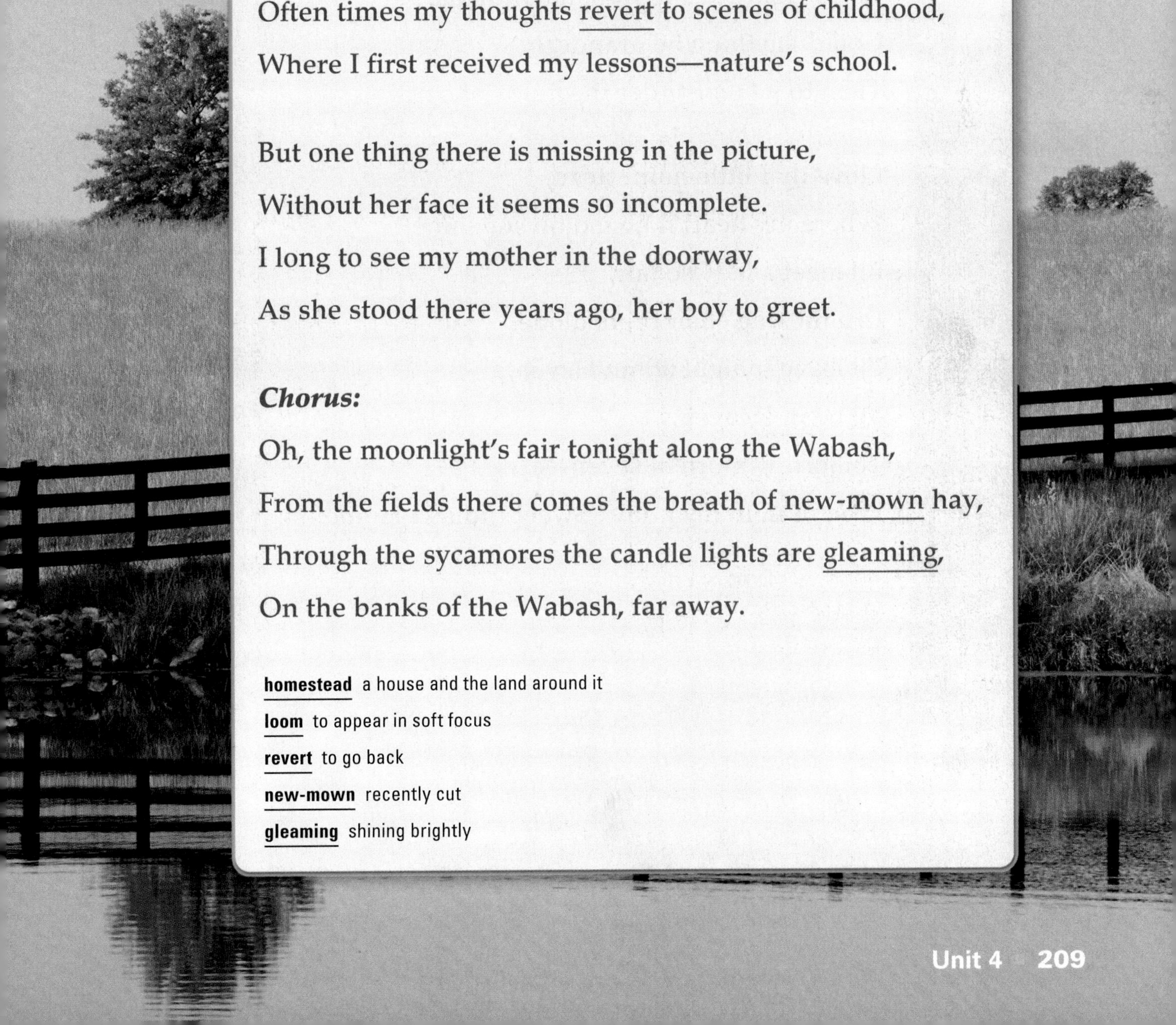

'Round my Indiana homestead wave the cornfields,

In the distance loom the woodlands clear and cool,

Often times my thoughts revert to scenes of childhood,

Where I first received my lessons—nature's school.

But one thing there is missing in the picture,

Without her face it seems so incomplete.

I long to see my mother in the doorway,

As she stood there years ago, her boy to greet.

Chorus:

Oh, the moonlight's fair tonight along the Wabash,

From the fields there comes the breath of new-mown hay,

Through the sycamores the candle lights are gleaming,

On the banks of the Wabash, far away.

homestead a house and the land around it

loom to appear in soft focus

revert to go back

new-mown recently cut

gleaming shining brightly

Sweet Indiana Home

lyrics and music by
Walter Donaldson

Chorus:

Down in Indiana, Indiana,

In my dreams I'm roamin',

Thru the shady gloamin',

Where I was born.

I'll go right back to Indiana, Indiana,

Could anything be grander,

Than to just meander the fields of corn.

I love that little homestead,

Where my heart'll be fed on sunshine,

I'll meet a lady so fair,

In a rocking chair there alone.

I'll leave tonight about eleven,

I'll be in Heaven,

Tomorrow morn at seven,

When I'm in my home, Sweet Indiana Home.

roamin' wandering

gloamin' twilight

meander wander

Can't Get Indiana Off My Mind

Lyrics by Robert De Leon   music by Hoagy Carmichael

Can't Get Indiana Off My Mind

That's the place I long to see,

Back in Indiana I will find

All the folks so dear to me.

How I'd love to see that lazy river stop and
    give "her" my love,

In my dreams I see a lady knittin' for the
    one she's thinking of.

Can't Get Indiana Off My Mind,

Anywhere I chance to roam

The moonlight on the Wabash that I left behind

Calls me back home.

Response Corner

1. **Focus Skill** **Compare and Contrast** How are the three songs alike? How are they different?

2. **Make It Relevant** How do these songs make you feel about Indiana? What are some things about Indiana that you would want to celebrate in a song?

Indiana Industries

WHAT TO KNOW
What industries are important to Indiana's economy?

VOCABULARY
economy p. 213
gross state product p. 213
productivity p. 213
surplus p. 214
competition p. 215
ethanol p. 216
tourism p. 217

PLACES
Gary
Hammond
Whiting
South Bend
Fort Wayne
Indianapolis
Lafayette
Marion
Kokomo
Evansville
New Albany

COMPARE AND CONTRAST

YOU ARE THERE Today is Career Day in your class. The parents of some of your classmates have come to talk about their jobs. You have listened to them talk about being nurses, factory workers, farmers, artists, business owners, computer programmers, and more. You are surprised to learn how many different kinds of jobs there are in Indiana. Then you wonder what job you might have one day and what you can do to prepare for that job.

> **TRANSPORTATION INDUSTRY**
Indiana is a leading producer of automobile parts.

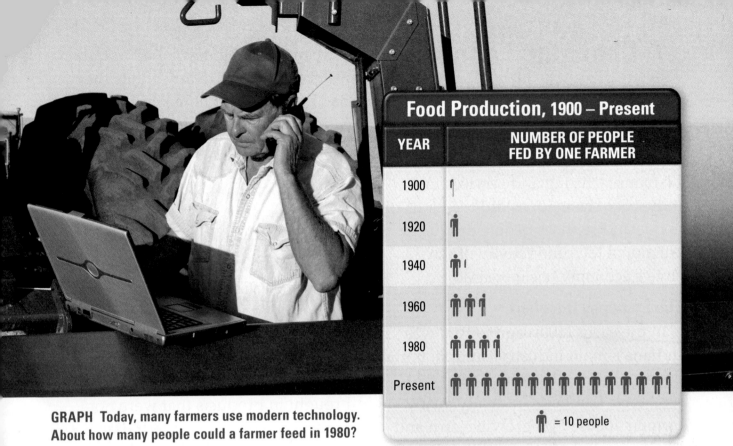

Food Production, 1900 – Present

YEAR	NUMBER OF PEOPLE FED BY ONE FARMER
1900	👤
1920	👤
1940	👤
1960	👤👤👤
1980	👤👤👤👤
Present	👤👤👤👤👤👤👤👤👤👤👤👤👤👤

👤 = 10 people

GRAPH Today, many farmers use modern technology. About how many people could a farmer feed in 1980?

Indiana's Economy

Indiana has a diverse economy. An **economy** is the way in which people of a state, region, or country use resources to meet their needs. In Indiana, people produce, sell, and buy many different products and services.

The Gross State Product

To better understand the economy of a state, people often discuss its GSP, or **gross state product**. This number is the total value of all the goods and services produced by the workers of the state in one year. For example, Indiana's GSP in 2006 was about $215 billion. This means that workers in Indiana produced a total of about $215 billion worth of goods and services that year.

Productivity

Productivity is another important number for measuring an economy. **Productivity** is the amount of goods and services produced in a period of time divided by the resources used to produce them. Some examples of resources include workers, equipment, and money.

The productivity of agriculture has increased dramatically over the years. New technologies, such as improved farming equipment, have allowed farmers to produce more food with fewer workers. For example, in 1900, one Indiana farmer fed about 2 people. Today, one can feed about 143 people!

READING CHECK ⬡**COMPARE AND CONTRAST**
How has the productivity of agriculture changed over the years?

A Changing Economy

In the past, Indiana's economy was an economy based mostly on agriculture. Over the years, the state's economy has changed to one based mostly on manufacturing and services. As industries changed, so did the kinds of goods and services people produced. All along, the productivity of the state's economy has increased.

The Economy Develops

In the early 1800s, agriculture was Indiana's main industry. At first, farmers produced only enough food to feed their families. Gradually, many farmers focused on growing corn and raising hogs. This allowed them to produce a **surplus**, or extra, amount of corn and hogs. They sold the surplus to earn money.

Manufacturing developed in Indiana as farmers began to buy goods they had once made at home. In towns, farmers bought clothing, household items, and some foods. People in towns made these and other products. Mills that ground corn into flour and factories that processed pork were centers of activity.

As manufacturing grew, so did the need for services. Two important services needed were those of merchants and banks. Merchants, or traders, helped sell Indiana's farming surplus to markets outside the state. They also brought in products that were not made, grown, or raised in Indiana. Banks provided safe places for people and businesses to keep their money. They also loaned money to people and to new and growing businesses.

PRODUCTIVITY IN INDIANA

> AGRICULTURE Indiana's early economy was based on agriculture.

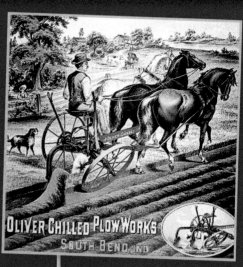

> SURPLUS Producing a surplus of food helped Indiana's economy grow.

Growth Continues

Indiana's economy continued to grow during the late 1800s. Towns provided more goods and services to the state's farming areas. Industries used more of the state's resources, including its timber, coal, and oil.

With a growing economy, Indiana's towns needed more workers with education. Workers needed skills to help run businesses and be more productive. To meet this need, more people attended schools.

During the early 1900s, productivity increased greatly in Indiana. New technologies helped bring about this change. Farmers used tractors instead of horse-drawn plows. Factories used electricity instead of steam to power machines. Huge machines performed the tasks that once required many workers to do by hand and with tools.

New Industries

By 1920, manufacturing replaced agriculture as Indiana's main industry. Huge factories produced iron and steel, automobiles, railroad cars, and electric machinery. Even so, farming remained important. Service industries also continued to grow.

The 1970s and 1980s were difficult times for Indiana's economy. At that time, Indiana factories began to face more competition from factories in other places. **Competition** is the effort among similar businesses to sell the most products. To better compete, Indiana's factories and other businesses began to add new technologies, such as computers and robots.

READING CHECK **CAUSE AND EFFECT**
What caused manufacturing to develop in Indiana?

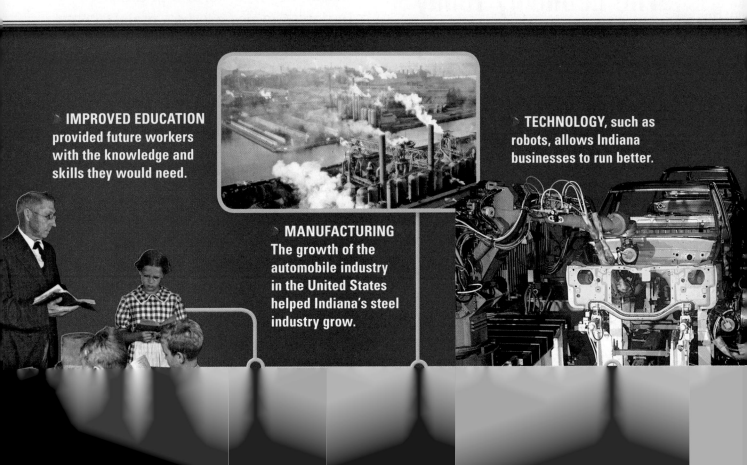

> IMPROVED EDUCATION provided future workers with the knowledge and skills they would need.

> MANUFACTURING The growth of the automobile industry in the United States helped Indiana's steel industry grow.

> TECHNOLOGY, such as robots, allows Indiana businesses to run better.

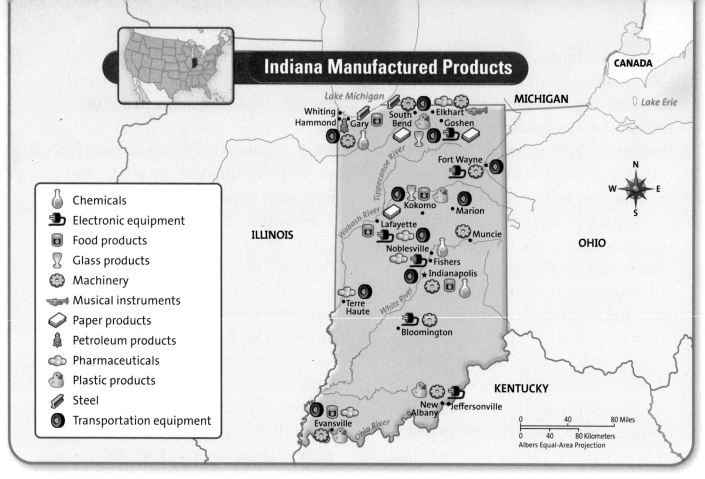

Indiana Manufactured Products

Chemicals
Electronic equipment
Food products
Glass products
Machinery
Musical instruments
Paper products
Petroleum products
Pharmaceuticals
Plastic products
Steel
Transportation equipment

Lake Michigan
Whiting
Hammond Gary
South Bend
Elkhart
Goshen
MICHIGAN
CANADA
Lake Erie
Fort Wayne
ILLINOIS
Kokomo
Marion
Lafayette
Muncie
Noblesville
Fishers
Indianapolis
OHIO
Terre Haute
Bloomington
New Albany Jeffersonville
KENTUCKY
Evansville

Tippecanoe River
Wabash River
White River
Ohio River

0   40   80 Miles
0   40   80 Kilometers
Albers Equal-Area Projection

MAP SKILL ❯ **HUMAN-ENVIRONMENT INTERACTIONS** Which Indiana city is a manufacturing center for musical instruments?

The Economy Today

Today, Indiana's economy has become more diverse. Hoosiers work in a variety of industries that produce many different products and services.

Agriculture and Mining

Agriculture and mining are both major industries in Indiana. However, few Hoosiers work in these industries. Machines perform most of the work.

Corn is Indiana's main crop. It provides feed for farm animals and food for people. Some corn is made into **ethanol**, a liquid that can be used as a fuel in automobiles. Other important farming products include soybeans,

wheat, hogs, cattle, and poultry. Indiana's mines produce mainly coal, limestone, sand, and gravel.

Manufacturing

Indiana factories employ nearly one-fourth of the state's workers. Important products include automobiles, automobile parts, steel, plastics, and chemicals.

Indiana has many manufacturing centers. In northern Indiana are **Gary**, **Hammond**, **Whiting**, **South Bend**, and **Fort Wayne**. In central Indiana are **Indianapolis**, **Lafayette**, **Marion**, and **Kokomo**. Both **Evansville** and **New Albany** are manufacturing centers in southern Indiana.

Service Industries

Service industries are the fastest-growing part of Indiana's economy. They employ nearly two-thirds of the state's workers. They include salespeople, teachers, doctors, mechanics, government workers, and others.

Tourism, or the business of serving visitors, is a growing service industry in Indiana. The tourism industry includes people who work in hotels, museums, and restaurants.

Life Sciences

The life sciences industry has grown in Indiana. It includes companies that perform medical research, sell health insurance, and make pharmaceuticals. Indiana companies, such as WellPoint, Eli Lilly, Zimmer, and Biomet, are leaders in the life sciences industry.

READING CHECK **SUMMARIZE**

What are five goods and services being produced in Indiana today?

❯ **CAREERS** Hoosiers do many kinds of jobs. This researcher works in a life sciences industry.

Summary

Indiana has a diverse economy. Over the years, the economy has changed from mainly agriculture to more manufacturing and service industries. Today, Hoosiers work in all these industries. Service industries make up the fastest-growing part of Indiana's economy.

REVIEW

1. **WHAT TO KNOW** What industries are important to Indiana's economy?

2. **VOCABULARY** Use the term **productivity** in a sentence about Indiana's economy.

3. **ECONOMICS** What was Indiana's main industry in the past? Which industry is growing most quickly today?

4. **CRITICAL THINKING** What has made productivity change in Indiana during the past 100 years?

5. **WRITE A JOB DESCRIPTION** Write a paragraph describing the duties of a job.

6. **COMPARE AND CONTRAST** (Focus Skill) On a separate sheet of paper, copy and complete this graphic organizer.

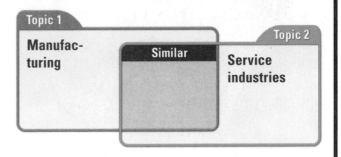

Topic 1
Manufacturing
Similar
Topic 2
Service industries

Make an Economic Choice

Why It Matters When you make a decision about what to buy, you are making an economic choice.

❯ LEARN

Sometimes you want to buy two items but have enough money for only one. If you give up one item to buy the other, you make a **trade-off**. The item you do not buy is the **opportunity cost**. Follow these steps to make good economic choices.

Step 1 List two items that you would like to buy, and write down the cost of each one.

Step 2 Think about how much money you have, and decide how much you want to spend and to save.

Step 3 Decide what you can buy with the money. Think about the trade-offs and opportunity costs.

Step 4 Make an economic choice. Then think about why your decision was the best choice.

❯ **ECONOMIC CHOICES** People make economic choices when they use banks (left) or buy products (right).

▶ **DAILY DECISIONS** Making a decision to buy a ticket to a museum is an economic choice.

▶ PRACTICE

Imagine that your class is visiting an Indiana museum. At the museum gift shop, you want to buy a shirt, which costs $10. You also want to buy a DVD about Indiana history. It costs $14. You have $15 to spend. Use these steps to make your economic choice.

1. What are your choices? How much does each one cost?

2. How much money do you have? How much do you want to spend? How much do you want to save?

3. What are the trade-offs and opportunity costs?

4. Make your choice, and explain it.

▶ APPLY

Make It Relevant Think of two items that you would like to buy, and recall the price of each item. Suppose that you have enough money to buy one item, but not both. First, explain to a partner the trade-off and the opportunity cost of each choice. Next, tell which economic choice you would make and why. Then make a plan for saving money. A savings plan will allow you to buy the other choice later on.

FIELD TRIP

READ ABOUT

The Indianapolis Motor Speedway is where the famous Indianapolis 500 race, or Indy 500, is run. The speedway was built in 1909 as a test track for the state's growing automobile industry.

The first Indy 500 was held in 1911. At that time, the speedway was paved with bricks. A small strip of those bricks, called the yard of bricks, remains near the starting line.

The Indy 500 has been held at the speedway every year except during the two world wars. Today, the speedway holds other big races each year, including the Brickyard 400.

FIND

INDIANA

Indianapolis

Indianapolis Motor Speedway

THE FIRST INDIANAPOLIS 500 RACE IN 1911

THE YARD OF BRICKS

THE RACE IS ON

INDIANAPOLIS MOTOR SPEED-
WAY HALL OF FAME MUSEUM

THE 2007 WINNER!

RACING FANS More than
250,000 people attend the
Indy 500 each year.

A VIRTUAL TOUR

GO ONLINE For more resources, go to
www.harcourtschool.com/ss1

Lesson 2

Indiana's Entrepreneurs

WHAT TO KNOW
In what ways have entrepreneurs changed life in Indiana?

VOCABULARY
entrepreneur p. 223
profit p. 223
investor p. 225

PEOPLE
Eli Lilly
Ball brothers
Studebaker brothers
Madame C. J. Walker
Marie Webster
Clessie Lyle Cummins
Orville Redenbacher

PLACES
Indianapolis
Muncie
South Bend
Marion
Columbus
Brazil

COMPARE AND CONTRAST

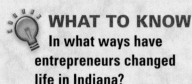

YOU ARE THERE A farmers' market opened recently near your neighborhood. There, farmers sell their fresh fruits and vegetables. The farmers live in nearby farming communities. Every Saturday, they haul their crops to the market in the city. You and your family stop at the market to make a purchase. You learn that the farmers set up the market because they wanted a place to sell their crops. They chose this area because no such market was there. You are grateful that people take the risk to open businesses that sell products you want.

SMALL BUSINESSES Each fruit and vegetable stand at this farmers' market in Indianapolis is a small business.

ILLUSTRATION Most entrepreneurs follow steps similar to the ones described below. Where might an entrepreneur get money for starting a business?

BUSINESS IDEA
An entrepreneur tries to fill a need or want.

BUSINESS PLAN
A business plan includes the products or services to be offered and prices.

OPEN THE BUSINESS
An entrepreneur finds a business location, hires workers, and advertises the products or services.

STARTUP COSTS
An entrepreneur might use his or her own money or borrow money from other people or a bank.

Entrepreneurs

Throughout Indiana's history, new businesses have been started by entrepreneurs (ahn•truh•pruh•NERZ). An **entrepreneur** is a person who takes a risk to start a new business. Entrepreneurs can start any kind of business they like.

Risk and Profit

Being an entrepreneur can be risky. A business may not succeed. In fact, many new businesses fail. However, some do quite well and can bring a great deal of profit to business owners. **Profit** is the money that is left over after all a business's expenses have been paid. The possibility of making a profit is why entrepreneurs are willing to take the risk to start a business.

An entrepreneur's business is more likely to succeed if it is based on the wants of people. The people might be in a local community or across a state, a nation, or the world. For example, people living in a community that already has four pet stores probably do not want more. If there are no car repair shops nearby, though, people would probably be happy to have one.

READING CHECK ☼COMPARE AND CONTRAST
What is one difference between a business that succeeds and one that fails?

Early Entrepreneurs

Many early entrepreneurs influenced Indiana. They created needed products and services and provided jobs for Hoosiers. They helped the state's economy grow.

Eli Lilly

In 1876, **Eli Lilly** bought a small drug laboratory in **Indianapolis**. One early success was making pills that were easy to swallow. Today, Eli Lilly and Company is one of the world's largest pharmaceutical companies.

The Ball Brothers

In 1880, the **Ball brothers** borrowed $200 to start the Ball Corporation in **Muncie**. The five brothers made glass jars for canning fruits and vegetables. Now located in Colorado, the company makes products ranging from food containers to space equipment.

The Studebaker Brothers

In the late 1800s, the **Studebaker brothers** began building wagons. The company of these five brothers was among the best-known wagon makers in the country. It built wagons by following the company's motto:

> **"Always give the customer more than you promise . . ."**

In 1902, the Studebaker brothers began building cars mainly at a factory in **South Bend**. Their cars were popular for many years. However, competition from other automobile makers caused the Studebaker Corporation to close in 1966.

Early Entrepreneurs in Indiana

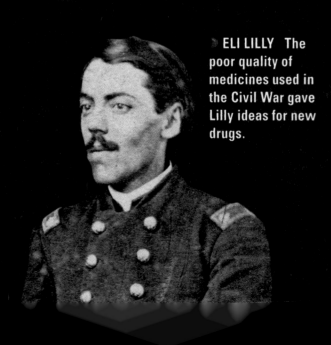

▶ ELI LILLY The poor quality of medicines used in the Civil War gave Lilly ideas for new drugs.

▶ THE STUDEBAKER BROTHERS supplied many of the wagons that settlers used to move west. Over time, they switched from building wagons to cars.

Madame C. J. Walker

In 1905, **Madame C. J. Walker** saw a need for cosmetic and hair products, especially for African-American women. At first, she made and sold products as a part-time business. By 1910, she had many salespeople and had opened a factory in Indianapolis.

Marie Webster

Marie Webster loved making quilts. In 1911, a magazine began featuring her quilts. Soon people wanted her quilting patterns. Webster began selling her patterns by mail order out of her home.

Today, a granddaughter runs a quilt pattern company that features Webster's designs. Webster's home in **Marion** is now the location of the Quilters Hall of Fame.

Clessie Lyle Cummins

Clessie Lyle Cummins was both an entrepreneur and inventor. As an inventor, he developed diesel engines. In 1919, he founded the Cummins Engine Company in **Columbus** with the help of an investor. An **investor** is someone who puts his or her money at risk in hopes of making a profit. Today, Cummins Incorporated sells diesel engines around the world.

Orville Redenbacher

A native of **Brazil**, Indiana, **Orville Redenbacher** set out to create better popcorn. After much testing, he developed an improved corn kernel. Today, Redenbacher's popcorn is one of the best-selling popcorns.

`READING CHECK` **MAIN IDEA AND DETAILS**
What want did Eli Lilly's company fulfill?

▷ **MARIE WEBSTER** wrote the first quilting book printed in the United States.

QUILTS
THEIR STORY AND HOW TO MAKE THEM
MARIE D. WEBSTER

NEW EDITION
of America's first Quilt book
with a biography of the author by
Rosalind Webster Perry

▷ **CLESSIE LYLE CUMMINS** was not only an entrepreneur but also an inventor.

▶ **INDIANA ENTREPRENEURS** Tim and Margi Griffith own and run a nature store in Evansville called Wild Birds Unlimited.

Entrepreneurs Today

Entrepreneurs continue to help Indiana's economy grow. Today, the state has more than 430,000 businesses. These businesses range from small neighborhood stores to giant global corporations.

Every day, Hoosiers open new businesses. Patricia Miller and Barbara Bradley Baekgaard formed Vera Bradley Designs. Based in Fort Wayne, their company makes women's bags. Mark Tarner founded the South Bend Chocolate Company. Sam Kwon runs Vesta Pharmaceuticals in Indianapolis. Indiana has many other entrepreneurs as well.

READING CHECK **MAIN IDEA AND DETAILS**
What kinds of businesses can be found in Indiana?

Summary

An entrepreneur is a person who takes a risk to start a new business. Indiana has had many famous and successful entrepreneurs. Today, Indiana's entrepreneurs continue to help the state's economy grow.

REVIEW

1. WHAT TO KNOW In what ways have entrepreneurs changed life in Indiana?

2. VOCABULARY Write a definition of an **entrepreneur**.

3. ECONOMICS Why do entrepreneurs take the risk of starting new businesses?

4. CRITICAL THINKING How did Indiana's early entrepreneurs make it possible for today's entrepreneurs to succeed?

5. CREATE A HALL OF FAME Draw pictures of Indiana's entrepreneurs from the past, and include captions.

6. COMPARE AND CONTRAST On a separate sheet of paper, copy and complete this graphic organizer.

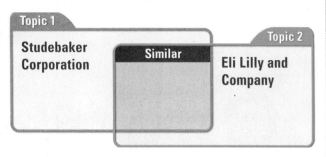

Topic 1
Studebaker Corporation

Similar

Topic 2
Eli Lilly and Company

William G. Mays

Biography

Trustworthiness
Respect
Responsibility
Fairness
Caring
Patriotism

"*I was . . . trying to help plant a more stable minority business community so more black-owned businesses would participate in the growth of Indianapolis.*"

William G. Mays was born in Indiana in 1946. His father was a chemistry professor. Mays earned degrees in chemistry and business from Indiana University.

In 1980, Mays started his own company. Today, Mays Chemical Company provides chemicals to the food and beverage, automotive, and pharmaceutical industries. Mays also owns *The Indianapolis Recorder*, the fourth-oldest African American newspaper in the country.

Over the years, Mays has used his success to give back to the community. He serves on the boards of many organizations, including the United Way of Central Indiana, the Indiana University Foundation, and the Indianapolis Chamber of Commerce. He works to encourage minority-owned businesses.

Why Character Counts

How do William G. Mays's actions show responsibility?

Time

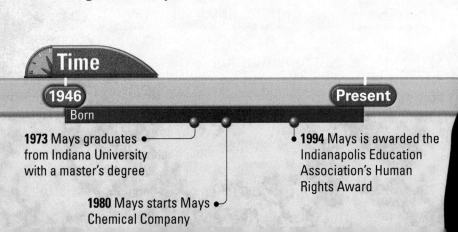

1946 Born

1973 Mays graduates from Indiana University with a master's degree

1980 Mays starts Mays Chemical Company

Present

1994 Mays is awarded the Indianapolis Education Association's Human Rights Award

THE COMMON GOOD

"I want my agents [sales women] to feel that their first duty is to humanity."

—Madame C. J. Walker

❯ **MADAME WALKER attended the opening ceremony for a YMCA in Indianapolis she gave money to help build.**

Successful entrepreneurs often improve their communities. They work for the common good, or the good of everyone in the community.

Indiana has a proud history of entrepreneurs who have helped their local communities. Eli Lilly presented ideas to Indianapolis for creating a water supply to the city. The Ball brothers provided money for Ball Memorial Hospital and Ball State University in Muncie.

Madame C. J. Walker also shared her success by helping her community. She gave money to charity groups and to Indiana schools. She built a center for the arts in downtown Indianapolis.

❯ **THE WALKER THEATRE in Indianapolis was started by Walker before she died in 1919. Walker's daughter went on to finish the project.**

Like Madame Walker, you can work for the common good of your community. This work can be something quite simple. For example, you might shovel the snow from your sidewalk so that your neighbors can walk more easily.

Young people in Indiana are eager to volunteer in ways that help their community. Some youth groups volunteer to help clean up neighborhood parks or beaches. Others may help by recycling goods that can be used again, such as plastic, newspapers, and aluminum cans. Some students donate their time to help other students with their homework. All these things contribute to the common good and make Indiana a better place to live.

Make It Relevant Why do you think people have a responsibility to work for the common good?

❯ **COMMUNITY CENTERS** provide for the common good of Hoosiers.

❯ **WORKING FOR THE COMMON GOOD** A young boy (right) volunteers to help build homes for the poor. Recycling (below) is another way that students can help in their communities.

Lesson  3

Trade in Indiana

WHAT TO KNOW
How does Indiana trade?

VOCABULARY
supply p. 231
demand p. 231
interdependence p. 233
export p. 234
import p. 234

PLACES
Port of Indiana-
   Jeffersonville
Great Lakes
Midwest
Illinois
Wisconsin
Ohio
Michigan
St. Lawrence Seaway

COMPARE AND CONTRAST

YOU ARE THERE Huge barges float at the ends of concrete piers. Giant cranes load steel, grain, and other cargo onto the ships. Workers are busy using cell phones and handheld computers.

You and your class are visiting the **Port of Indiana-Jeffersonville**. The port is located on the Ohio River. It is one of Indiana's largest, busiest ports. The port handles between 2 million and 3 million tons of cargo each year. Hundreds of people come to work here each day. Watching a barge depart, you wonder where in the world Indiana's products will end up.

▷ **MOVING CARGO** Barges are loaded at the Port of Indiana-Jeffersonville.

How Supply and Demand Can Affect Prices

Prices Usually Rise
• high demand
• low supply

• low demand
• high supply
Prices Usually Fall

CHART Changes in the supply and demand of products affect their prices. What factors cause prices to fall?

Supply and Demand

Business owners only want to provide products or services that people will want to buy. They will not make a profit if there is no demand for the product or service.

Business owners think about supply and demand when deciding what to make and what to sell. **Supply** is the amount of a product or service that is available. **Demand** is the amount of a product or service that people, as buyers, want and are willing to buy.

Prices Change

The prices of products and services change because of changes in supply and demand. For example, when more people want a product, the demand for the product increases. When the demand for the product increases, the price will increase. In contrast, the price will decrease when the demand decreases.

In the same way, the supply of a product or service affects prices. For example, when a business produces more of a product, the supply of the product increases. When the supply increases, the price will decrease. In contrast, the price will increase when the supply decreases.

Competition among businesses that sell similar products also causes prices to decrease. However, the business that offers the lowest price to buyers often sells more of its products.

READING CHECK ☼COMPARE AND CONTRAST
How does the price of a product change when the supply of the product decreases?

▶ **MODERN HIGHWAYS** support Indiana's trade within the state and with other states.

▶ **RAILROADS** in Indiana carry mostly freight, or transported goods.

Trading Within Indiana

Trade is an important part of every economy. It allows people to sell their surpluses of products and services so that they can buy those they do not produce. In this way, both sides of the exchange can benefit.

Trade in the Past

Trade has long been important in Indiana. Early Native Americans traded with one another. By the early 1700s, they traded with Europeans. They traded furs for European goods, such as metal tools and weapons.

Trade often took place along the **Great Lakes** and on Indiana's rivers. Over time, Europeans built trading posts along trade routes. Some posts became towns.

For settlers, towns built along rivers became important trading centers. Farmers carried their farming products by boat to towns located along rivers or by wagon on rough roads. At towns, they traded their products for many goods, including clothing and tools.

Trade Today

Today, people move products by land, water, and air within Indiana. Trucks carry the farming products of northern and central Indiana all over the state. Manufactured goods move by boat, truck, and airplane from places where they are made to places where they are sold.

READING CHECK ☼COMPARE AND CONTRAST
How is trade within Indiana today similar to trade in the past?

▶ **MAJOR PORTS** in Indiana include one on Lake Michigan and two on the Ohio River.

▶ **AIRPLANES** provide a fast way for people to send freight and mail.

Trading with Other States

Indiana depends on trade with other states. This trade benefits both Indiana and its trading partners.

Trading with the Midwest

Indiana's biggest trading partners in the **Midwest** are **Illinois**, **Wisconsin**, **Ohio**, and **Michigan**. Its trade with these states takes place mainly by interstate highways, railroads, and the **St. Lawrence Seaway**.

Indiana's trade with neighboring states makes up an important part of the state's economy. About two-fifths of all goods shipped out of Indiana go to neighboring states. Almost one-half of all goods coming into Indiana come from other states in the Midwest.

Interdependence

Trade creates interdependence between states in the Midwest. **Interdependence** means that people in each place depend on people in other places for resources, products, and services. For example, Indiana ships steel from its ports to Illinois each year. It then receives goods made with the steel back from Illinois.

Trade also creates interdependence between Indiana and states outside the Midwest. Indiana ships automobiles across the nation. It then imports from other states goods it does not produce. For example, Indiana gets citrus fruit, such as oranges and grapefruit, from Florida and California.

READING CHECK **MAIN IDEA AND DETAILS**
Which states are Indiana's biggest trading partners in the Midwest?

Trading with the World

Indiana's economy is made up of more than trade within the United States. It is connected to economies around the world.

World Trade

The world's economies have become more global. For example, the United States sells many **exports**, or goods shipped from one country to be sold in another. It also buys many **imports**, or goods brought into one country from another country.

Global trade means that many countries are interdependent. It allows them to exchange resources, products, and services. A country might have just one major export, such as oil. It must then depend on imports from other countries for almost everything else. Some countries have many different products to export.

Indiana's Global Connections

Indiana businesses trade with about 200 countries each year. In 2006, Indiana's exports totaled more than $22 billion. Major exports include automobiles, trucks, machinery, chemicals, and pharmaceuticals.

Indiana's connections to the global economy are growing. More international companies, or those that do business around the world, are coming to Indiana. They include automobile makers Toyota, Honda, Subaru, and Daimler and the medical equipment manufacturer Roche Diagnostics.

Indiana Exports

ILLUSTRATION Which two countries are Indiana's top export markets?

Indiana's Top Export Markets, 2006

RANK	COUNTRY
❶	Canada
❷	Mexico
❸	United Kingdom
❹	France
❺	Germany
❻	China
❼	Netherlands
❽	Australia

North America

South America

Several Indiana companies are international companies. They include pharmaceutical company Eli Lilly of Indianapolis, medical equipment manufacturer Biomet of Warsaw, and engine maker Cummins Incorporated of Columbus.

READING CHECK MAIN IDEA AND DETAILS
What are Indiana's major exports?

Summary

Indiana's business owners think about supply and demand when deciding what to make and sell. Indiana's economy is made up of trade within the state and with other states. It also includes trade with countries around the world.

1. **WHAT TO KNOW** How does Indiana trade?

2. **VOCABULARY** Use **supply** and **demand** in a sentence to describe how prices change.

3. **ECONOMICS** How do both parties benefit from trade?

4. **CRITICAL THINKING** Why do you think waterways have always been important to Indiana's trade?

5. **WRITE A SUMMARY** Write several paragraphs summarizing Indiana's trade. Include information about trade in the past and present and trading within the state, between states, and with other countries.

6. **COMPARE AND CONTRAST** On a sheet of paper, copy and complete this graphic organizer.

Topic 1
Trade with other states
Similar
Topic 2
Trade with other countries

Europe

Asia

Africa

INDIANA EXPORTS

Read a Double-Bar Graph

Why It Matters Graphs can help you compare numbers. A **double-bar graph** makes it easy to compare two sets of numbers.

❯ LEARN

Suppose you want to see the changes over time in the value of Indiana's exports to other countries. The double-bar graph on page 237 compares the values of Indiana's exports to four countries in 2005 and 2006.

Step 1 Read the graph's title, the labels, and the information in the key. The left side of the graph shows the value of exports in billions of dollars. Countries to which Indiana exports are listed along the bottom. Each green bar shows the total value of exports to a country in 2005. Each purple bar shows the total value of exports to the same country in 2006.

Step 2 Read the double-bar graph. Run your finger up to the top of each bar and then left to the dollar amount.

Step 3 Compare the numbers for a certain country. A taller bar stands for a larger value of exports. Look at the difference between the heights of the green bar and the purple bar. This shows the difference in the export values for the two years.

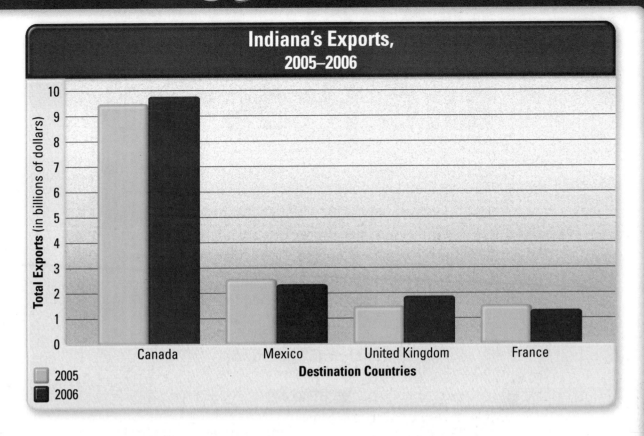

Indiana's Exports, 2005–2006

Total Exports (in billions of dollars)

Destination Countries: Canada, Mexico, United Kingdom, France

2005
2006

▶ PRACTICE

Use the double-bar graph to answer these questions.

1 By about how much did the value of Indiana's exports to the United Kingdom change between 2005 and 2006?

2 What can you tell about the value of Indiana's exports to Mexico and France between 2005 and 2006?

▶ APPLY

Make a double-bar graph that compares the values of Indiana's exports to four more countries in 2005 and 2006. Use the export values listed in the paragraph below. Then write a paragraph that describes each comparison.

Indiana's exports to Japan were $770 million in 2005 and $830 million in 2006. Exports to Germany were $690 million in 2005 and $735 million in 2006. Exports to the Netherlands were $425 million in 2005 and $470 million in 2006. Exports to China were $420 million in 2005 and $475 million in 2006.

Chart and Graph Skills

Money, Past and Present

Background People in Indiana, in the United States, and across the world have used many kinds of things as money. Money has several important uses. It can be used to buy goods and services. Without money, people would have to trade goods and services for other goods and services. Money lets people use prices to set certain values on goods and services. Money can also be saved to be used when it is needed.

DBQ **Document-Based Question** Study these primary sources, and answer the questions.

WAMPUM BELTS

Some Native Americans in what is now Indiana used wampum belts as money. These belts were made of tiny shell beads.

DBQ ❶ What other uses do you think wampum belts had?

SHELLS

The ancient Chinese used shells as money. They later used metal copies of shells.

DBQ ❷ Why do you think the Chinese of long ago used shells as money?

FURS

During the 1600s, settlers in many parts of North America, including what is now Indiana, used goods such as metal tools and cloth to trade with Native Americans for furs.

DBQ ❸ Which do you think was easier for Native Americans to use for trade—wampum belts or furs?

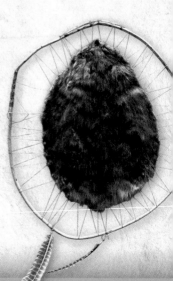

CIVIL WAR MONEY

During the Civil War, metal coins were scarce. The United States government made paper bills that could be used anywhere.

DBQ ④ Why do you think metal coins were scarce during the Civil War?

PAPER MONEY AND COINS

The United States uses the dollar as its unit of money. Many countries in Europe use the euro.

DBQ ⑤ How are coins and paper bills alike? How are they different?

ELECTRONIC MONEY

Today, more and more people use computers to move money. They use credit cards to pay for purchases. They use bankcards to put money into their banks and take it out.

DBQ ⑥ Why might some people prefer using bankcards?

WRITE ABOUT IT

Write a paragraph that compares and contrasts two different things that have been used as money over the years.

GO ONLINE For more resources, go to www.harcourtschool.com/ss1

4 Indiana's State Government

WHAT TO KNOW
What are the branches of Indiana's state government?

VOCABULARY
legislative branch p. 242
bill p. 242
executive branch p. 243
budget p. 243
veto p. 243
appoint p. 243
judicial branch p. 243
appeal p. 243

PEOPLE
Mitch Daniels
Becky Skillman
Todd Rokita
Randall T. Shepard
Richard Lugar
Evan Bayh
Dan Burton
Julia Carson
John Roberts

PLACES
Indianapolis

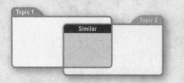

COMPARE AND CONTRAST

YOU ARE THERE

Your class is visiting the Indiana Statehouse in **Indianapolis**. Your tour begins in the rotunda. The tour guide points out the magnificent statues and stained-glass windows. Then you all walk by the governor's office. Next, you visit the House and Senate chambers. You get to sit where Indiana's lawmakers sit when the government is at work. You also visit the Supreme Court chamber and view pictures of judges of the past and present.

Office of the Governor

Indiana's Constitution

The Indiana Constitution in use today was written in 1851. It replaced an earlier version of 1816. Since 1851, Indiana's constitution has been amended many times. Some parts of the original constitution have been taken out, and new ideas have been added.

The Preamble, or introduction, to the Indiana Constitution states that its purposes are to establish justice, keep public order, and make sure freedom lasts. It begins

> **"TO THE END, that justice be established, public order maintained, and liberty perpetuated. . . . "**

Bill of Rights

Most articles, or sections, of the Indiana Constitution deal with how the government should be run. The state constitution divides Indiana's government into branches and tells what powers each branch has.

The first article of the constitution is the Bill of Rights. Unlike the other articles, the Bill of Rights outlines the rights and freedoms of Indiana citizens. It includes the right to public education, to gather freely, and to a speedy and fair trial. The Bill of Rights also grants Indiana citizens freedom of religion and speech.

READING CHECK ♂ **COMPARE AND CONTRAST**
How does the first article of the Indiana Constitution differ from the other articles?

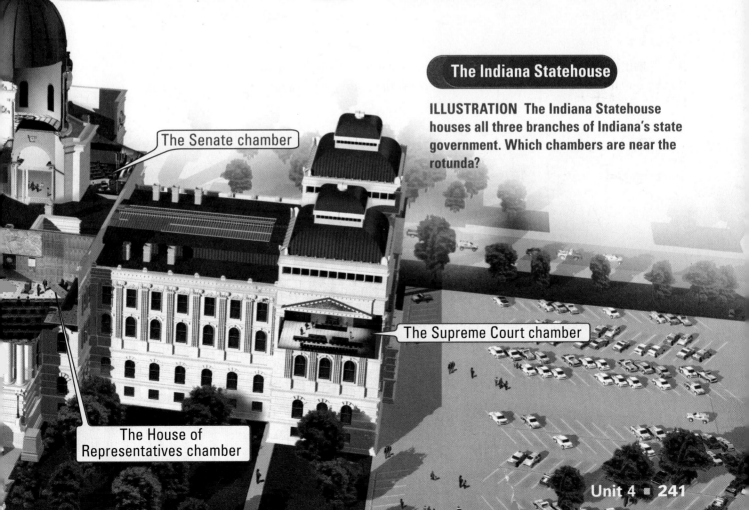

The Indiana Statehouse

ILLUSTRATION The Indiana Statehouse houses all three branches of Indiana's state government. Which chambers are near the rotunda?

The Senate chamber

The Supreme Court chamber

The House of Representatives chamber

Branches of Government

Like the United States Constitution, the Indiana Constitution divides the state government into three branches. These branches are the legislative branch, the executive branch, and the judicial branch. Leaders of all three branches of the state government have offices in Indiana's Statehouse.

The Indiana Constitution describes the main responsibilities and powers of each branch of state government. Like the United States Constitution, it gives each branch of government different powers. It also sets up a system of checks and balances so that no one branch can become too powerful or misuse its power.

The Legislative Branch

Indiana's **legislative branch** writes state laws. The state legislature is called the General Assembly.

The General Assembly has two parts, known as houses—the Senate and the House of Representatives. The Senate has 50 members who serve four-year terms. The House of Representatives has 100 members who serve two-year terms. Members are elected by voters in their districts, or voting areas.

Members of each house can present **bills**, or plans for new laws. Each house first works on bills by itself. Bills that are passed, or agreed to, by one house are sent on to the other house. If both houses pass a bill, it can become state law.

▶ THE INDIANA GOVERNMENT CENTER includes the Indiana Statehouse (background) and buildings of offices that support the state government.

Branches of Indiana's State Government

LEGISLATIVE BRANCH	EXECUTIVE BRANCH	JUDICIAL BRANCH
General Assembly	Governor	Supreme Court Judges
The Indiana Senate and House of Representatives present bills and write state laws.	The governor and other leaders enforce state laws, or make sure they are carried out.	Courts decide whether state laws have been broken or whether they go against the Indiana Constitution.

TABLE According to the Indiana Constitution, the state government is divided into three branches. What is the main responsibility of the judicial branch?

The Executive Branch

The **executive branch** makes sure that state laws are carried out. The governor is the leader of the executive branch. Indiana's voters elect the governor to serve a four-year term.

The governor has many duties and powers. One job is to create the yearly state **budget**, or written plan for how to spend money. The governor can either approve or **veto**, or reject, bills the legislature passes.

The governor shares the work of the executive branch with other leaders. The lieutenant governor is elected as part of the governor's team. Other leaders run various departments such as the Department of Agriculture. The governor can **appoint**, or choose, people to lead these departments.

The Judicial Branch

The **judicial branch** decides whether state laws agree with Indiana's constitution. It also makes sure that laws are carried out fairly. This branch is made up of all the state's judges and courts. The governor appoints state judges.

Indiana has several levels of courts, including the court of appeals, circuit courts, and county and city courts. A person not satisfied with the result of a trial can **appeal**, or ask that it be judged again in a higher court.

The Indiana Supreme Court is the state's highest court. This court is made up of a chief justice, or head judge, and four justices.

READING CHECK ⟳COMPARE AND CONTRAST
How are the roles of the legislative branch and executive branch different?

State Leaders

Indiana's state government is made up of many officials, or leaders, working together. Voters elect some of these officials. The governor also appoints, or chooses, officials. Groups of leaders appoint officials as well.

State Offices

The governor is the top official in the state. Governor **Mitch Daniels** took office in 2005. He is known for having balanced the state's budget.

The lieutenant governor is the state's second-highest official. He or she takes over the governor's duties if necessary. The lieutenant governor also serves as the leader of the Senate in the legislative branch. In 2005, **Becky Skillman** became lieutenant governor.

The secretary of state is the third-highest official. This leader oversees elections and the state's economy. In 2007, voters reelected **Todd Rokita** as Indiana's secretary of state.

The chief justice of the supreme court is the top official of the judicial branch. The governor appoints the court's five justices, and a group of leaders appoints one of them as the chief justice. Former governor Robert D. Orr appointed **Randall T. Shepard** as a justice in 1985. Two years later, Shepard became the chief justice.

READING CHECK ☼COMPARE AND CONTRAST
How is the selection of the supreme court's five justices different from the selection of its chief justice?

MITCH DANIELS

BECKY SKILLMAN

TODD ROKITA

The Federal System

Indiana is part of the country's federal system of government. In the federal system, the national and state governments share power.

Indiana voters elect leaders to represent them in the United States Congress. Each state elects two senators to the United States Senate. Senators **Richard Lugar** and **Evan Bayh** have long represented Indiana.

The number of representatives a state elects to the United States House of Representatives is based on the state's population. Indiana voters elect nine representatives to the House. Representative **Dan Burton** has served in office since 1983. **Julia Carson** served for more than ten years.

READING CHECK SUMMARIZE
How are Hoosiers represented in Congress?

▶ **JOHN ROBERTS**, who grew up in Indiana, is the Chief Justice of the United States Supreme Court.

Summary

The Indiana Constitution provides the plan for state government. It divides the state government into three branches—legislative, executive, and judicial. Each branch has different powers and responsibilities.

REVIEW

1. **WHAT TO KNOW** What are the branches of Indiana's state government?

2. **VOCABULARY** Use the terms **legislative branch** and **bill** in a sentence.

3. **CIVICS AND GOVERNMENT** What are some of the rights given to citizens in the Indiana Bill of Rights?

4. **CRITICAL THINKING** Why do you think the Indiana Constitution is modeled after the United States Constitution?

5. **MAKE A TABLE** Create a table that describes one leader from each branch of Indiana's state government. Include the office, how the leader is chosen, and the duties of the office.

6. **COMPARE AND CONTRAST** (Focus Skill) On a separate sheet of paper, complete this graphic organizer.

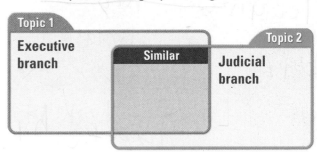

Topic 1
Executive branch

Similar

Topic 2
Judicial branch

Indiana's Local Governments

WHAT TO KNOW
What are the different local governments of Indiana?

VOCABULARY
county seat p. 247
municipal p. 247
income p. 249

PLACES
Rochester
Fulton County
Indianapolis
Marion County

 **COMPARE AND CONTRAST**

YOU ARE THERE
Today your class is visiting the courthouse in **Rochester**, where you have lived all your life. You have ridden your bike by the courthouse a thousand times. Until today, though, you did not know that the courthouse was the workplace of people who help govern **Fulton County**. You also learn that Fulton County was named after Robert Fulton, inventor of the steamboat.

> **THE FULTON COUNTY COURTHOUSE** is located in the city of Rochester. County courthouses are often located in the largest city in the county.

▶ **UNIGOV** The city-county council of Unigov discusses issues that affect the citizens of Indianapolis and Marion County.

Local Governments

Indiana has different kinds of local governments. Each kind takes care of the needs of the people who live there.

From Counties to Districts

Indiana is divided into 92 counties. Most counties are led by three county commissioners and a county council. These officials are elected by the voters of the county in which they serve.

Most county governments meet at county courthouses or nearby offices. The city in which the county courthouse is located is the **county seat**.

Each county is further divided into townships. Each township is led by a township trustee and board.

Also within each county are cities and towns. The governments of cities and towns are called **municipal** governments. Cities and towns are usually led by elected mayors. In cities, the legislature is the city council. In towns, it is the town council.

Indianapolis and **Marion County** have a unique government called Unigov. A city-county council makes laws for both the city and the county.

Special districts are also found throughout the state. Special districts are usually set up to handle a single issue, such as flooding or schools.

READING CHECK ☼**COMPARE AND CONTRAST**
How are the ways in which county and municipal governments are led different?

Government Services

The state and local governments in Indiana provide many services for citizens. These services range from building roads to collecting trash.

Providing Services

The state government is responsible for a wide variety of services across the state. For example, it builds and repairs state roads and highways. It maintains state parks and museums. It provides state police protection.

County governments provide many services within the county. They build and repair county roads and provide county police and fire protection. They also collect trash, run county courts, and organize elections.

▶ SOUTH BEND CITY SEAL

Township responsibilities include fire protection and help for people who do not have enough money for food or shelter. They also handle weed control and fence disputes.

Cities and towns offer many services as well. They provide city police and fire protection, city street repair, city water, city parks, and much more.

Usually, special districts provide one service, such as schools, libraries, or fire protection. These districts overlap with county and city governments.

In addition to services, the state and local governments also provide goods for citizens. These goods include printed materials, such as brochures and pamphlets, and items

▶ FIRE PROTECTION is just one of the many services that local governments provide. Taxes help pay for the salaries and equipment of firefighters.

for those in need, such as food and medicines.

Paying for Government

To pay for the goods and services they provide, the state and local governments collect taxes. This money that each citizen must give supports the government. The state government gives local governments some of the money it collects from state taxes.

Taxes can be collected in many ways. Governments tax people's **income**, or the money they earn. The state also collects sales tax. The sales tax is an amount added to the cost of items people buy. Local governments collect property taxes from people who own buildings or land. People also pay taxes on the vehicles they own and the gasoline they use.

READING CHECK MAIN IDEA AND DETAILS
How do local governments pay for the services they provide?

▶ **TAXES** help pay for building and repairing roads.

Summary

Local governments in Indiana include counties, townships, cities and towns, and special districts. The state and local governments provide important services to citizens, such as road repair and trash collection. They pay for such services by collecting taxes.

REVIEW

1. **WHAT TO KNOW** What are the different local governments of Indiana?

2. **VOCABULARY** Use the term **municipal** in a sentence about governments of cities and towns.

3. **CIVICS AND GOVERNMENT** How do state and local governments use tax money to help citizens?

4. **CRITICAL THINKING** Why do you think local governments are needed?

5. ✎ **WRITE A LIST** Write a list of five or more services your local governments provide.

6. ⭐(Focus Skill) **COMPARE AND CONTRAST** On a separate piece of paper, copy and complete this graphic organizer.

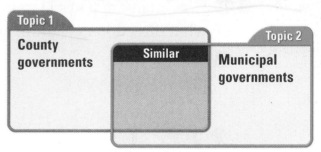

Topic 1
County governments
Similar
Topic 2
Municipal governments

Use a Road Map and Mileage Table

Why It Matters Road maps show us how far one place is from another. By knowing the distance between two places, people can choose the best route for travel.

▶ LEARN

A **mileage table** tells how far apart two places on a map are. Look at the Indiana mileage table on page 251. Put your finger on *Indianapolis* in the lefthand column. Move your finger three boxes to the right across the table. The *125* in that box is in the column with *Fort Wayne* at the top. This tells you that Indianapolis is 125 miles from Fort Wayne.

You can also use the **scale** on a map to measure distances. The scale at the bottom center of the Indiana road map shows that 1 inch equals about 50 miles. The length in inches between two places on a map lets you figure out the miles between them. For cities listed on a mileage table, however, using the table is much faster.

▶ PRACTICE

Use the road map and mileage table on page 251 to answer the questions.

1 How many miles is Hammond from Indianapolis? In what direction is Hammond from Indianapolis?

2 What is the distance between Evansville and Bloomington?

▶ APPLY

Use a road map and mileage table to plan a trip between two Indiana cities. Figure out the distance in miles.

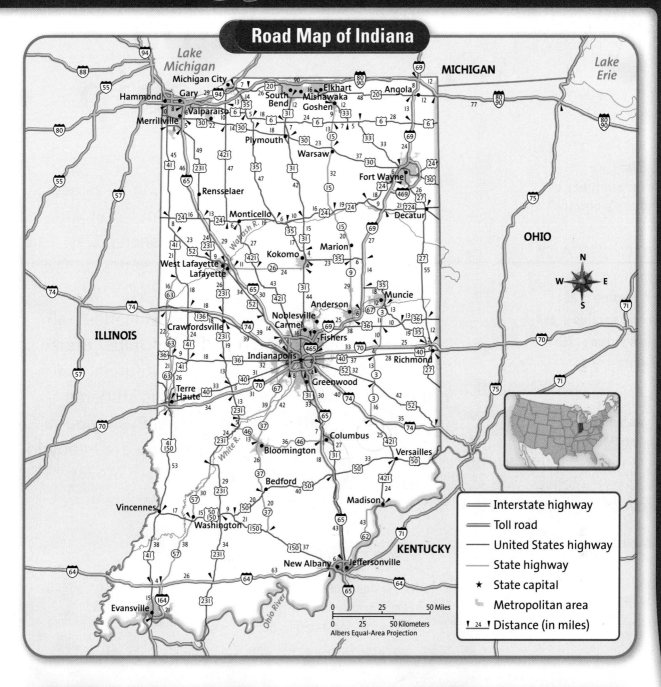

Road Map of Indiana

Map and Globe Skills

Indiana Road Mileage

	BLOOMINGTON	EVANSVILLE	FORT WAYNE	HAMMOND	INDIANAPOLIS
Bloomington		139	178	208	51
Evansville	139		310	285	182
Fort Wayne	178	310		140	125
Hammond	208	285	140		158
Indianapolis	51	182	125	158	

Indiana Citizenship

WHAT TO KNOW

What are the responsibilities of Indiana's citizens?

VOCABULARY

register p. 253
citizenship p. 254
public service p. 254
civic virtue p. 255
civility p. 255

PEOPLE

Ryan White
Raven Peterson

COMPARE AND CONTRAST

YOU ARE THERE

Today is September 17. Your class sits in the Indiana Supreme Court to take part in Constitution Day and Citizenship Day. This yearly holiday honors the signing of the United States Constitution on September 17, 1787.

During the event, several Indiana leaders talk about the importance of both the United States Constitution and the Indiana Constitution. Later, the Indiana secretary of state helps students 18 years old or older sign up to vote. Even though you are not old enough to vote, you are happy to be part of this important event.

FAST FACT

A large chandelier hangs from the ceiling in the Supreme Court. It is 24 feet tall and 6 feet wide, and it weighs 500 pounds.

Hoosier Rights and Responsibilities

Earlier, you learned that Hoosiers have many rights guaranteed by the Indiana Constitution. These rights include the right to vote and the right to hold office.

Citizen Responsibilities

With the rights guaranteed to Hoosiers come many responsibilities. A responsibility is something that a person should do.

Some responsibilities are stated in laws. Both United States and Indiana laws say that citizens are responsible for paying taxes and obeying laws. Citizens who are 18 years of age or older are also required to serve on juries when called to do so.

Citizens of Indiana have other responsibilities that are not required by law. Voting is an important responsibility. By voting, citizens participate in their government. A democracy can work only when citizens take part in the process.

In Indiana, a citizen 18 years old or older must **register**, or sign up, to vote before an election. Registered voters in Indiana may vote to elect the President of the United States, the governor of Indiana, county and city leaders, and others.

With voting comes the responsibility of being an informed citizen. Before an election, voters should prepare by learning about important issues and about the candidates.

READING CHECK ⭮**COMPARE AND CONTRAST**
How is voting a right and a responsibility?

> **CONSTITUTION DAY AND CITIZENSHIP DAY** Students visit the Indiana Supreme Court to learn about the United States and Indiana Constitutions.

Taking Part

All citizens of Indiana and the United States enjoy the rights of citizenship. To have **citizenship** is to be a full member of a community or country. Many Indiana citizens work to make their community a better place.

Volunteering

Some Hoosiers help others in their communities by volunteering. In doing this, they show compassion, or an understanding of people who suffer. Some volunteers collect food and clothing for people who are in need. Others help out at animal shelters.

Indiana has a variety of volunteer organizations. Some are related to education, health care, and the arts. Others help protect the environment or provide help for the homeless.

Public Service

People in **public service** work for the good of the community. Being a government leader is one kind of public service. Some government leaders, such as the governor, are elected. Others, such as the chief of police, are appointed.

Active citizens communicate with their government officials. They go to meetings, write letters, and call or e-mail leaders to give their opinions.

Patriotism

Hoosiers also help their community and nation through their patriotism, or love of country. Displaying the flag and reciting the Pledge of Allegiance are both ways of showing patriotism.

READING CHECK **MAIN IDEA AND DETAILS**
How can citizens help their communities?

▶ CITIZENSHIP Students can take part in citizenship in different ways. A young girl (left) shows her patriotism at a parade. A boy (below) volunteers to carry sandbags used to hold back floodwaters.

Children IN HISTORY

Ryan White

Ryan White of Kokomo learned that he had gotten AIDS from a medical procedure in 1984. He was 13 years old. Little was known about the disease at that time. Ryan was not allowed to go to school because parents were afraid their children might catch it from him. Ryan and his family fought for his right to attend school and won.

People admired Ryan's bravery and his patience with those who did not understand. He educated people about AIDS through his appearances on television and his speeches to crowds. He helped them understand how to be caring and respectful toward people who have the disease.

Make It Relevant Why do you think people found Ryan so inspiring?

Civic Virtues

Communities in Indiana depend on their citizens to show certain civic virtues. **Civic virtues** are actions that contribute to the smooth running of a democracy.

Respect for Others

Many civic virtues relate to respect. Politeness, or **civility**, is an important trait needed to work with others in a community. Citizens need to respect the rights and dignity, or worth, of other people. It is also important to respect the right of others to have opinions different from your own.

Citizens must also respect the law. They must obey laws and settle their disagreements peacefully.

Individual Responsibility

For a democracy to work well, all citizens must be willing to take individual responsibility. This means that each person takes responsibility for his or her own actions.

Good citizens show self-discipline. They obey laws and are honest and fair without having to be told by others how to act. They also have the courage to stand up for what they believe in.

The Common Good

Another responsibility involved in being a good citizen is working for the common good. One way of working for the common good is to help clean up a community park. Another way is to help the homeless.

Demonstrating Civic Virtues

Young people can practice civic virtues by volunteering in their communities. Young people can practice civic virtues every day in school, at home, and in the community.

Raven Peterson began volunteering when she was a sixth-grade student in Carmel, Indiana. She helps School on Wheels provide an education to homeless children. She received a national award for her volunteer service when she was 12 years old.

READING CHECK **SUMMARIZE**
What are civic virtues?

▶ **RAVEN PETERSON,** shown with Senator Richard Lugar, traveled to Washington, D.C., to receive a national award for her volunteer work.

Summary

Hoosiers are guaranteed certain rights by the United States and Indiana Constitutions. Those rights come with responsibilities. People can be good citizens and show civic virtues.

REVIEW

1. **WHAT TO KNOW** What are the responsibilities of Indiana's citizens?

2. **VOCABULARY** Describe how **civic virtues** and **civility** are related.

3. **CIVICS AND GOVERNMENT** What are four examples of civic virtues?

4. **CRITICAL THINKING** Why do you think it is important for citizens to take part in government?

5. ✎ **WRITE A NEWSPAPER ARTICLE** Research an issue that affects Indiana. Find out the different opinions people have on the issue. Then write a newspaper article explaining the different sides of the issue.

6. ⭐ (Focus Skill) **COMPARE AND CONTRAST** On a separate sheet of paper, copy and complete this graphic organizer.

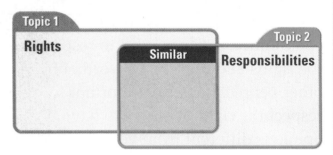

Topic 1 — Rights
Similar
Topic 2 — Responsibilities

Yvonne Shaheen

Biography

Trustworthiness
Respect
Responsibility
Fairness
Caring
Patriotism

"I don't want to be the biggest. I just want to be the best."

Yvonne Shaheen has been described as the perfect example of someone who gives back to the community. For years, she has helped Hoosiers in Indianapolis.

Shaheen developed a leadership role in her work and her community after tragedy struck in 1987. With little experience, Shaheen took over the company she owned with her husband after he died. She worked 16 hours a day, 6 days a week to grow the company. Yet, she found time to take part in 16 non-profit and civic groups.

Since retiring in 2004, Shaheen has continued to give back to her community. She is active in helping Junior Achievement, Boy Scouts of America, the Children's Museum of Indianapolis, the Arts Council of Indiana, and many others. Shaheen has received several awards for her community work, including the 2006 Michael A. Carroll Award and the 1999 Charles L. Whistler Award.

Why Character Counts

How has Yvonne Shaheen shown she cares about people?

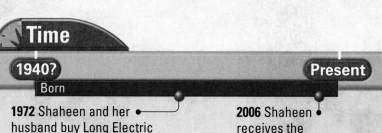

Time

1940? — Present
Born

1972 Shaheen and her husband buy Long Electric Company in Indianapolis

2006 Shaheen receives the Michael A. Carroll Award

Symbols of Indiana

Background Symbols are images that stand for important ideas. The symbols on these pages remind people of what it means to live in Indiana and why Hoosiers can be proud of their state.

DBQ **Document-Based Question** Study these primary sources, and answer the questions.

INDIANA STATE SONG

The state song of Indiana is "On the Banks of the Wabash, Far Away."

DBQ **1** What are some reasons Hoosiers might like to hear songs about their state?

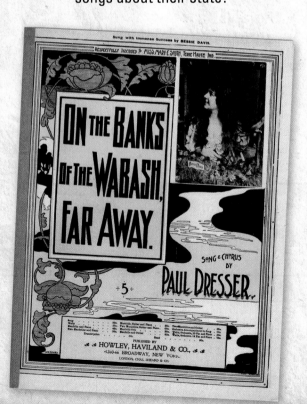

INDIANA QUARTER

The Indiana quarter shows the year in which Indiana became a state and the state's motto. It also features a race car to stand for the Indianapolis 500 race.

DBQ **2** Why are coins good places on which to show state symbols?

THE STATE FLAG AND THE SEAL OF INDIANA

Indiana's state seal shows a pioneer scene and the year Indiana became a state. The state's flag shows a torch, which stands for liberty and learning. It also has 19 stars because Indiana was the nineteenth state to join the United States.

DBQ ❸ Why do you think the state's seal shows a pioneer scene?

STATE NICKNAME

Indiana's state nickname is "The Hoosier State." No one is certain of how the word *Hoosier* came into use or what it means. Even so, the nickname has been used since the 1830s.

DBQ ❹ Why do you think the term *Hoosier* has remained popular?

STATE MOTTO

Indiana's state motto is "The Crossroads of America." This motto means that many important transportation routes cross the state.

DBQ ❺ Why is Indiana's motto meaningful?

WRITE ABOUT IT

How do these symbols make you feel about living in Indiana? Write a paragraph to tell how you feel.

GO ONLINE For more resources, go to www.harcourtschool.com/ss1

Fun with Social Studies

What does a person who provides money need?
????? protector

If people want bigger lawns, what do they have?
land ?????

What did the plan for a new law catch when it was left outdoors in a blizzard?
????? chill

Rhyme Time

Answer each question using a vocabulary word from the unit. For example: What do you call a wild story about someone who pays for goods and services?
consumer rumor

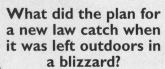

How did the tidy governor reject a suggested law?
with a neat-o ?????

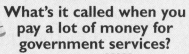

What's it called when you pay a lot of money for government services?
a max ?????

Vacation Souvenirs

Where did the tourist buy each of these shirts?

What cars those Studebakers built, near a BEND in the river!

write this city's name in CAPITAL letters!

Indiana Tic-Tac-Toe

Play Indiana Tic-Tac-Toe. Find three items in a row that are closely related.

Tic-Tac-Toe

	agriculture	
constitution		mayor
entrepreneur	soybeans	BILL

Online Adventures

GO ONLINE

Our first stop is the Indiana Statehouse. Before we go, we need to fill up the gas tank.

▶ GO ON!

Eco is running for state senator. Join the campaign, and try to convince voters that Eco will be a good state leader. Before people vote for Eco, they will want to make sure both of you know enough about Indiana's economy and government. Do you think you can do it? Play now at **www.harcourtschool.com/ss1**

Visual Summary

Indiana's economy is based mostly on manufacturing and services

Summarize the Unit

(Focus Skill) Compare and Contrast Complete this graphic organizer to show that you understand how to compare and contrast information about Indiana's state government.

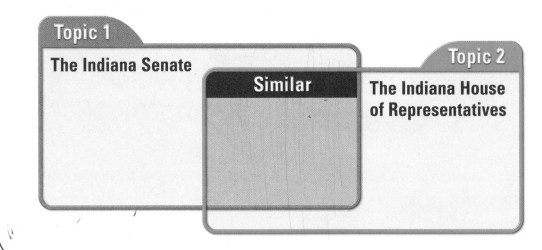

Topic 1

The Indiana Senate

Similar

Topic 2

The Indiana House of Representatives

Vocabulary

Write a definition for each term. Then use each term in a sentence that explains its meaning.

1. **economy** p. 213
2. **productivity** p. 213
3. **entrepreneur** p. 223
4. **profit** p. 223
5. **interdependence** p. 233
6. **budget** p. 243
7. **veto** p. 243
8. **municipal** p. 247
9. **income** p. 249
10. **civic virtue** p. 255

Each branch of Indiana's state government has its own responsibilities

Hoosiers show civic virtues in many ways

Facts and Main Ideas

Answer these questions.

11. How do changes in supply and demand affect the prices of products?

12. What is the Indiana Bill of Rights?

13. What are three examples of services that local governments provide?

Write the letter of the best choice.

14. Which of the following is a list of some of Indiana's top products?
    A citrus fruit, books, bottled water
    B corn, automobiles, pharmaceuticals
    C cotton, steel, clothing
    D corn, toys, bottled water

15. For what is Eli Lilly best known?
    A He started what is now one of the largest pharamaceutical companies.
    B He invested in a company that made cosmetic and hair products for African-American women.
    C He started a company that built wagons and automobiles.
    D He started a company that manufactured and sold the diesel engines he invented.

16. Which of the following is a list of state government officials?
    A governor, mayor, state senator
    B governor, mayor, commissioner
    C governor, lieutenant governor, secretary of state
    D mayor, city council member, town council member

Critical Thinking

Answer these questions.

17. What are some reasons a person might want to be an entrepreneur?

18. Give an example of a civic virtue. Why is this characteristic an important one for citizens of a democracy?

Skills

Use a Road Map and Mileage Table

Use the road map and mileage table on page 251 to answer these questions.

19. Using the mileage table, how far is Fort Wayne from Evansville?

20. If you travel Interstate Highway 65 from New Albany to Columbus, and then take State Highway 46 to Bloomington, about how many miles will you have traveled?

writing

Write a Report Write a report that describes Indiana's global trade.

Write a Persuasive Letter Research an issue that affects the citizens of Indiana today, and decide what your point of view about the issue is. Then write a persuasive letter to the governor explaining possible actions that can be taken on the issue.

Show What You Know

Unit Writing Activity

Write a Report Find out how your local government works, and write a report about it.

- Explain how your local government is organized.
- Identify local leaders.
- List goods and services that your local government provides.

Unit Project

Make a Bulletin Board Make a bulletin board about Indiana's economy and government.

- Include pictures and drawings of industries, entrepreneurs, and the state and local government.
- Write labels and short captions for the pictures and drawings displayed on your bulletin board.

Read More

- *Hoosier Heart* by Luke Messer. Eva Publishing.

- *Madam C. J. Walker* by Susan Bivin Aller. Lerner Publications.

- *Indiana (It's My State!)* by Kathleen Derzipilski. Benchmark Books.

For more resources, go to
www.harcourtschool.com/ss1

For Your Reference

ATLAS/ALMANAC

RESEARCH HANDBOOK

BIOGRAPHICAL DICTIONARY

GAZETTEER

GLOSSARY

INDEX

For Your Reference

ATLAS/ ALMANAC

RESEARCH HANDBOOK

BIOGRAPHICAL DICTIONARY

GAZETTEER

GLOSSARY

INDEX

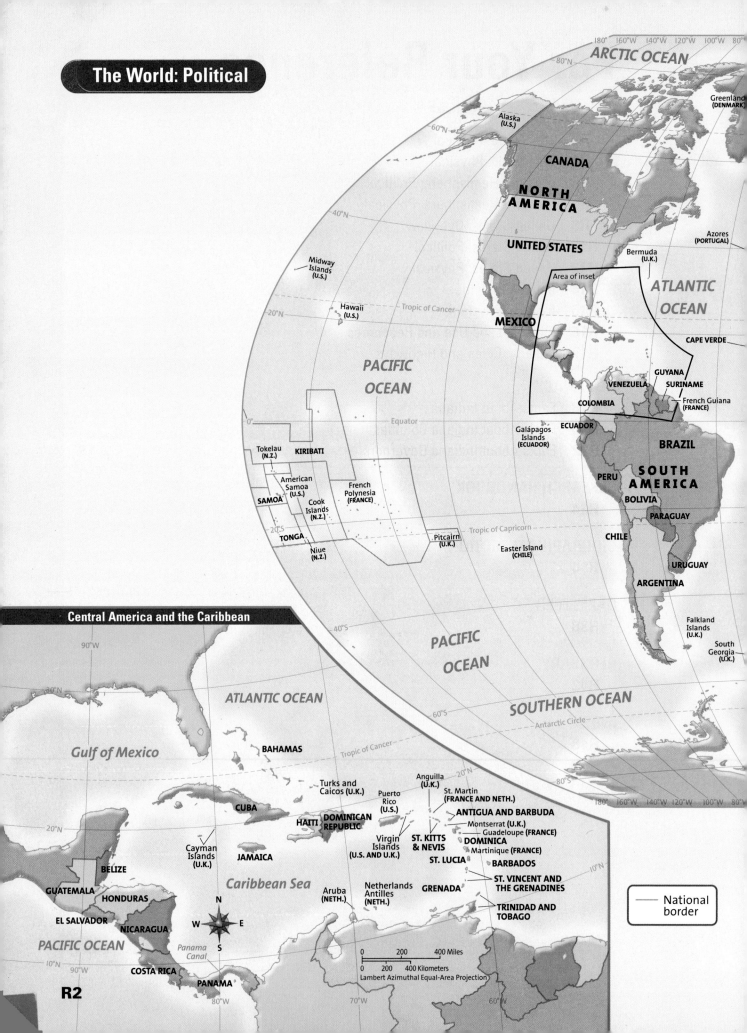

The World: Political

ARCTIC OCEAN

Greenland (DENMARK)

Alaska (U.S.)

CANADA

NORTH AMERICA

UNITED STATES

Bermuda (U.K.)

Azores (PORTUGAL)

ATLANTIC OCEAN

Midway Islands (U.S.)

Area of inset

MEXICO

CAPE VERDE

Hawaii (U.S.)

Tropic of Cancer

PACIFIC OCEAN

VENEZUELA

GUYANA

SURINAME

French Guiana (FRANCE)

COLOMBIA

Galápagos Islands (ECUADOR)

ECUADOR

BRAZIL

Equator

Tokelau (N.Z.)

KIRIBATI

PERU

SOUTH AMERICA

American Samoa (U.S.)

French Polynesia (FRANCE)

BOLIVIA

SAMOA

Cook Islands (N.Z.)

PARAGUAY

TONGA

CHILE

Pitcairn (U.K.)

Tropic of Capricorn

Easter Island (CHILE)

URUGUAY

Niue (N.Z.)

ARGENTINA

PACIFIC OCEAN

Falkland Islands (U.K.)

South Georgia (U.K.)

SOUTHERN OCEAN

Antarctic Circle

Central America and the Caribbean

90°W

ATLANTIC OCEAN

Gulf of Mexico

BAHAMAS

Turks and Caicos (U.K.)

Anguilla (U.K.)

St. Martin (FRANCE AND NETH.)

CUBA

Puerto Rico (U.S.)

ANTIGUA AND BARBUDA

HAITI

DOMINICAN REPUBLIC

Montserrat (U.K.)

Guadeloupe (FRANCE)

Cayman Islands (U.K.)

JAMAICA

Virgin Islands (U.S. AND U.K.)

ST. KITTS & NEVIS

DOMINICA

Martinique (FRANCE)

ST. LUCIA

BELIZE

Caribbean Sea

BARBADOS

GUATEMALA

Aruba (NETH.)

Netherlands Antilles (NETH.)

GRENADA

ST. VINCENT AND THE GRENADINES

HONDURAS

TRINIDAD AND TOBAGO

EL SALVADOR

NICARAGUA

PACIFIC OCEAN

Panama Canal

N
W   E
S

0   200   400 Miles

0   200   400 Kilometers

Lambert Azimuthal Equal-Area Projection

COSTA RICA

PANAMA

National border

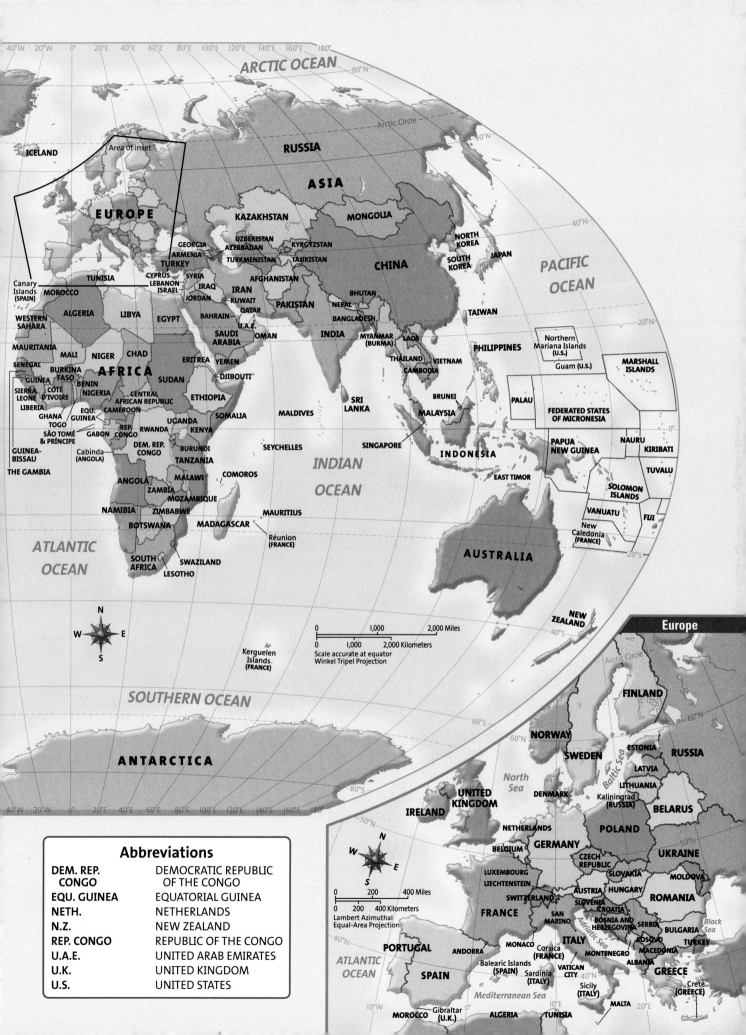

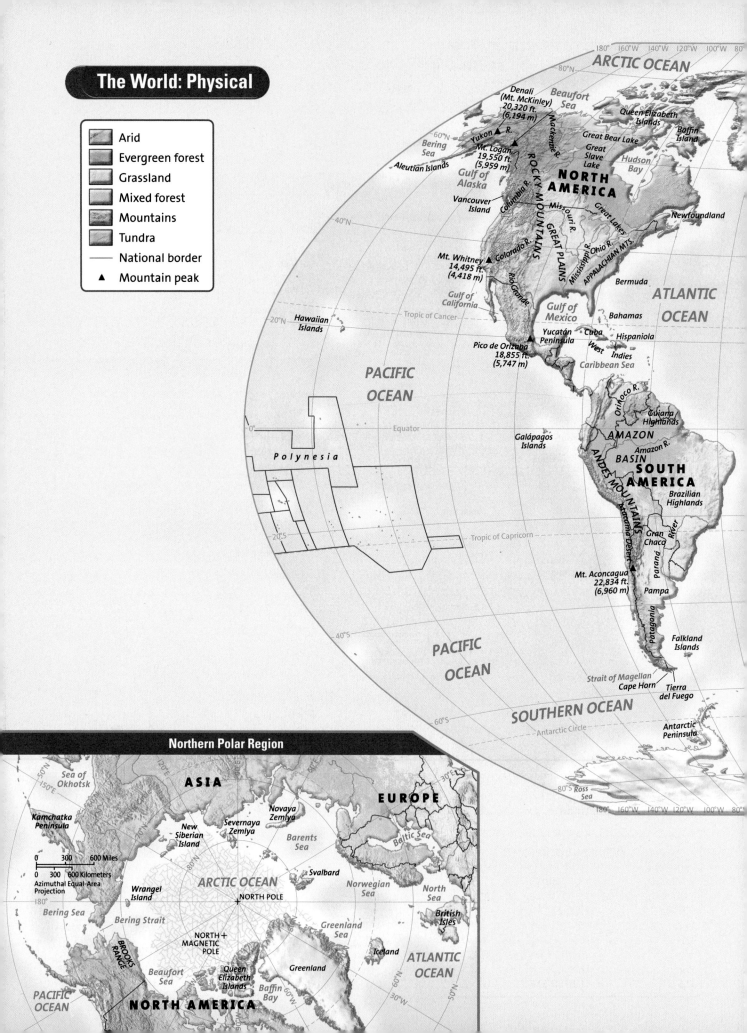

The World: Physical

Legend
- Arid
- Evergreen forest
- Grassland
- Mixed forest
- Mountains
- Tundra
- ⎯ National border
- ▲ Mountain peak

ARCTIC OCEAN

80°N

Beaufort Sea

Queen Elizabeth Islands

Baffin Island

Denali (Mt. McKinley) 20,320 ft. (6,194 m)

Mackenzie R.

Great Bear Lake

Great Slave Lake

Hudson Bay

Yukon R.

60°N

Mt. Logan 19,550 ft. (5,959 m)

Bering Sea

ROCKY MOUNTAINS

NORTH AMERICA

Aleutian Islands

Gulf of Alaska

GREAT PLAINS

Columbia R.

Missouri R.

Great Lakes

Newfoundland

Vancouver Island

40°N

Mississippi R.

Ohio R.

APPALACHIAN MTS.

Bermuda

ATLANTIC OCEAN

Mt. Whitney 14,495 ft. (4,418 m)

Colorado R.

Rio Grande

Gulf of California

20°N

Tropic of Cancer

Hawaiian Islands

Gulf of Mexico

Bahamas

Cuba

Hispaniola

Yucatán Peninsula

West Indies

Caribbean Sea

Pico de Orizaba 18,855 ft. (5,747 m)

PACIFIC OCEAN

0°

Equator

Orinoco R.

Guiana Highlands

Galápagos Islands

AMAZON BASIN

Amazon R.

SOUTH AMERICA

Polynesia

ANDES MOUNTAINS

Brazilian Highlands

20°S

Tropic of Capricorn

Madeira River

Gran Chaco

Paraná River

Mt. Aconcagua 22,834 ft. (6,960 m)

Pampa

40°S

Patagonia

Falkland Islands

PACIFIC OCEAN

Strait of Magellan

Cape Horn

Tierra del Fuego

SOUTHERN OCEAN

60°S

Antarctic Circle

Antarctic Peninsula

80°S

Ross Sea

180° 160°W 140°W 120°W 100°W 80°

Northern Polar Region

Sea of Okhotsk

ASIA

EUROPE

Kamchatka Peninsula

New Siberian Island

Severnaya Zemlya

Novaya Zemlya

Barents Sea

Baltic Sea

Svalbard

Norwegian Sea

North Sea

ARCTIC OCEAN

NORTH POLE

Wrangel Island

British Isles

0 300 600 Miles

0 300 600 Kilometers

Azimuthal Equal-Area Projection

180°

Bering Sea

Bering Strait

NORTH + MAGNETIC POLE

Greenland Sea

Greenland

Iceland

ATLANTIC OCEAN

BROOKS RANGE

Beaufort Sea

Queen Elizabeth Islands

Baffin Bay

PACIFIC OCEAN

NORTH AMERICA

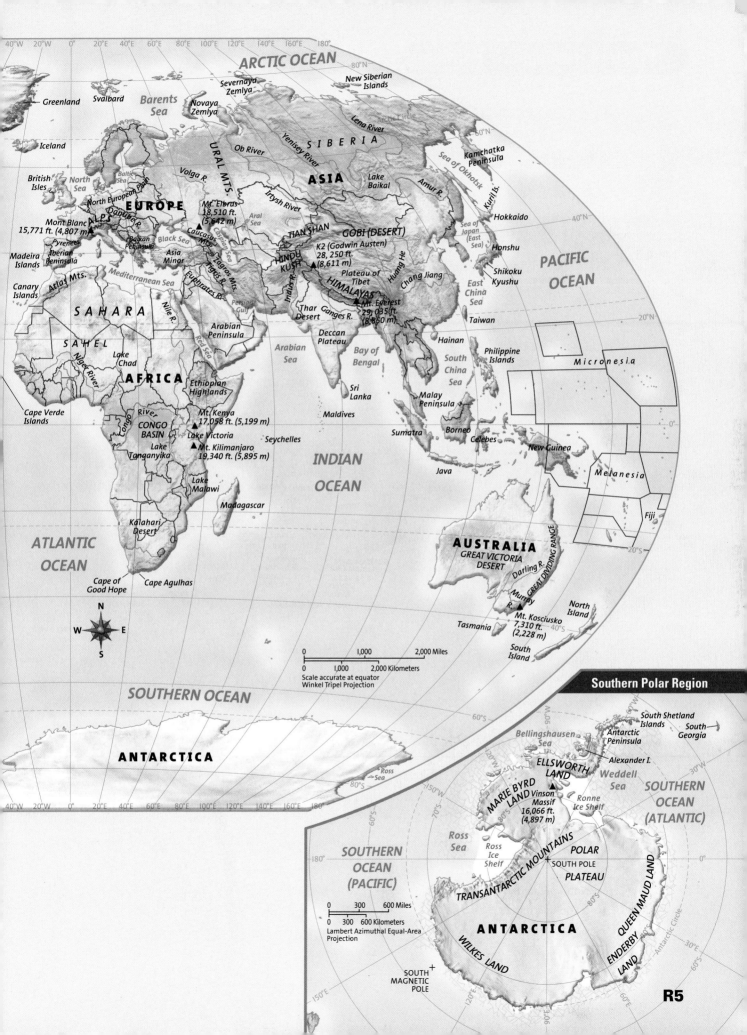

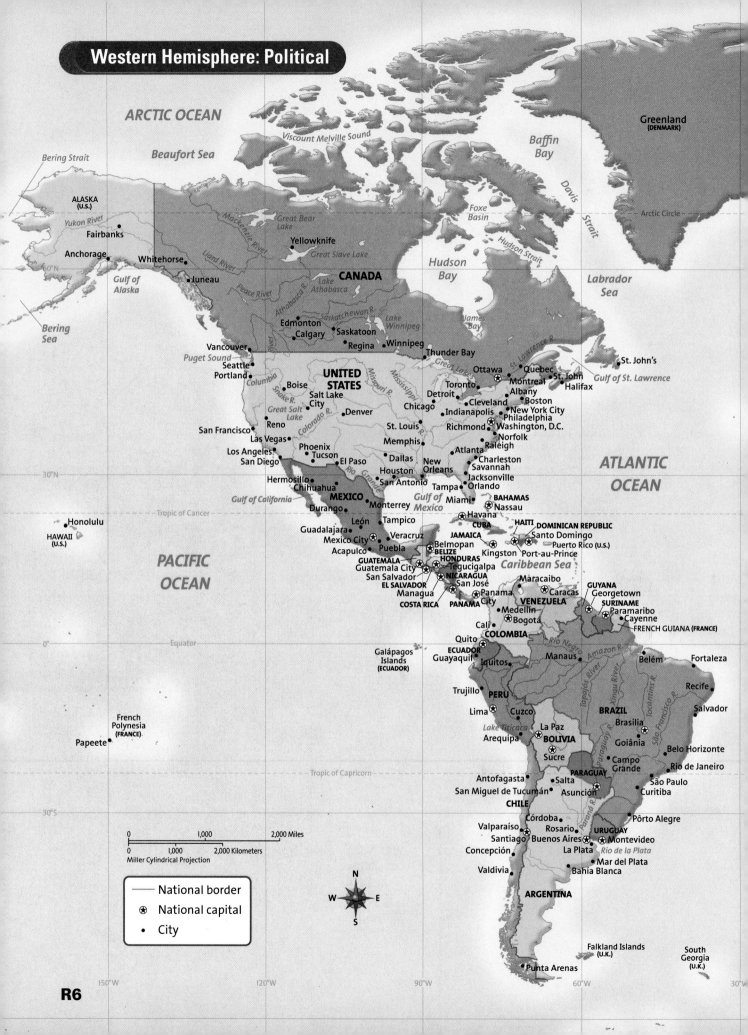

Western Hemisphere: Political

ARCTIC OCEAN

Bering Strait

Beaufort Sea

Viscount Melville Sound

Baffin Bay

Greenland
(DENMARK)

ALASKA
(U.S.)

Yukon River

Fairbanks

Anchorage

Whitehorse

Juneau

Gulf of Alaska

Bering Sea

60°N

Mackenzie River

Great Bear Lake

Yellowknife

Great Slave Lake

Liard River

Peace River

Lake Athabasca

CANADA

Edmonton
Calgary

Saskatoon

Athabasca R.

Saskatchewan R.

Lake Winnipeg

Regina

Winnipeg

Thunder Bay

James Bay

Hudson Bay

Hudson Strait

Foxe Basin

Davis Strait

Arctic Circle

Labrador Sea

Vancouver

Puget Sound

Seattle

Portland

UNITED STATES

Columbia

Boise

Snake R.

Missouri R.

Mississippi

Great Lakes

Ottawa

Toronto

Detroit

Cleveland

St. Lawrence R.

Quebec

Montreal

St. John

Albany

Boston

St. John's

Gulf of St. Lawrence

Halifax

Salt Lake City

Great Salt Lake

Denver

Colorado R.

Chicago

Indianapolis

New York City

Philadelphia

Washington, D.C.

San Francisco

Reno

Las Vegas

Los Angeles

San Diego

Phoenix

Tucson

St. Louis

Memphis

Richmond

Norfolk

Raleigh

Atlanta

Charleston

Savannah

ATLANTIC OCEAN

El Paso

Dallas

Houston

New Orleans

Jacksonville

Orlando

Hermosillo

San Antonio

Tampa

30°N

Chihuahua

Rio Grande

MEXICO

Durango

Monterrey

Gulf of Mexico

Miami

BAHAMAS

Nassau

Gulf of California

Tropic of Cancer

Honolulu

HAWAII
(U.S.)

PACIFIC OCEAN

León

Guadalajara

Tampico

Havana

CUBA

HAITI

DOMINICAN REPUBLIC

Santo Domingo

Puerto Rico (U.S.)

Mexico City

Veracruz

Acapulco

Puebla

JAMAICA

Belmopan

BELIZE

Kingston

Port-au-Prince

GUATEMALA

Guatemala City

San Salvador

EL SALVADOR

Managua

HONDURAS

Tegucigalpa

NICARAGUA

San José

COSTA RICA

Caribbean Sea

Panama

PANAMA

City

Maracaibo

Caracas

VENEZUELA

GUYANA

Georgetown

SURINAME

Paramaribo

Cayenne

FRENCH GUIANA (FRANCE)

Medellín

Bogotá

Cali

COLOMBIA

Quito

ECUADOR

Guayaquil

Galápagos Islands
(ECUADOR)

0° Equator

Iquitos

Manaus

Rio Negro

Amazon River

Belém

Fortaleza

Trujillo

PERU

Lima

Cuzco

Lake Titicaca

La Paz

Arequipa

BOLIVIA

Sucre

BRAZIL

Brasília

Tapajós River

Xingu R.

Tocantins R.

São Francisco R.

Recife

Salvador

Goiânia

Belo Horizonte

Rio de Janeiro

French Polynesia
(FRANCE)

Papeete

Tropic of Capricorn

Antofagasta

San Miguel de Tucumán

Salta

PARAGUAY

Campo Grande

São Paulo

Curitiba

Asunción

Paraguay R.

Pôrto Alegre

CHILE

Valparaíso

Santiago

Concepción

Valdivia

30°S

Córdoba

Rosario

Buenos Aires

La Plata

URUGUAY

Montevideo

Rio de la Plata

Mar del Plata

Bahía Blanca

ARGENTINA

0   1,000   2,000 Miles

0   1,000   2,000 Kilometers

Miller Cylindrical Projection

N
W   E
S

Falkland Islands
(U.K.)

South Georgia
(U.K.)

Punta Arenas

— National border

⊛ National capital

• City

150°W   120°W   90°W   60°W

R6

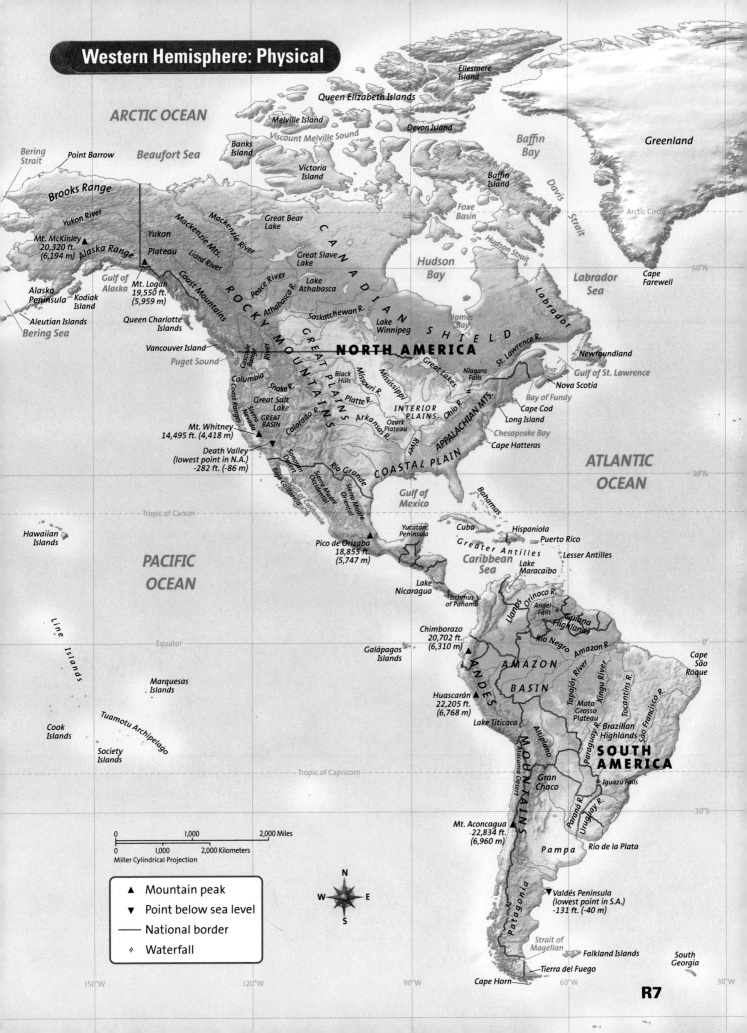

Western Hemisphere: Physical

ARCTIC OCEAN

Ellesmere Island

Queen Elizabeth Islands

Melville Island

Viscount Melville Sound

Devon Island

Baffin Bay

Greenland

Bering Strait

Point Barrow

Beaufort Sea

Banks Island

Victoria Island

Baffin Island

Davis Strait

Arctic Circle

60°N

Brooks Range

Yukon River

Mackenzie Mts.

Mackenzie River

Great Bear Lake

Foxe Basin

Hudson Strait

Cape Farewell

Mt. McKinley 20,320 ft. (6,194 m)

Alaska Range

Yukon Plateau

Liard River

Great Slave Lake

Hudson Bay

Labrador Sea

Alaska Peninsula

Gulf of Alaska

Mt. Logan 19,550 ft. (5,959 m)

Coast Mountains

Peace River

Athabasca R.

Lake Athabasca

James Bay

Labrador

Kodiak Island

Queen Charlotte Islands

Saskatchewan R.

Lake Winnipeg

CANADIAN SHIELD

Aleutian Islands

Bering Sea

Vancouver Island

Puget Sound

Cascade Range

Columbia River

GREAT PLAINS

NORTH AMERICA

Great Lakes

Niagara Falls

St. Lawrence R.

Newfoundland

Gulf of St. Lawrence

Coast Ranges

Snake R.

Black Hills

Missouri R.

Mississippi R.

Nova Scotia

Bay of Fundy

Great Salt Lake

GREAT BASIN

Platte R.

INTERIOR PLAINS

Ohio R.

APPALACHIAN MTS.

Cape Cod

Long Island

Sierra Nevada

Mt. Whitney 14,495 ft. (4,418 m)

Colorado R.

Arkansas R.

Ozark Plateau

Chesapeake Bay

Cape Hatteras

Death Valley (lowest point in N.A.) -282 ft. (-86 m)

Sonoran Desert

Rio Grande

COASTAL PLAIN

ATLANTIC OCEAN

30°N

Sierra Madre Occidental

Sierra Madre Oriental

Gulf of Mexico

Bahamas

Tropic of Cancer

Baja California

Gulf of California

Yucatán Peninsula

Cuba

Hispaniola

Puerto Rico

Hawaiian Islands

Pico de Orizaba 18,855 ft. (5,747 m)

Greater Antilles

Lesser Antilles

PACIFIC OCEAN

Lake Nicaragua

Caribbean Sea

Lake Maracaibo

Line Islands

Lake Nicaragua

Isthmus of Panama

Llanos

Orinoco R.

Angel Falls

Guiana Highlands

Equator

Galápagos Islands

Chimborazo 20,702 ft. (6,310 m)

Rio Negro

Amazon R.

Cape São Roque

0°

Marquesas Islands

AMAZON BASIN

Tapajós River

Xingu River

Tocantins R.

Tuamotu Archipelago

Huascarán 22,205 ft. (6,768 m)

Mato Grosso Plateau

São Francisco R.

Cook Islands

ANDES

Lake Titicaca

Paraguay R.

Brazilian Highlands

Society Islands

Altiplano

Atacama Desert

SOUTH AMERICA

Tropic of Capricorn

Gran Chaco

Iguazú Falls

Mt. Aconcagua 22,834 ft. (6,960 m)

MOUNTAINS

Paraná R.

Uruguay R.

30°S

Pampa

Rio de la Plata

Patagonia

Valdés Peninsula (lowest point in S.A.) -131 ft. (-40 m)

0   1,000   2,000 Miles

0   1,000   2,000 Kilometers

Miller Cylindrical Projection

N W E S

▲ Mountain peak

▼ Point below sea level

— National border

⁄ Waterfall

Strait of Magellan

Falkland Islands

South Georgia

Tierra del Fuego

Cape Horn

150°W   120°W   90°W   60°W   30°W

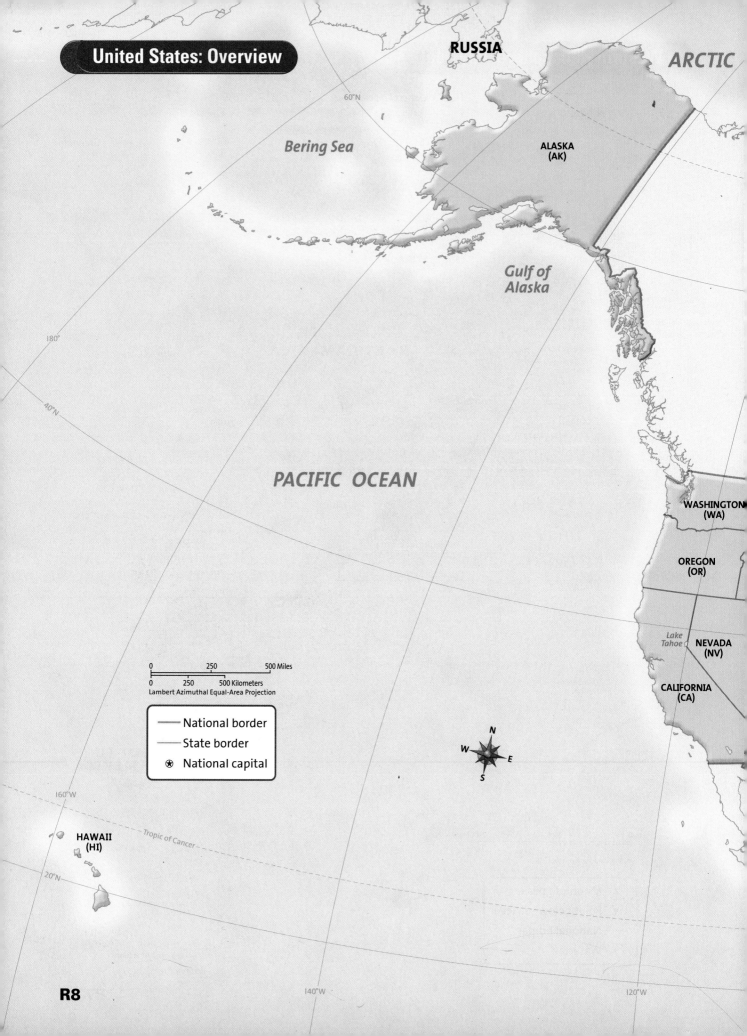

RUSSIA

ARCTIC

60°N

Bering Sea

**ALASKA
(AK)**

*Gulf of
Alaska*

180°

40°N

PACIFIC OCEAN

**WASHINGTON
(WA)**

**OREGON
(OR)**

*Lake
Tahoe*

**NEVADA
(NV)**

**CALIFORNIA
(CA)**

0   250   500 Miles
0   250   500 Kilometers
Lambert Azimuthal Equal-Area Projection

——— National border
——— State border
⊛ National capital

N
W   E
S

160°W

Tropic of Cancer

**HAWAII
(HI)**

20°N

R8

140°W   120°W

OCEAN

Baffin
Bay

ICELAND

Greenland
(DENMARK)

Labrador
Sea

Hudson
Bay

James
Bay

CANADA

Lake of
the Woods

Lake Superior

MONTANA
(MT)

NORTH
DAKOTA
(ND)

MINNESOTA
(MN)

MICHIGAN

Lake Huron

VERMONT
(VT)

MAINE
(ME)

IDAHO
(ID)

WYOMING
(WY)

SOUTH
DAKOTA
(SD)

WISCONSIN
(WI)

MICHIGAN
(MI)

Lake
Ontario

Lake
Champlain

NEW
YORK
(NY)

NEW HAMPSHIRE
(NH)

MASSACHUSETTS
(MA)

RHODE ISLAND (RI)

Great
Salt Lake

IOWA
(IA)

Lake
St. Clair

Lake Erie

PENNSYLVANIA
(PA)

NEW
JERSEY
(NJ)

CONNECTICUT
(CT)

NEBRASKA
(NE)

ILLINOIS
(IL)

INDIANA
(IN)

OHIO
(OH)

Washington, D.C.

DELAWARE (DE)

UTAH
(UT)

COLORADO
(CO)

KANSAS
(KS)

MISSOURI
(MO)

WEST
VIRGINIA
(WV)

KENTUCKY
(KY)

VIRGINIA
(VA)

MARYLAND (MD)

Chesapeake Bay

ARIZONA
(AZ)

NEW MEXICO
(NM)

OKLAHOMA
(OK)

ARKANSAS
(AR)

TENNESSEE
(TN)

NORTH
CAROLINA
(NC)

SOUTH
CAROLINA
(SC)

ATLANTIC OCEAN

TEXAS
(TX)

MISSISSIPPI
(MS)

ALABAMA
(AL)

GEORGIA
(GA)

Gulf of California

LOUISIANA
(LA)

FLORIDA
(FL)

Lake
Okeechobee

MEXICO

Gulf of Mexico

BAHAMAS

CUBA

DOMINICAN
REPUBLIC

Puerto
Rico
(U.S.)

HAITI

100°W

80°W

20°N

Arctic Circle

60°N

40°W

60°W

40°N

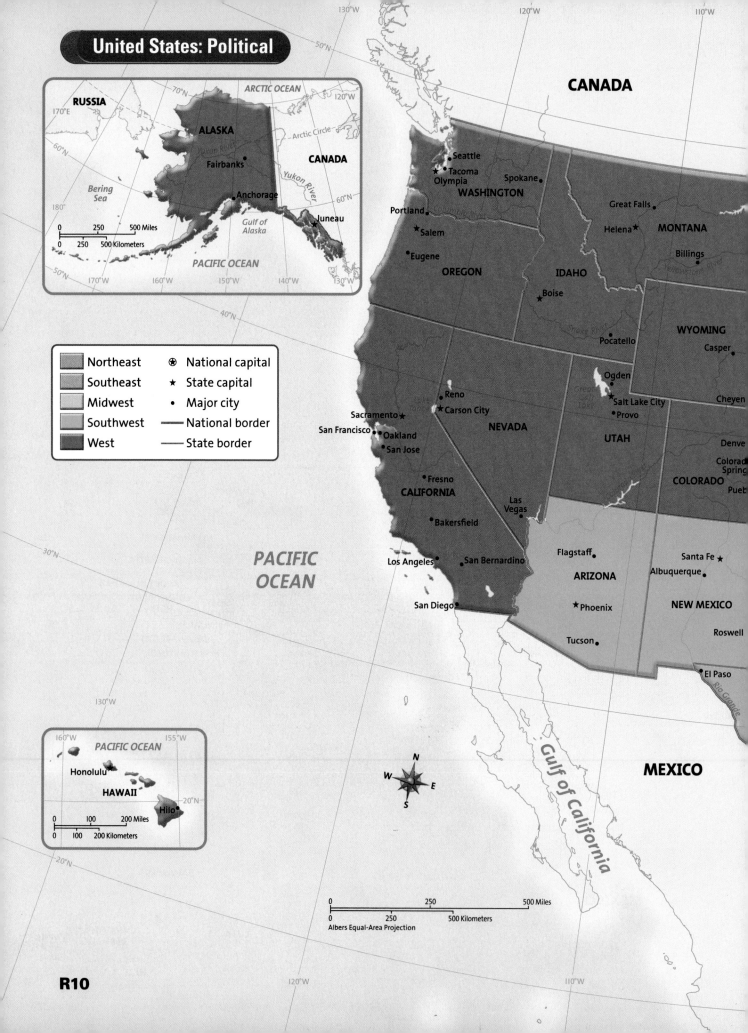

United States: Political

RUSSIA

ALASKA

ARCTIC OCEAN

CANADA

Fairbanks •

Bering
Sea

• Anchorage

Yukon River

Gulf of
Alaska

Juneau ★

PACIFIC OCEAN

| 0 | 250 | 500 Miles |
| 0 | 250 | 500 Kilometers |

Northeast
Southeast
Midwest
Southwest
West

⊛ National capital
★ State capital
• Major city
— National border
— State border

CANADA

Seattle •
Tacoma •
Olympia ★
WASHINGTON

Spokane •

Great Falls •

Helena ★
MONTANA

Portland •

Salem ★

Billings •

Eugene •

OREGON

IDAHO

Boise ★

Pocatello •

WYOMING

Casper •

Ogden •

Cheyen

Reno •
Carson City ★

Salt Lake City ★
Provo •

Sacramento ★

San Francisco •
• Oakland
• San Jose

NEVADA

UTAH

Denve

Colorad
Spring

Fresno •

CALIFORNIA

COLORADO

Pueb

Las
Vegas •

Bakersfield •

**PACIFIC
OCEAN**

Flagstaff •

Santa Fe ★
Albuquerque •

Los Angeles •

• San Bernardino

ARIZONA

San Diego •

★ Phoenix

NEW MEXICO

Roswell •

Tucson •

El Paso •

Rio Grande

Gulf of California

MEXICO

N
W   E
S

PACIFIC OCEAN

Honolulu •

HAWAII

Hilo •

| 0 | 100 | 200 Miles |
| 0 | 100 | 200 Kilometers |

| 0 | 250 | 500 Miles |
| 0 | 250 | 500 Kilometers |
Albers Equal-Area Projection

100°W · · · 90°W · · · 80°W · · · 70°W

50°N

Lake of the Woods

Grand Forks
NORTH DAKOTA
Fargo
Bismarck

Duluth

Lake Superior

Sault Sainte Marie

CANADA

St. Lawrence River

MAINE
★ Augusta

MINNESOTA
St. Paul ★
Minneapolis ★

WISCONSIN
Green Bay
Madison ★
Milwaukee

MICHIGAN
Lake Michigan
Grand Rapids
Lansing ★
Flint
Detroit
Lake Huron
Lake St. Clair

Burlington
Lake Champlain
VERMONT
Montpelier ★
NEW HAMPSHIRE
Concord ★
Manchester

Portland

SOUTH DAKOTA
Pierre ★
Rapid City

Sioux Falls
Sioux City

IOWA
Cedar Rapids
Rockford
Chicago
Davenport ★
Des Moines ★

Peoria
ILLINOIS
Decatur
Springfield

Gary
South Bend

Toledo

Cleveland
Lake Erie
Akron

NEW YORK
Albany ★
Rochester
Syracuse
Buffalo

Worcester ★
MASSACHUSETTS
Hartford
★ Boston
Providence ★
RHODE ISLAND
CONNECTICUT
Bridgeport
Newark
New York City

70°W

NEBRASKA
Platte River
Omaha
Lincoln ★

Missouri River

OHIO
Columbus ★
Dayton
Cincinnati
Ohio River

Wheeling
Pittsburgh

PENNSYLVANIA
Harrisburg ★
Philadelphia
★ Trenton
NEW JERSEY
Wilmington
★ Dover
DELAWARE

Topeka ★
Kansas City
KANSAS
Wichita

Jefferson City ★
St. Louis
MISSOURI
Springfield

INDIANA
Indianapolis ★

WEST VIRGINIA
Charleston ★

Baltimore
Annapolis ★
Washington, D.C. ★
MARYLAND

VIRGINIA
Richmond ★

Chesapeake Bay

Newport News
Norfolk
Virginia Beach

Arkansas River

Louisville
Frankfort ★
Lexington
Evansville
KENTUCKY

Roanoke

OKLAHOMA
Tulsa
Oklahoma City ★

ARKANSAS
Fort Smith
Little Rock ★

Arkansas River

Memphis

Knoxville
Nashville ★
TENNESSEE
Chattanooga
Huntsville

Tennessee River

Winston-Salem
Charlotte

Greensboro
Raleigh ★
NORTH CAROLINA

Amarillo
Lubbock

Red River
Lake Texoma

MISSISSIPPI
Meridian
Jackson ★

Birmingham
ALABAMA
Montgomery ★

Atlanta ★
GEORGIA
Macon
Columbus

SOUTH CAROLINA
Columbia ★

Charleston

Savannah

ATLANTIC OCEAN

Odessa
Abilene
Fort Worth
Dallas
TEXAS

Shreveport
LOUISIANA

Mississippi River

Biloxi
Mobile

Tallahassee ★

Jacksonville

30°N

Austin ★
San Antonio
Beaumont
Houston

Baton Rouge ★
New Orleans

FLORIDA
Orlando
Tampa
St. Petersburg
Lake Okeechobee
West Palm Beach

BAHAMAS

Laredo
Corpus Christi

Rio Grande

Gulf of Mexico

Miami

CUBA

20°N

100°W · · · 90°W · · · 80°W

R11

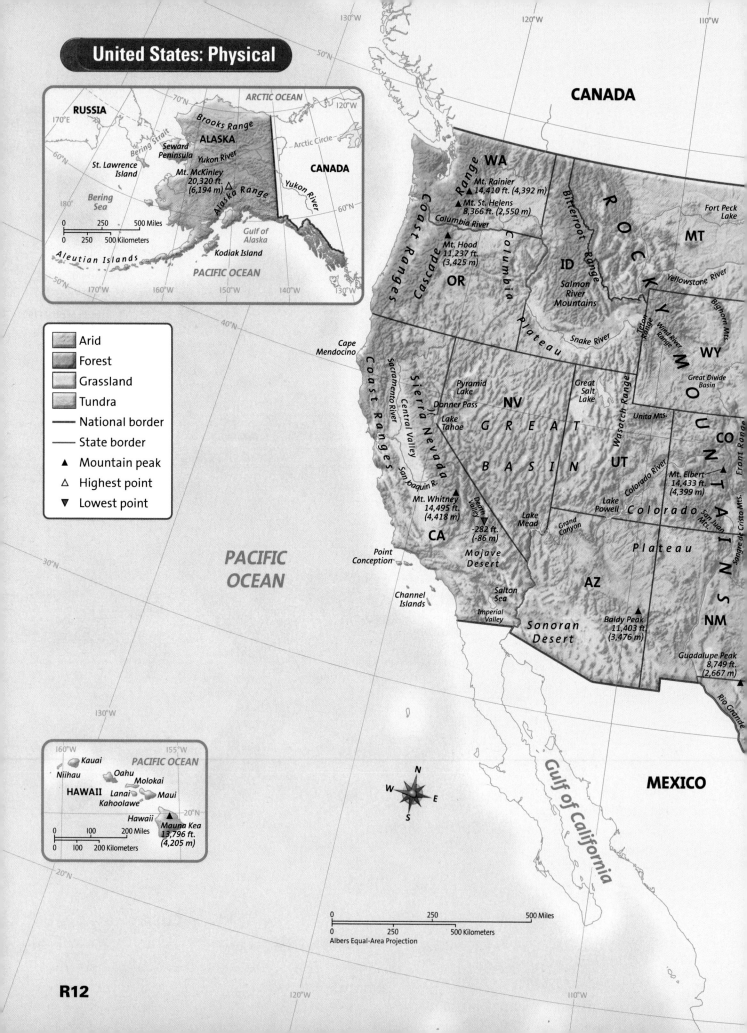

United States: Physical

RUSSIA

ARCTIC OCEAN

Brooks Range

ALASKA

Seward Peninsula

Yukon River

CANADA

Arctic Circle

St. Lawrence Island

Mt. McKinley 20,320 ft. (6,194 m)

Alaska Range

Yukon River

Bering Sea

Bering Strait

Gulf of Alaska

Kodiak Island

Aleutian Islands

PACIFIC OCEAN

0   250   500 Miles
0   250   500 Kilometers

CANADA

WA

Coast Ranges

Cascade Range

Mt. Rainier 14,410 ft. (4,392 m)

Mt. St. Helens 8,366 ft. (2,550 m)

Columbia River

Mt. Hood 11,237 ft. (3,425 m)

Columbia Plateau

OR

Bitterroot Range

ID

Salmon River Mountains

Snake River

MT

Fort Peck Lake

Yellowstone River

Bighorn Mts.

Teton Range

Wind River Range

WY

Great Divide Basin

R O C K Y   M O U N T A I N S

Cape Mendocino

Coast Ranges

Sacramento River

Central Valley

Sierra Nevada

San Joaquin R.

Pyramid Lake

Donner Pass

Lake Tahoe

NV

G R E A T   B A S I N

Great Salt Lake

Wasatch Range

Uinta Mts.

UT

CO

Colorado River

Mt. Elbert 14,433 ft. (4,399 m)

San Juan Mts.

Sangre de Cristo Mts.

Front Range

Mt. Whitney 14,495 ft. (4,418 m)

Death Valley -282 ft. (-86 m)

Lake Mead

Lake Powell

Colorado Plateau

CA

Point Conception

PACIFIC OCEAN

Channel Islands

Mojave Desert

Salton Sea

Imperial Valley

Grand Canyon

Sonoran Desert

Baldy Peak 11,403 ft (3,476 m)

AZ

NM

Guadalupe Peak 8,749 ft. (2,667 m)

Rio Grande

Gulf of California

MEXICO

Legend

- Arid
- Forest
- Grassland
- Tundra
- ― National border
- — State border
- ▲ Mountain peak
- △ Highest point
- ▼ Lowest point

HAWAII

Kauai

Niihau

Oahu

Molokai

Lanai

Kahoolawe

Maui

Hawaii

Mauna Kea 13,796 ft. (4,205 m)

PACIFIC OCEAN

0   100   200 Miles
0   100   200 Kilometers

N W E S

0   250   500 Miles
0   250   500 Kilometers
Albers Equal-Area Projection

CANADA

Mt. Katahdin
5,269 ft.
(1,606 m) ▲

Lake of
the Woods

Lake
Sakakawea

ND

Lower
Red Lake

Upper
Red Lake

Mesabi
Range

Leech
Lake

Mille
Lacs
Lake

Isle
Royale

Lake Superior

Keweenaw
Peninsula

Upper Peninsula

Moosehead
Lake

ME

Mt. Washington
6,288 ft. (1,917 m) ▲

G
R
E
A
T

P
L
A
I
N
S

SD

Lake
Oahe

Black
Hills

MN

WI

Wisconsin River

Lake
Winnebago

Lake Michigan

Lower Peninsula

Lake Huron

MI

Lake
St. Clair

VT

Lake
Champlain

Green Mts.

White Mts.

NH

Connecticut R.

Cape Ann

MA

Cape Cod

Missouri River

Mississippi River

IA

NY

Adirondack
Mountains

Lake Ontario

Niagara Falls

Finger
Lakes

Hudson R.

CT

RI

Long
Island

Sand Hills

NE

North Platte R.

South Platte R.

Platte River

I N T E R I O R

P L A I N S

Illinois River

IL

Wabash River

IN

CENTRAL PLAINS

OH

Ohio River

PA

Allegheny Mts.

A
P
P
A
L
A
C
H
I
A
N

M
O
U
N
T
A
I
N
S

NJ

MD

Potomac R.

DE

Delaware Bay

Smoky Hills

KS

Harry S. Truman
Reservoir

Arkansas River

Red Hills

Missouri River

Lake of
the Ozarks

MO

WV

KY

Lake
Barkley

Cumberland
Gap

Cumberland R.

Mt. Mitchell
6,684 ft.
(2,037 m) ▲

James R.

VA

Roanoke R.

Cape Charles

Chesapeake Bay

Albemarle Sound

Cape Hatteras

Llano
Estacado

OK

Canadian River

Red River

Ozark Plateau

Arkansas River

Ouachita
Mountains

AR

TN

Tennessee River

Tombigbee R.

P
I
E
D
M
O
N
T

NC

Cape Fear River

Clark Hill
Lake

SC

Cape Fear

C
O
A
S
T
A
L

P
L
A
I
N

Lake
Texoma

TX

Edwards
Plateau

Pecos
River

Brazos River

Colorado River

Rio Grande

Sabine River

Sam
Rayburn
Reservoir

LA

Toledo Bend
Reservoir

C O A S T A L   P L A I N

Lake
Maurepas

Lake
Pontchartrain

Galveston
Bay

Mississippi River

MS

AL

Alabama R.

Stone ▲
Mountain

Chattahoochee R.

Savannah River

Oconee R.

Ocmulgee R.

GA

Altamaha R.

Okefenokee
Swamp

Mobile
Bay

Mississippi
Delta

St. Johns River

FL

Lake
Okeechobee

Tampa
Bay

Cape
Canaveral

Everglades

Cape Sable

Florida Keys

ATLANTIC
OCEAN

Gulf of Mexico

Straits of Florida

BAHAMAS

CUBA

St. Lawrence River

50°N

40°N

70°W

30°N

20°N

100°W

90°W

80°W

70°W

R13

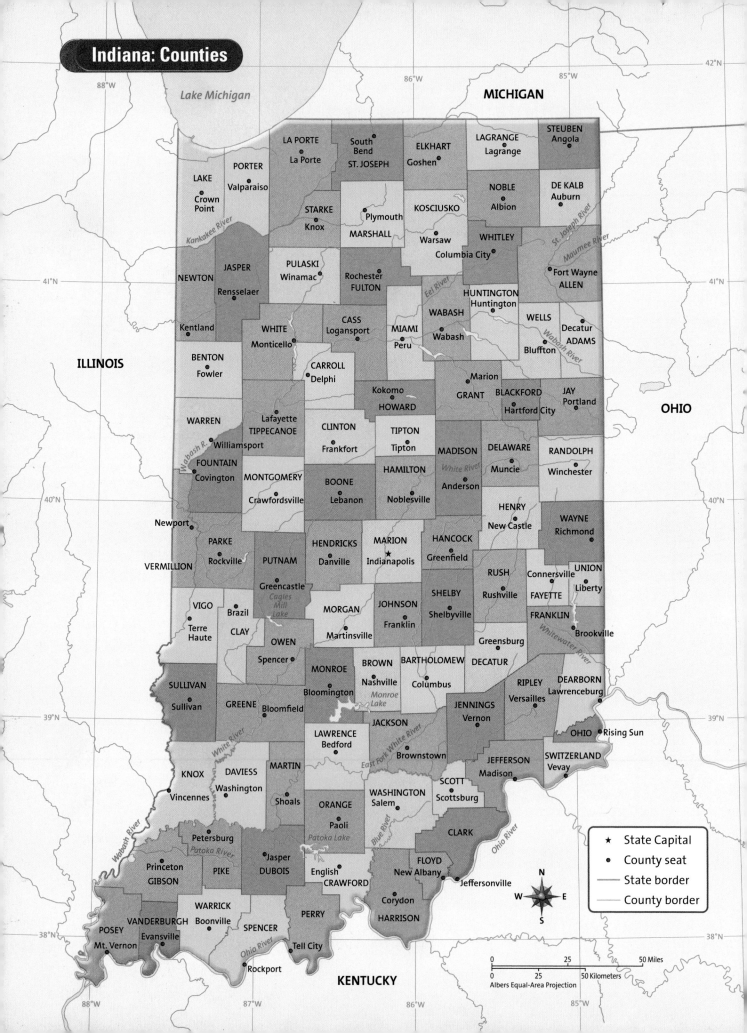

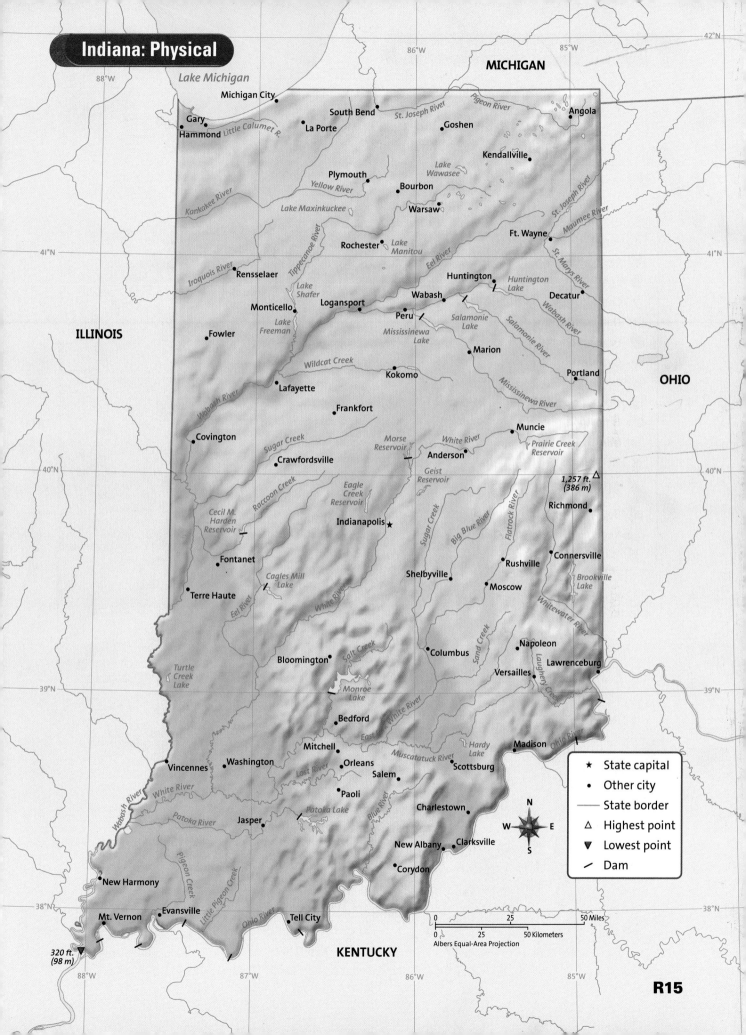

Indiana: Physical

MICHIGAN

Lake Michigan

Michigan City
Gary
Hammond
Little Calumet R.
La Porte
South Bend
St. Joseph River
Goshen
Pigeon River
Angola

Kendallville

Plymouth
Yellow River
Bourbon
Lake Wawasee

Kankakee River
Lake Maxinkuckee
Warsaw

Tippecanoe River
Rochester
Lake Manitou
Eel River
Ft. Wayne
St. Joseph River
Maumee River

ILLINOIS

Iroquois River
Rensselaer
Lake Shafer
Logansport
Huntington
Huntington Lake
St. Marys River
Decatur

Monticello
Wabash
Peru
Salamonie Lake
Wabash River

Fowler
Lake Freeman
Mississinewa Lake
Salamonie River

Wildcat Creek
Kokomo
Marion
Mississinewa River
Portland

Lafayette
Wabash River

Frankfort

Covington
Sugar Creek
Muncie
White River
Prairie Creek Reservoir
OHIO

Crawfordsville
Morse Reservoir
Anderson
1,257 ft. △
(386 m)

Raccoon Creek
Geist Reservoir
Sugar Creek
Big Blue River
Flatrock River
Richmond

Cecil M. Harden Reservoir
Eagle Creek Reservoir
Indianapolis ★
Connersville
Brookville Lake

Fontanet
Shelbyville
Rushville

Cagles Mill Lake
Moscow
Whitewater River

Terre Haute
Eel River
White River

Turtle Creek Lake
Salt Creek
Columbus
Sand Creek
Napoleon
Lawrenceburg

Bloomington
Versailles
Laughery Creek
Ohio River

Monroe Lake

Bedford
East Fork White River
Madison

Mitchell
Muscatatuck River
Hardy Lake
Scottsburg

Vincennes
Washington
Orleans
Salem

White River
Paoli
Blue River
Charlestown

Wabash River
Lost River
Patoka Lake

Jasper
Patoka River
New Albany
Clarksville

New Harmony
Pigeon Creek
Corydon

Mt. Vernon
Evansville
Little Pigeon Creek
Ohio River
Tell City

320 ft. ▼
(98 m)

KENTUCKY

Legend	
★	State capital
●	Other city
—	State border
△	Highest point
▼	Lowest point
⁄	Dam

N
W E
S

0   25   50 Miles
0   25   50 Kilometers
Albers Equal-Area Projection

R15

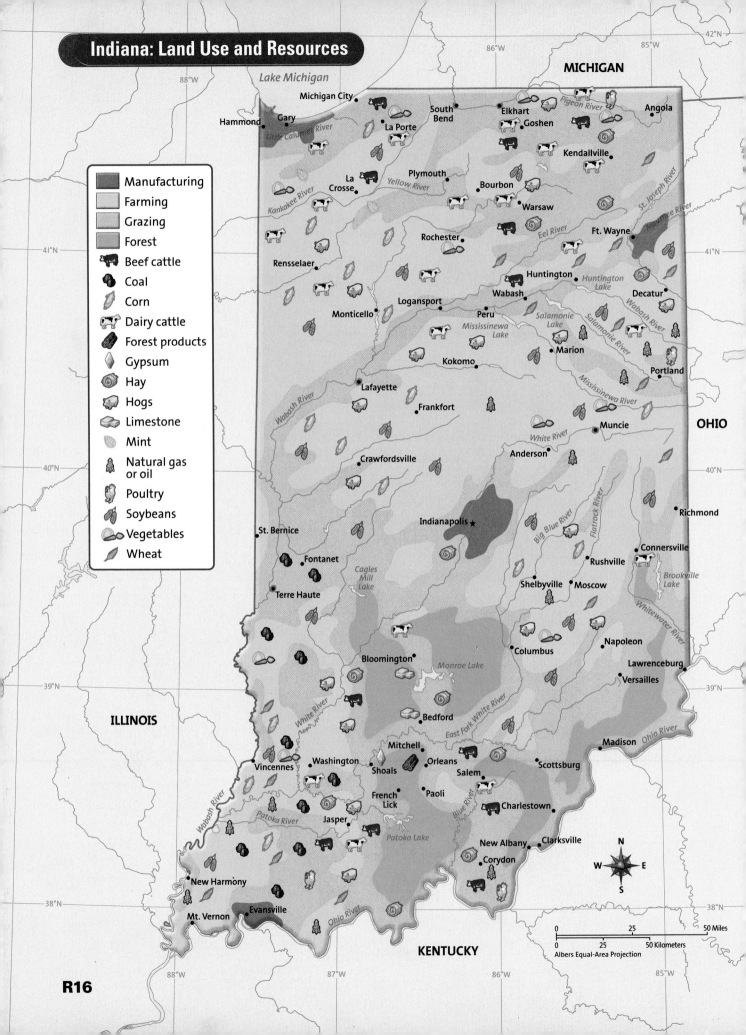

Indiana: Land Use and Resources

Legend:
- Manufacturing
- Farming
- Grazing
- Forest
- Beef cattle
- Coal
- Corn
- Dairy cattle
- Forest products
- Gypsum
- Hay
- Hogs
- Limestone
- Mint
- Natural gas or oil
- Poultry
- Soybeans
- Vegetables
- Wheat

MICHIGAN

Lake Michigan

Michigan City
Hammond
Gary
South Bend
La Porte
Elkhart
Goshen
Angola
Pigeon River
Little Calumet River
Kendallville
La Crosse
Plymouth
Bourbon
Kankakee River
Yellow River
Warsaw
St. Joseph River
Rensselaer
Rochester
Ft. Wayne
Eel River
Maumee River
Huntington
Huntington Lake
Decatur
Monticello
Logansport
Wabash
Peru
Salamonie Lake
Salamonie River
Wabash River
Mississinewa Lake
Marion
Portland
Kokomo
Mississinewa River
Lafayette
Frankfort
White River
Muncie
OHIO
Crawfordsville
Anderson
Richmond
Indianapolis ★
Big Blue River
Flatrock River
Connersville
St. Bernice
Rushville
Brookville Lake
Fontanet
Shelbyville
Moscow
Cagles Mill Lake
Whitewater River
Terre Haute
Napoleon
Columbus
Bloomington
Monroe Lake
Lawrenceburg
Versailles
ILLINOIS
Bedford
Madison
East Fork White River
Ohio River
Mitchell
Orleans
Scottsburg
Vincennes
Washington
Shoals
Salem
White River
Paoli
French Lick
Charlestown
Blue River
Jasper
Patoka River
Clarksville
New Albany
Patoka Lake
Corydon
New Harmony
Evansville
N
W   E
S
Mt. Vernon
Ohio River
KENTUCKY

0   25   50 Miles
0   25   50 Kilometers
Albers Equal-Area Projection

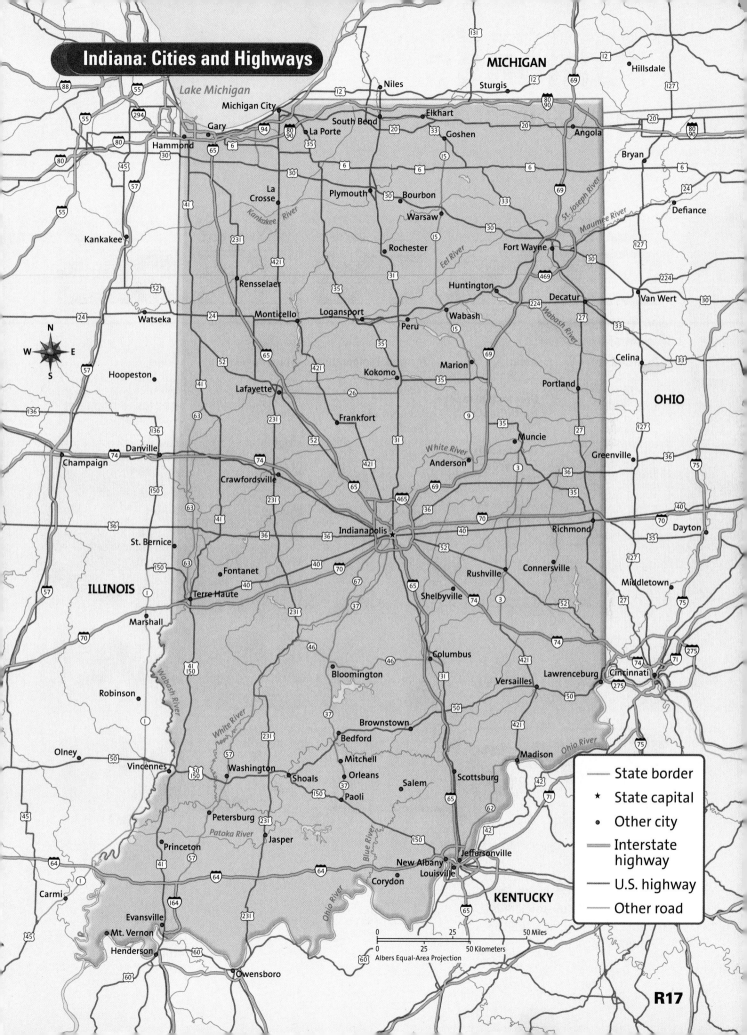

Indiana: Cities and Highways

MICHIGAN

OHIO

ILLINOIS

KENTUCKY

Lake Michigan

Kankakee River
St. Joseph River
Maumee River
Eel River
Wabash River
White River
White River
Wabash River
Patoka River
Blue River
Ohio River
Ohio River

Cities:
Hillsdale, Niles, Sturgis, Bryan, Michigan City, Gary, South Bend, Elkhart, Goshen, Angola, Hammond, La Porte, Defiance, Kankakee, La Crosse, Plymouth, Bourbon, Warsaw, Van Wert, Watseka, Rensselaer, Rochester, Fort Wayne, Huntington, Decatur, Hoopeston, Monticello, Logansport, Peru, Wabash, Celina, Danville, Lafayette, Frankfort, Kokomo, Marion, Portland, Champaign, Crawfordsville, Muncie, Greenville, Anderson, St. Bernice, Fontanet, Terre Haute, Indianapolis, Richmond, Dayton, Marshall, Rushville, Connersville, Middletown, Shelbyville, Robinson, Bloomington, Columbus, Lawrenceburg, Cincinnati, Olney, Vincennes, Washington, Bedford, Mitchell, Orleans, Salem, Versailles, Madison, Scottsburg, Shoals, Paoli, Petersburg, Jasper, Princeton, New Albany, Louisville, Corydon, Carmi, Evansville, Mt. Vernon, Henderson, Owensboro, Jeffersonville, Brownstown

Legend:
— State border
★ State capital
• Other city
— Interstate highway
— U.S. highway
— Other road

0   25   50 Miles
0   25   50 Kilometers
Albers Equal-Area Projection

R17

Almanac

FACTS ABOUT INDIANA

LAND

INDIANA

Highest Point:
Hoosier Hill
Franklin County,
1,257 feet (383 m)

Lowest Point:
Ohio River in Posey
County, 320 feet
(98 m)

SIZE

Area:
36,418 square miles

**Greatest Distance
North/South:**
270 miles

**Greatest Distance
East/West:**
140 miles

Water Area:
550 square miles

CLIMATE

Average Temperature:
26°F in January
74°F in July

**Average Yearly
Rainfall:**
40 inches

POPULATION

Total Population:
6,313,520*

**Population
Density:**
170 people per
square mile

**Population
Distribution:**
Urban: 71 percent
Rural: 29 percent

*U.S. Census estimate
2006 population
figures

LEADING PRODUCTS AND RESOURCES

Crops:
corn, soybeans, hay,
wheat, tomatoes, cucumbers, apples, blueberries,
melons, pumpkins

Livestock:
hogs, chickens, cattle, turkeys, dairy products, eggs

Timber:
hickory, oak

Manufacturing:
transportation equipment,
chemicals, steel, iron,
aluminum, metal products,
machinery, appliances,
food products

Mining:
coal, crushed stone, sand,
gravel

Indiana is the thirty-eighth-largest state among all the states. It is the smallest state west of the Appalachian Mountains.

The lowest recorded temperature in Indiana was –36°F at New Whiteland on January 19, 1994. The highest temperature ever recorded in Indiana was 116°F on July 14, 1936, at Collegeville.

Indiana has the fifteenth-largest population of any state. Hoosiers come from many different cultural backgrounds.

GOVERNMENT

STATE SYMBOLS

Elected Officials:
4-year terms: Governor,
Lieutenant Governor,
Secretary of State,
Attorney General,
Treasurer,
State Auditor

State Senate:
50 members
4-year terms

**State House of
Representatives:**
100 members
2-year terms

Counties: 92

United States Senators:
2 senators, 6-year terms

**United States
Representatives:**
9 representatives,
2-year terms

Bird: cardinal

Flower: peony

Tree: yellow poplar (tulip tree)

Motto: The Crossroads of
America

River: Wabash River

Song: "On the Banks of the
Wabash, Far Away"

Stone: Limestone

Nickname: The Hoosier State

The cardinal was
adopted as the
state bird in 1933 by
the Indiana General
Assembly.

The limestone for the Soldiers and
Sailors monument came from Owen
County, Indiana. The monument
stands 284 feet high, only 15 feet
shorter than the Statue of Liberty.

In 2002, Indiana was the
second-largest producer of
popcorn in the United States.
Every year, people worldwide
enjoy popcorn.

The Indiana Constitution of
1851 set up the basic form of
government that Indiana still
has today. The constitution
that Hoosiers have today
also reflects changes, or
amendments, that have been
added to the constitution
since 1851.

Almanac
Facts About Indiana Counties

ATLAS/
ALMANAC

County Name	County Seat	Population*	County Name	County Seat	Population*
Adams	Decatur	33,719	Franklin	Brookville	23,373
Allen	Fort Wayne	347,316	Fulton	Rochester	20,622
Bartholomew	Columbus	74,444	Gibson	Princeton	33,396
Benton	Fowler	9,050	Grant	Marion	69,825
Blackford	Hartford City	13,603	Greene	Bloomfield	33,360
Boone	Lebanon	53,526	Hamilton	Noblesville	250,979
Brown	Nashville	15,071	Hancock	Greenfield	65,050
Carroll	Delphi	20,526	Harrison	Corydon	36,992
Cass	Logansport	39,902	Hendricks	Danville	131,204
Clark	Jeffersonville	103,569	Henry	New Castle	46,947
Clay	Brazil	27,021	Howard	Kokomo	84,500
Clinton	Frankfort	34,217	Huntington	Huntington	38,026
Crawford	English	11,137	Jackson	Brownstown	42,404
Daviess	Washington	30,220	Jasper	Rensselaer	32,296
Dearborn	Lawrenceburg	49,663	Jay	Portland	21,605
Decatur	Greensburg	24,948	Jefferson	Madison	32,668
DeKalb	Auburn	41,902	Jennings	Vernon	28,473
Delaware	Muncie	114,879	Johnson	Franklin	133,316
Dubois	Jasper	41,212	Knox	Vincennes	38,241
Elkhart	Goshen	198,105	Kosciusko	Warsaw	76,541
Fayette	Connersville	24,648	LaGrange	LaGrange	37,291
Floyd	New Albany	72,570	Lake	Crown Point	494,202
Fountain	Covington	17,486	LaPorte	LaPorte	110,479

*Population Estimates for July 1, 2006

County Name	County Seat	Population*
Lawrence	Bedford	46,413
Madison	Anderson	130,575
Marion	Indianapolis	865,504
Marshall	Plymouth	47,295
Martin	Shoals	10,340
Miami	Peru	35,552
Monroe	Bloomington	122,613
Montgomery	Crawfordsville	38,173
Morgan	Martinsville	70,290
Newton	Kentland	14,293
Noble	Albion	47,918
Ohio	Rising Sun	5,826
Orange	Paoli	19,659
Owen	Spencer	22,741
Parke	Rockville	17,021
Perry	Tell City	18,843
Pike	Petersburg	12,855
Porter	Valparaiso	160,105
Posey	Mount Vernon	26,765
Pulaski	Winamac	13,861
Putnam	Greencastle	36,978
Randolph	Winchester	26,581
Ripley	Versailles	27,748

County Name	County Seat	Population*
Rush	Rushville	17,684
St. Joseph	South Bend	266,678
Scott	Scottsburg	23,704
Shelby	Shelbyville	44,114
Spencer	Rockport	20,596
Starke	Knox	23,069
Steuben	Angola	33,683
Sullivan	Sullivan	21,542
Switzerland	Vevay	9,721
Tippecanoe	Lafayette	156,169
Tipton	Tipton	16,377
Union	Liberty	7,291
Vanderburgh	Evansville	173,356
Vermillion	Newport	16,645
Vigo	Terre Haute	103,009
Wabash	Wabash	33,559
Warren	Williamsport	8,701
Warrick	Boonville	57,090
Washington	Salem	28,062
Wayne	Richmond	68,846
Wells	Bluffton	28,199
White	Monticello	24,396
Whitley	Columbia City	32,556

*Population Estimates for July 1, 2006

Almanac
Facts About Indiana Governors

Governor	Term	Governor	Term
Jonathan Jennings	1816–1822	Isaac P. Gray	1885–1889
Ratliff Boon	1822	Alvin P. Hovey	1889–1891
William Hendricks	1822–1825	Ira J. Chase	1891–1893
James B. Ray	1825–1831	Claude Matthews	1893–1897
Noah Noble	1831–1837	James A. Mount	1897–1901
David Wallace	1837–1840	Winfield T. Durbin	1901–1905
Samuel Bigger	1840–1843	James F. Hanly	1905–1909
James Whitcomb	1843–1848	Thomas R. Marshall	1909–1913
Paris C. Dunning	1848–1849	Samuel M. Ralston	1913–1917
Joseph A. Wright	1849–1857	James P. Goodrich	1917–1921
Ashbel P. Willard	1857–1860	Warren T. McCray	1921–1924
Abram A. Hammond	1860–1861	Emmett F. Branch	1924–1925
Henry S. Lane	1861	Edward L. Jackson	1925–1929
Oliver P. Morton	1861–1867	Harry G. Leslie	1929–1933
Conrad Baker	1867–1873	Paul V. McNutt	1933–1937
Thomas A. Hendricks	1873–1877	Maurice C. Townsend	1937–1941
James D. Williams	1877–1880	Henry F. Schricker	1941–1945
Isaac P. Gray	1880–1881	Ralph F. Gates	1945–1949
Albert G. Porter	1881–1885	Henry F. Schricker	1949–1953

Governor	Term
George N. Craig	1953–1957
Harold W. Handley	1957–1961
Matthew E. Welsh	1961–1965
Roger D. Branigin	1965–1969
Edgar D. Whitcomb	1969–1973
Otis R. Bowen	1973–1981

Governor	Term
Robert D. Orr	1981–1989
Evan Bayh	1989–1997
Frank O'Bannon	1997–2003
Joseph E. Kernan	2003–2005
Mitch E. Daniels, Jr.	2005–

Research Handbook

Before you can write a report or complete a project, you must gather information about your topic. You can find information from many sources, including maps, photos, illustrations, and artifacts. You can also find information in your textbook. Other sources of information are technology resources, print resources, and community resources.

Technology Resources

- Internet
- Computer disk
- Television and radio

Print Resources

- Almanac
- Atlas
- Dictionary
- Encyclopedia
- Nonfiction book
- Periodical
- Thesaurus

Community Resources

- Teacher
- Museum curator
- Community leader
- Older citizen

Technology Resources

The main technology resources you can use for researching information are the Internet and computer disks. Your school or local library may have CD-ROMs or DVDs that contain information about your topic. Other media, such as television and radio, can also be good sources of current information.

Using the Internet

The Internet contains vast amounts of information. By using a computer to go online, you can read letters and documents, see pictures and artworks, listen to music, take a virtual tour of a place, and read about current events.

Information that you find online is always changing. Keep in mind that some websites might contain mistakes or incorrect information. To get accurate information, be sure to visit only trusted websites, such as museum and government sites. Also, try to find two or more websites that give the same facts.

❭ Plan Your Search
- Identify the topic to be researched.
- Make a list of questions that you want to answer about your topic.
- List key words or groups of words that can be used to write or talk about your topic.
- Look for good online resources to find answers to your questions.
- Decide if the information you find is relevant, reliable, and accurate.

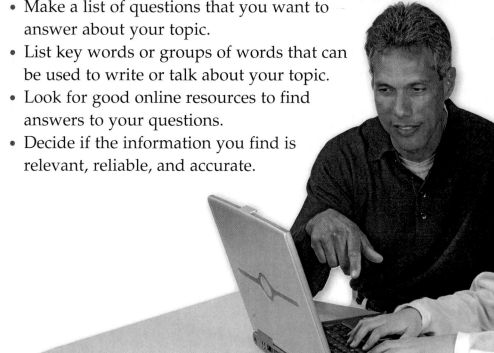

Use a Search Engine

A search engine is an online collection of websites that can be sorted by entering a key word or group of words. There are many different search engines available. You may want to ask a librarian, a teacher, or a parent for suggestions on which search engine to use.

◗ **Search by Subject**   To search by subject, or topic, use a search engine. Choose from the list of key words that you made while planning your search, and enter a key word or group of words in the search engine field on your screen. Then click SEARCH or GO. You will see a list of available websites that have to do with your topic. Click on the site or sites you think will be most helpful. If you do not find enough websites listed, think of other key words or related words, and search again.

◗ **Search by Address**   Each website has its own address, called a Uniform Resource Locator, or URL for short. To get to a website using a URL, simply type the URL in the LOCATION/GO TO box on your screen and hit ENTER or click GO.

◗ **Use Bookmarks**   The bookmark feature is an Internet tool for keeping and organizing URLs. If you find a website that seems especially helpful, you can save the URL so that you can quickly and easily return to it later. Click BOOKMARKS or FAVORITES at the top of your screen, and choose ADD. Your computer makes a copy of the URL and keeps a record of it.

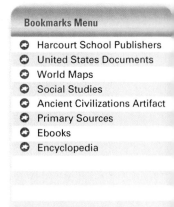

Print Resources

Books in libraries are organized through a system of numbers. These traditional resources have their own title and a number called a call number. The call number tells where in the library the book can be found.

You can locate information in the book by using its table of contents and index. Some reference books, such as encyclopedias, are usually kept in a separate section of a library. Each book there has R or RE—for *reference*—on its spine. Most reference books can only be used in the library. Most libraries also have a special section for periodicals, which include magazines and newspapers.

▶ Almanac

An almanac is a book or electronic resource that contains facts about different subjects. The subjects are listed in alphabetical order in an index, and many number-based facts are shown in tables or charts. New almanacs are published each year, so they have the most current information.

▶ Atlas

An atlas is a book of maps that gives information about places. Different kinds of atlases show different places at different times. Your teacher or librarian can help you find the kind of atlas you need for your research.

▶ Dictionary

A dictionary gives the correct spelling of words and their definitions, or meanings. It also gives the words' pronunciations, or how to say the words aloud. In addition, many dictionaries have lists of foreign words, abbreviations, well-known people, and place names.

> **de•mand\di-´mand***n* **1:** to ask with authority **2:** the desire or need for a product or service
> **de•pend\di-´pend***vi* **1:** to be undecided **2:** to rely on for help
> **de•pos•it\di-´pä-zit***vb* **1:** to put money into a bank account **2:** to place for safekeeping or as a pledge

Dictionary entry

◗ Encyclopedia

An encyclopedia is a book or set of books that gives information about many different topics. The topics are arranged alphabetically. An encyclopedia is a good source to use when beginning your research. In addition to words, electronic encyclopedias often have sound and video clips as well.

◗ Nonfiction Books

A nonfiction book gives facts about real people, places, and things. All nonfiction books in a library are arranged in order and by category according to their call numbers. To find a book's call number, you use a library's card file or computer catalog. You can search for a book in the catalog by subject, author, or title.

◗ Periodicals

A periodical is published each day, each week, or each month. Periodicals are good resources for current information on topics not yet found in books. Many libraries have a guide that lists magazine articles by subject. Two such guides are the *Children's Magazine Guide* and the *Readers' Guide to Periodical Literature*. The entries in guides are usually in alphabetical order by subject, author, or title.

◗ Thesaurus

A thesaurus (thih•SAWR•uhs) gives synonyms, or words that mean the same or nearly the same as another word. A thesaurus also gives antonyms, or words that have the opposite meanings. Using a thesaurus can help you find words that better describe your topic and make your writing more interesting.

Capitol, United States, houses the United States legislative branch, or Congress. The Capitol building is in Washington, D.C., on Capitol Hill. The Capitol is a government building and a symbol of the United States. Visitors from different countries visit the Capitol each year. The public can go inside and see where the House of Representatives and the Senate meet.

In 1792 the government held a special contest. Architects from around the country competed to see whose design for the Capitol would be chosen. Amateur architect and doctor William Thornton submitted the winning entry. In 1793, construction of the Capitol began. Congress held its first meeting in the new Capitol in 1800. During the War of 1812, British troops set fire to the building in the year 1814. Congress could not return to the Capitol until 1819.

The Capitol is modeled on the architecture used by Romans. The Capitol's 540 rooms include offices and reception rooms. In these rooms are keepsakes from United States history and works of art from memorable artists. The center of the Capitol, also known as the Rotunda, is beneath the dome. It is more than 95 feet in diameter and 185 feet high. The large center dome is painted white to match the rest of the marble building. On top of the dome is the Statue of Freedom. The statue is a woman with a headdress of eagle feathers, holding a shield and sword.

Many state funerals for famous United States citizens, such as Abraham Lincoln and Ronald Reagan, have been held in the Rotunda under the dome ceiling. Painted in 1865, *The Apotheosis of George Washington* by an Italian painter Constantino Brumidi, decorates the dome ceiling.

To the north of the Rotunda is the Senate wing of the Capitol. This wing has rooms open to the public where visitors can watch the Senate in session. The old Supreme court chamber is also housed in this wing. The chamber looks much like it did in 1859. This is where the court met during 1810 to 1859. The President's room is also located on the Senate side. It is one of the most decorated rooms. Portraits of George Washington and a large bronze chandelier decorate this room.

South of the Rotunda is the House of Representatives' wing. Located in this wing are the House Chamber and the Statuary Hall. The House Chamber has rooms open to the public for viewing. The Statuary Hall contains statues of notable Americans. In 1857, an extension to the House wing was completed. Thomas Ustick Walter, co-founder of the American Institute of Architects, built it. Walter is responsible for the fireproof cast-iron dome on top of the building's center completed in 1866. It replaced the small wood-constructed dome built in 1824.

In 1962, architect J. George Stewart completed the eastward expansion of the Capitol's center. Today, the Capitol covers 4 acres and has five levels. It is part of the Capitol Complex.

The Capitol Complex consists of the United States Botanical Garden Conservatory, United States Supreme Court, office buildings for the House of Representatives and Senate, and the Library of Congress.

Chapter 1 · **217**

Encyclopedia article

Community Resources

People in your community can share oral histories or information about your research topic. You can learn facts, opinions, or points of view by asking these people thoughtful questions. Before you talk to any of them, always ask a teacher or a parent for permission.

Listening to Find Information

It is important to plan ahead whenever you talk with people as part of your research. Planning ahead will help you gather the information you need. Follow these tips as you gather information from people in your community.

❯ Before
- Find out more about the topic you want to discuss.
- Think about the kind of information you still need.
- Consider the best way to gather the information you need.
- List the people you want to talk to.
- Make a list of useful questions you want to ask. Make sure your questions are clear and effective.

❯ During
- Speak clearly and loudly enough when asking questions.
- Listen carefully. Make sure you are getting the information you need, and revise your questions based on what you hear. You may also think of new questions to ask.
- Think about the speaker's perspective, tone of voice, and word choice. Use these clues to evaluate whether the speaker is a good source of information about your topic.
- Be polite. Do not interrupt or argue with the person who is speaking.
- Take notes to help you remember important ideas and details.
- Write down the person's exact words if you think you will want to quote them in your report. If possible, use a tape recorder. Be sure to ask the speaker for permission in advance.

❯ After
- Thank the person you spoke with.
- Follow up by writing a thank-you note.

Writing to Get Information

You can also write to people in your community to gather information. You can write an e-mail or a letter. Keep these ideas in mind as you write:

- Write neatly or use a computer.
- Say who you are and why you are writing. Be clear and specific about what you want to know.
- Carefully check your spelling and punctuation.
- If you are writing a letter, provide a self-addressed, stamped envelope for the person to send you a response.
- Thank the person.

222 Central Avenue
Dover, NJ 07801
October 25, 20- -

Regional Tourism Division
Attn: Ms. Stephanie Nguyen
123 Main Street
Cape May, NJ 08204

Dear Ms. Nguyen:

My name is David Thomas, and I am writing this letter to see if you can send me some information about scenic attractions in southern New Jersey. My family is planning a vacation next month, and we would like to visit some of the attractions in the southern part of the state. Please send a brochure listing the scenic attractions and a highway map. I understand this is a service you provide for those planning vacations in the area. I am excited about visiting your part of the state.

Thank you for your help.

Sincerely,

David Thomas

David Thomas
222 Central Avenue
Dover, NJ 07801

Bureau of Tourism
Attn: Stephanie Nguyen
123 Main Street
Cape May, NJ 08204

Reporting

❱ Written Reports

Your teacher may ask you to write a report about the information you find. Knowing how to write a report will help you make good use of the information. The following tips will help you write your report.

❱ Before Writing

- Choose a main idea or topic.
- Think of questions about your topic. Questions should be clear and focus on specific ideas about your topic.
- Gather information from two or more sources. You may use print resources, technology resources, or community resources. Be sure to look for answers to your questions.
- Take notes that paraphrase or summarize the information.
- Review your notes to be sure you have the information you need. Write down ideas and details about your topic to put in your report.
- Use your notes to make an outline of the information you found. Organize your ideas in a way that is easy to understand.

❱ Citing Sources

An important part of research and writing is citing sources. When you cite a source, you keep a written record of where you got your information. The list of sources will be presented as a bibliography. A bibliography is a list of the books, periodicals, and other sources that you used to find the information in your report.

Outline

Little Rock, Arkansas

I. The History of Little Rock, Arkansas

   A. Little Rock is the state capital of Arkansas.

      1. The site was explored and named by a French trapper in 1722.

      2. Little Rock became the capital of the Arkansas Territory in 1820.

   B. During the Civil War, Little Rock was in the Confederacy.

      1. In 1861, the Confederacy took over a Union arsenal in Little Rock.

      2. In 1863, Little Rock was captured by the Union.

   C. Little Rock became an economic center.

      1. Railroads were built to link industries and natural resources around Little Rock in the 1880s.

      2. In 1969, dams and canals were built to link Little Rock with the Mississippi River.

   D. Important events happened in Little Rock during the Civil Rights movement.

      1. In 1957, nine African American children became students at a previously all-white school.

      2. The school later became a national historic site.

Bibliography

Hernandez, Elizabeth. *Little Rock Through the Years.* San Antonio, Texas: Old Alamo Press, 2004

Wyatt, Adam. *The History of Arkansas.* Philadelphia, Pennsylvania: Scenic River Publishing, 2003

Bibliography Card

Wyatt, Adam. *The History of Arkansas.* Philadelphia, Pennsylvania: Scenic River Publishing, 2003, page 25.

Little Rock became the state capital of the Arkansas territory in 1820.

LITTLE ROCK, ARKANSAS

Reading Notes	Class Notes
• Little Rock was named after a nearby rock formation on the Arkansas River • Little Rock is located in the central part of the state of Arkansas • Little Rock expanded economically in the 1940s • Timber and coal are found in Arkansas • Farmers from all around Arkansas sell their produce in Little Rock • The University of Arkansas is located in Little Rock	• Little Rock is in Arkansas, a state in the South • After the Civil War, many states in the South were still segregated • Segregation is the practice of keeping people in separate groups based on their race or culture • In 1954, the Supreme Court decided that segregation was unconstitutional • In 1957, nine African American students, known as the Little Rock Nine, were sent to Central High School, a previously all-white school • Today, Central High School is a national historic site

Marta Berzina
Social Studies

A History of Little Rock, Arkansas

Little Rock is the capital of the state of Arkansas. The city has a rich history. In 172
the site where Little Rock is located was explored by a french trapper. He named the ar
Little Rock after a rock formation that he saw there. About 100 years later, in 1820, Littl
Rock became the capital of the Arkansas Territory. During the Civil War Arkansas was o
of the states in the Confederacy. In 1861, Confederate troops took over a Union arsenal
Little Rock. The Union captured Little Rock in 1863.

After the Civil War, Little Rock's economy grew. In the 1880s, railroads began to
connect the industries in Little Rock with the natural resources around Arkansas. Timbe
and coal, especially, were important natural resources for Little Rock. Also, farmers fro
around the state of Arkansas sold their produce in markets in Little Rock. After that
In 1969, a network of canals and dams linked Little Rock to the Mississippi River bringi
more trade.

Little Rock is also famous for what happened there during the Civil Rights
movement. After the Civil War, Arkansas like most other states in the South, became
segregated. Segregation meant that African Americans and whites were separated. Th
ate in different restaurants used different restrooms, and attended different schools. In
1954, the Supreme Court decided that segregation was against the Constitution. The L
Rock Nine were nine African American students from Little Rock who, in 1957, were the
first to be sent to a school that before had only allowed white students to attend. Centr
High School, the school where this took place, is now a national historic site.

Write a First Draft
- Use your notes and your outline to write a draft of your report. Keep in mind that your purpose is to share information.
- Write in paragraph form. Develop your topic with facts, details, examples, and explanations. Each paragraph should focus on one new idea.
- Get all your ideas down on paper. You can revise your draft and correct errors in the next step.

Revise
- Read over your draft. Does it make sense? Does your report have a beginning, a middle, and an end? Have you answered all your questions?
- Rewrite sentences that are unclear or poorly worded. Move sentences that seem out of place.
- Add details when needed to support your ideas.
- If too many sentences are alike, make some sentences shorter or longer to keep your report interesting.
- Check any quotations to be sure you have shown someone's exact words and that you have noted the source correctly.

Marta Berzina
Social Studies

A History of Little Rock, Arkansas

Little Rock is the capital of the state of Arkansas. The city has a rich history. In 172
the site where Little Rock is located was explored by a French trapper. He named the ar
Little Rock after a rock formation that he saw there. About 100 years later, in 1820, Littl
Rock became the capital of the Arkansas Territory.

During the Civil War, Arkansas was one of the states in the Confederacy. In 1861,
Confederate troops took over a Union arsenal in Little Rock. The Union captured Little
Rock in 1863.

After the Civil War, Little Rock's economy grew. In the 1880s, railroads began to
connect the industries in Little Rock with the natural resources around Arkansas. Timbe
and coal, especially, were important natural resources for Little Rock. Also, farmers fro
around the state of Arkansas sold their produce in markets in Little Rock. In 1969, a
network of canals and dams linked Little Rock to the Mississippi River, bringing more
trade to the city.

Little Rock is also famous for what happened there during the Civil Rights
movement. After the Civil War, Arkansas, like most other states in the South, became
segregated. Segregation meant that African Americans and whites were separated. Th
ate in different restaurants, used different restrooms, and attended different schools. In
1954, the Supreme Court decided that segregation was unconstitutional. The Little Roc
Nine were nine African American students from Little Rock who, in 1957, were the first
be sent to a school that before had only allowed white students to attend. Central High
School, the school where this took place, is now a national historic site.

Proofread and Edit
- Proofread your report, checking for errors.
- Correct any errors in spelling, capitalization, or punctuation. If you are writing your report on a computer, use the spell-check feature.
- Use a thesaurus to find words that better describe your topic or that make your report more interesting.

Publish
- Make a neat, clean copy of your report.
- Include graphs, tables, maps, or other illustrations to help explain your topic.

Proofreading marks and their meanings	
Mark	**Meaning**
∧	Insert word.
∧,	Insert comma.
¶	Start a new paragraph.
☰ cap	Use capital letter.
℮	Delete.
lc	Use lowercase letter.

Listening to Find Information

Sometimes in class you may be asked to give an oral presentation. Like a written report, the purpose of an oral presentation is to share information. These tips will help you prepare an oral presentation:

- Follow the steps described in Before Writing on page R31 to gather and organize information.
- Use your notes to plan and organize your presentation. Include an introduction and a conclusion in your report.
- Prepare note cards that you can refer to as you speak.
- Prepare visuals such as illustrations, diagrams, maps, graphs, tables, or other graphics to help listeners better understand your topic.
- Give your audience a controlling idea about your topic. A controlling idea is the main idea that you support with facts and details.
- Practice your presentation.
- Be sure to speak clearly and loudly enough. Keep your listeners interested in your report by using facial expressions and hand movements.

Biographical Dictionary

The Biographical Dictionary provides information about many of the people introduced in this book. Names are listed alphabetically by last name. Pronunciation guides are provided for hard-to-pronounce names. Following each name are the birth and death dates of that person. If the person is still alive, only the year of birth appears. A brief description of the person's main achievement is then given. The page number that follows tells where the main discussion of that person appears in this book. (You can check the Index for other page references.) Guide names at the top of each page help you quickly locate the name you need to find.

Ball brothers Edmund, William, Lucius, George, and Frank Ball owned one of the nation's largest glassmaking factories, in Muncie. They donated a campus to start Ball State University. p. 163

Bayh, Evan (BY, EV•uhn) *1955–* Indiana governor from 1989 to 1997 and a U.S. senator since 1999. p. 245

Bell, Joshua *1967–* Violinist from Bloomington who has played with major orchestras since he was 14 years old. p. 56

Bird, Larry *1956–* Former professional basketball player from French Lick. p. 53

Blue Jacket *1745?–1805?* Shawnee chief who led Native Americans against U.S. soldiers in the Battle of Fallen Timbers and signed the Treaty of Greenville. p. 111

Bolton, Sarah T. *1814–1893* Indianapolis poet who became well known for her popular poem "Paddle Your Own Canoe." p. 143

Buell, Dorothy (BOO•uhl) *1886–1977* Helped organize the Save the Dunes Council to protect the area that became the Indiana Dunes National Lakeshore. p. 42

Burton, Dan *1938–* Member of the United States House of Representatives from Indiana. p. 245

Bush, George W. *1946–* Forty-third President of the United States. p. 189

Carmichael, Hoagy (KAR•my•kuhl, HOH•gee) *1899–1981* Composer, pianist, actor, and bandleader from Bloomington. p. 58

Carson, Julia *1938–2007* U.S. representative who in 1996 became the first woman and first African American to be elected to Congress from Indianapolis. p. 245

Clark, George Rogers *1752–1818* Pioneer and leader of the American forces that defeated the British at Fort Sackville during the American Revolution. p. 102

Coffin, Catharine *1803–1881* With her husband Levi Coffin, she helped more than 2,000 enslaved people reach freedom. p. 152

Coffin, Levi *1792–1877* One of Indiana's best-known abolitionists. His house served as a station on the Underground Railroad. p. 152

Columbus, Christopher *1451–1506* Italian explorer working for Spain. In 1492, he reached the Americas, lands unknown to Europeans, while trying to find a western route to Asia. p. 93

Conner, William *1777–1855* Pioneer who settled in Indiana in 1823. Today, his house is part of the Conner Prairie Living History Museum. p. 148

Cummins, Clessie Lyle *1888–1968* Inventor of diesel engines and founder of the Cummins Engine Company. p. 225

Daniels, Mitch *1949–* Forty-ninth governor of Indiana. He became governor on January 10, 2005. p. 244

DeBaptiste, George *1814–1875* African American conductor on the Underground Railroad in Indiana. p. 152

Debs, Eugene V. *1855–1926* Railway union leader from Terre Haute. He ran for President of the United States five times. p. 164

Demoiselle *?–1752* Chief of the Piankeshaw branch of the Miami. He signed a treaty with the British during the French and Indian War. p. 96

Duesenberg brothers (DOOZ•uhn•berg) Fred and August Duesenberg built bicycles, motorcycles, and automobiles. In 1913, they started a company that made sports cars, some of which were used to race in the Indianapolis 500. p. 170

Evans, Mari *1923–* Poet who lives in Indianapolis. She has also taught college and written essays, plays, and children's books. p. 55

Forsyth, William *1854–1935* Artist from Indianapolis. He helped start the Herron School of Art, Indiana's oldest and largest art school. p. 55

Fulton, Robert *1765–1815* Built the first practical submarine and the first commercial steamboat, the *Clermont*. p. 144

Gary, Elbert H. *1846–1927* Chairman of the United States Steel Corporation when the company built a mill and a town in the Calumet region. The city of Gary is named for him. p. 163

George III *1738–1820* King of Great Britain during the American Revolution. He attempted to end the fighting between the colonists and the Native Americans. p. 97

Gibault, Father Pierre *1737–1802* A Jesuit missionary and priest for the people of Vincennes. He persuaded the city's French citizens to support the American cause. p. 102

Grissom, Virgil ("Gus") *1926–1967* Astronaut from Mitchell. He was the second American in space. p. 192

Hamilton, Henry *1734?–1796* British official who served as lieutenant governor at Fort Detroit. He was defeated at Fort Sackville by George Rogers Clark in the American Revolution. p. 102

Harper, Ida Husted *1851–1931* Activist in the woman's suffrage movement. p. 169

Harris, Chapman *1802–1890* African American conductor on the Underground Railroad in Indiana. p. 152

Harrison, Benjamin *1833–1901* Twenty-third President of the United States. Six new states were added during his presidency. p. 164

Harrison, William Henry *1773–1841* First governor of the Indiana Territory and later the ninth President of the United States. He led American soldiers at the Battle of Tippecanoe, in 1811. p. 111

Hatcher, Richard G. *1933–* Mayor of Gary from 1968 to 1988. He was one of the first African Americans elected as mayor of a large United States city. p. 184

Haynes, Elwood *1857–1925* Inventor from Kokomo. He invented one of the first successful gasoline-powered automobiles. p. 162

Henry, Patrick *1736–1799* Supporter of American independence. He served as governor of Virginia during the American Revolution. p. 102

Indiana, Robert *1928–* Artist associated with the pop art movement. p. 55

Jackson, Andrew *1767–1845* Seventh President of the United States. He signed the Indian Removal Act in 1830. p. 146

Jennings, Jonathan *1784–1834* The first governor of the state of Indiana. He represented the Indiana Territory in Congress and helped write Indiana's first constitution. p. 119

Kennedy, Robert F. *1925–1968* Served as United States attorney general and as a United States senator from New York. He ran for President in 1968 and was assassinated. p. 184

King, Jr., Dr. Martin Luther *1929–1968* African American civil rights leader who worked in nonviolent ways to end discrimination. He won the Nobel Peace Prize in 1964. p. 184

L

Lanier, James *1800–1881* Banker from Madison who lent money to the state during the Civil War. This money was used to outfit Union troops. p. 154

La Salle, René-Robert Cavelier, Sieur de (luh•SAL) *1643–1687* French explorer who explored the Great Lakes region and the Mississippi River. He was the first European to see what is today Indiana. p. 94

Letterman, David *1947–* Award-winning comedian and late-night talk-show host. He was born in Indianapolis. p. 58

Lilly, Eli *1838–1898* Business leader in Indianapolis. The pharmaceutical company he started in 1876 became one of the world's largest. p. 162

BIOGRAPHICAL DICTIONARY

Lincoln, Abraham *1809–1865* Sixteenth President of the United States. He spent part of his childhood in Indiana. p. 141

Lugar, Richard *1932–* U.S. senator from Indiana and former mayor of Indianapolis. p. 245

Madison, James *1751–1836* Fourth President of the United States. He signed the act that made Indiana the nineteenth state. p. 119

Mays, William G. *1945–* Entrepreneur who started the Mays Chemical Company. p. 227

McNutt, Paul V. *1891–1955* Governor of Indiana during the Great Depression. p. 176

Mellencamp, John *1951–* American rock singer and songwriter. p. 56

Michikinikwa (mih•chih•kin•EE•kwah) *1752?–1812* Miami chief, also known as Little Turtle. He led his people to several victories against the United States in the 1790s but called for peace in the years leading up to the War of 1812. p. 110

Montgomery, Wes *1925–1968* Was one of the greatest modern jazz guitarists. p. 56

Morgan, John Hunt *1825–1864* Confederate general who led raids into southern Indiana and Ohio during the Civil War. p. 155

Morton, Oliver P. *1823–1877* Governor of Indiana during the Civil War. He helped raise volunteers for the Union army. p. 154

Nelson, Julia D. *1863–1936* Politician from Mooresville. In 1920, she became the first woman to be elected to the Indiana state legislature. p. 169

O'Bannon, Frank *1930–2003* Governor of Indiana from 1997 to 2003. p. 189

Oliver, James *1823–1908* Inventor of the chilled-iron plow. He owned the largest plow factory in Indiana. p. 162

Owen, Robert *1771–1858* Welsh factory owner who started the town of New Harmony in 1825. He wanted the town to be a utopia. p. 142

Pauley, Jane *1950–* Long-time television journalist from Indianapolis. p. 58

Peterson, Raven *1994–* Student in Indiana who has volunteered with School on Wheels. In 2006, she received a national award for her volunteer service. p. 256

Pontiac *1720–1769* Ottawa chief who united tribes and led a rebellion against the British in 1763 to stop the loss of Native American lands. p. 97

Porter, Cole *1891–1964* Composer and songwriter from Peru, Indiana. p. 58

Pyle, Ernest Taylor ("Ernie") *1900–1945* Newspaper reporter from Dana. He wrote about the experiences of soldiers in World War II. p. 179

R

Ralston, Alexander *1771–1827* Architect who developed a plan for the city of Indianapolis. He had previously helped Pierre L'Enfant plan Washington, D.C. p. 143

Rapp, George *1757–1847* German preacher who started the town of Harmonie in 1814. p. 142

Redenbacher, Orville (RED•uhn•bah•ker) *1907–1995* Entrepreneur born in Brazil, Indiana. He began one of the most successful popcorn businesses in the United States. p. 225

Red Jacket *1750?–1830* Chief of the Seneca. He was originally against selling Native American lands but later ended his opposition. p. 116

Riley, James Whitcomb *1849–1916* Known as the Hoosier Poet, he wrote more than 1,000 poems about the state he loved, Indiana. He was born in Greenfield and lived in Indianapolis. p. 54

Roberts, John *1955–* The Chief Justice of the United States Supreme Court who grew up in Long Beach, Indiana. p. 245

Rokita, Todd *1966–* Became secretary of state of Indiana in 2003. p. 244

Roosevelt, Franklin D. *1882–1945* Thirty-second President of the United States. He began New Deal programs to help the nation out of the Great Depression and led the United States during World War II. p. 176

St. Clair, Arthur *1734?–1818* General in the Continental Army during the American Revolution and the first governor of the Northwest Territory. p. 110

Scudder, Janet *1869–1940* Sculptor from Terre Haute. p. 55

Sewall, May Wright *1844–1920* Leader from Indianapolis who worked to help women gain the right to vote. p. 169

Shaheen, Yvonne *1940?–* Former CEO of Long Electric Company in Indianapolis who is known for her community work. p. 257

Shepard, Randall T. *1947?–* Chief Justice of the Indiana Supreme Court since 1987. p. 244

Skelton, Red *1913–1997* Comedian from Vincennes who performed on the radio and on television. p. 58

Skillman, Becky *1950–* Fiftieth lieutenant governor of Indiana. She took office in 2005. p. 244

Slocum, Frances *1773–1847* Kidnapped as a young girl and lived most of her life among Native Americans. p. 109

Steele, T. C. *1847–1926* Artist from Owen County. He painted nine of the portraits in the Indiana Governors' Portraits collection. p. 55

Stratton-Porter, Gene *1863–1924* Author and photographer whose books show her love of nature and geography. p. 34

Studebaker brothers Clement and Henry Studebaker were wagon makers in South Bend starting in the 1850s. They later became leading manufacturers of automobiles. p. 170

Tecumseh (tuh•KUHM•suh) *1768?–1813* Shawnee leader of Native Americans in the Northwest Territory. He wanted to stop settlers from taking Native American lands. p. 111

Tenskwatawa (ten•SKWAH•tuh•wah) *1775–1836* Shawnee religious and political leader known as the Prophet. He worked with his brother, Tecumseh, to unite Native American tribes. p. 111

Tharp, Twyla *1941–* Dancer and choreographer from Portland, Indiana. She has won many awards for her work. p. 57

Tipton, John *1786–1839* Member of the Indiana House of Representatives. He served on the commission that chose the location of Indiana's new capital in 1820. Tipton County is named for him. p. 143

Vigo, Francis *1747–1836* Italian-born trader and merchant who provided supplies, money, and information to George Rogers Clark during the American Revolution. p. 103

Voss, Janice *1956–* Astronaut from South Bend. She graduated from Purdue University and took part in five spaceflights. p. 188

W

Walker, Madame C. J. *1867–1919* African American entrepreneur from Louisiana. She started a business in Indianapolis making hair-care products for women, and became one of the country's wealthiest women. p. 225

Wallace, Lew *1827–1905* Union general during the Civil War who helped recruit troops in Indiana. He later wrote a best-selling novel. p. 154

Wayne, Anthony *1745–1796* United States army general. He defeated Blue Jacket's forces at the Battle of Fallen Timbers in 1794 and set up the Treaty of Greenville. p. 111

Webster, Marie *1859–1956* Entrepreneur from Wabash who wrote the first quilting book published in the United States. p. 225

White, Ryan *1971–1990* High school student who died of AIDS, which he contracted through a blood transfusion. Before his death, he worked to educate people about the disease. p. 255

Wilson, Woodrow *1856–1924* Twenty-eighth President of the United States. He was President during World War I. p. 167

Gazetteer

The Gazetteer is a geographical dictionary that can help you locate places discussed in this book. Place names are listed alphabetically. Hard-to-pronounce names are followed by pronunciation guidelines. A description of the place is then given. The absolute location, or latitude and longitude, of each city and of some other places is provided. The page number that follows tells where each place is shown on a map or discussed in a lesson. Guide words at the top of each page help you locate the place name you need to find.

Adena (uh•DEE•nuh) An ancient settlement of a mound-building culture, in present-day Ohio. (40°N, 81°W) p. 79

Anderson The county seat of Madison County, in eastern Indiana. (40°N, 86°W) p. 19

Angel Mounds State Historic Site An ancient site of a mound-building culture; located near present-day Evansville. (42°N, 85°W) p. 80

Angola (an•GOH•luh) The county seat of Steuben County. (42°N, 85°W) p. 19

Bean Blossom A town in Brown County, in southern Indiana. (39°N, 87°W) p. 47

Benton County A county in northwestern Indiana. p. 45

Berne A city in Adams County, in northeastern Indiana. (41°N, 85°W) p. 47

Bloomington The county seat of Monroe County, in south-central Indiana. (39°N, 87°W) p. 19

Bluespring Caverns A cavern in southern Indiana. (39°N, 86°W) p. 7

Brazil The county seat of Clay County, in west-central Indiana. (40°N, 87°W) p. 225

Brookville Lake A lake in southern Indiana. p. 15

Brown County State Park Indiana's largest state park, in southern Indiana. (39°N, 86°W) p. 22

Cahokia (cuh•HOH•kee•uh) An ancient settlement of a mound-building culture; located in present-day southwestern Illinois. (39°N, 90°W) p. 103

Calumet region A region of Indiana near Lake Michigan. p. 163

Camp Morton An army camp and prison during the Civil War, located near Indianapolis. p. 155

Carmel A town in Hamilton County, in central Indiana. (40°N, 86°W) p. 41

Central Till Plain A natural region of flat, fertile land in the central part of Indiana. p. 22

Clarksville A town in Clark County, in southern Indiana. (38°N, 86°W) p. 109

Columbus The county seat of Bartholomew County, in southern Indiana. (39°N, 86°W) p. 19

Corydon The county seat of Harrison County, in southern Indiana. (38°N, 86°W) p. 118

Crooked Lake A lake in northeastern Indiana. p. 5

Decatur (dih•KAY•tuhr) The county seat of Adams County, in northeastern Indiana. (41°N, 85°W) p. 205

East Chicago A city in Lake County, in northern Indiana. (42°N, 87°W) p. 41

East Fork of the White River A tributary of the White River. p. 5

Eel River A tributary of the White River. p. 15

Elkhart A city in Elkhart County, in northern Indiana. (42°N, 86°W) p. 41

Emerald Mound An ancient settlement of a mound-building culture; located in present-day southwestern Mississippi. (32°N, 91°W) p. 79

Evansville The county seat of Vanderburgh County, in southern Indiana. (38°N, 88°W) p. 19

Fishers A city in Hamilton County, in central Indiana. (40°N, 86°W) p. 148

Fort Detroit A fort during the 1700s, in present-day Michigan. (42°N, 83°W) p. 103

Fort Massac A fort during the 1700s, in present-day southern Illinois. (37°N, 89°W) p. 103

GAZETTEER

Fort Miami An early trading post and fort built by the French in 1721, near present-day Fort Wayne. (41°N, 85°W) p. 96

Fort Ouiatenon (wee•AHT•uh•non) The first French trading post in Indiana, built in 1717 near present-day Lafayette. (40°N, 87°W) p. 96

Fort Pitt An American fort built in 1758, in present-day Pittsburgh, Pennsylvania. (40°N, 80°W) p. 103

Fort Sackville A fort during the American Revolution, in Vincennes. (39°N, 88°W) p. 103

Fort Wayne The county seat of Allen County, in northeastern Indiana; site of the early Miami settlement called Kekionga. (41°N, 85°W) p. 19

Fountain City A town in Wayne County, in eastern Indiana. (40°N, 85°W) p. 152

Gary A city in Lake County, in northwestern Indiana on Lake Michigan. (42°N, 87°W) p. 19

Geneva A town in Adams County, in northeastern Indiana. (41°N, 85°W) p. 39

Goshen (GOH•shuhn) The county seat of Elkhart County, in northern Indiana. (42°N, 86°W) p. 41

Great Lakes A group of five large lakes on or near the United States-Canadian border. p. 21

Great Mound An ancient settlement of a mound-building culture; located in present-day central Indiana. (40°N, 86°W) p. 79

Greenwood A city in Johnson County, in central Indiana. (40°N, 86°W) p. 41

Hammond A city in Lake County, in northwestern Indiana. (42°N, 87°W) p. 19

Harmonie A town founded in 1814; it was later renamed New Harmony. (38°N, 88°W) p. 142

Hobart A city in Lake County, in northern Indiana on Lake Michigan. (42°N, 87°W) p. 47

Hoosier Hill The highest point in Indiana, with an elevation of 1,257 feet. (40°N, 85°W) p. 22

Hoosier National Forest A national forest in southern Indiana; the state's largest forest. p. 24

Hopewell An ancient settlement of a mound-building culture; located in present-day southern Ohio. (39°N, 83°W) p. 79

Indiana A state located in the Midwest region of the United States. pp. 12–13

Indiana Dunes National Lakeshore A national park in north Indiana on Lake Michigan. p. 22

Indianapolis The state capital of Indiana and the county seat of Marion County, in central Indiana. (40°N, 86°W), p. 19

Indiana Territory Part of the Northwest Territory that was divided in 1800. p. 111

Jeffersonville The county seat of Clark County, in southeastern Indiana. (38°N, 86°W) p. 41

Kankakee River (kahng•kuh•KEE) A river that begins in northern Indiana and flows southwest into Illinois. p. 15

Kaskaskia (kas•KAS•kee•uh) A battle site of the American Revolution. (38°N, 90°W) p. 103

Kekionga (kee•kee•ohn•GUH) A settlement built by the Miamis on the Maumee River, where the city of Fort Wayne is today. (41°N, 85°W) p. 103

Knox County A county in southwestern Indiana; it originally took up most of the state's land. p. 143

Kokomo (KOH•kuh•moh) The county seat of Howard County, in north-central Indiana. (40°N, 86°W) p. 19

Lafayette (lah•fee•ET) The county seat of Tippecanoe County, in northern Indiana. (40°N, 87°W) p. 19

Lake Michigan One of the five Great Lakes; forms part of Indiana's northern border. pp. 14–15

Lake Wawasee (wah•wuh•SEE) A large lake in northern Indiana. pp. 14–15

Lawrence A city in Marion County, in central Indiana. (40°N, 86°W) p. 41

Limberlost State Historic Site A state historic site, in northeastern Indiana. (40°N, 84°W) p. 39

Loblolly Marsh A wetland in eastern Indiana. p. 34

Marengo Cave A cave in southern Indiana. p. 19

Marion The county seat of Grant County, in north-central Indiana. (41°N, 86°W) p. 216

Marion County A county in central Indiana. p. 187

Maumee River (maw•MEE) A river that begins in northeastern Indiana and flows into Ohio. p. 15

Merrillville A town in Lake County, in northern Indiana. (41°N, 87°W) p. 41

Michigan The state to the north of Indiana. p. 15

Michigan City A city in La Porte County, in northern Indiana. (42°N, 87°W) p. 41

Midwest A region in the United States; made up of 12 states, including Indiana. pp. 12–13

Mishawaka A city in Saint Joseph County, in northern Indiana. (42°N, 86°W) p. 41

Mississinewa Lake (mih•sih•SIH•nuh•weh) A lake in northern Indiana. p. 15

Mississinewa River (mih•sih•SIH•nuh•weh) A tributary of the Wabash River. p. 15

Mitchell A city in Lawrence County, in southern Indiana. (39°N, 86°W) p. 47

Monroe Lake A lake in southern Indiana. pp. 14–15

Monticello (mahnt•uh•SEL•oh) The county seat of White County, in northwestern Indiana. (41°N, 87°W) p. 22

Moundville An ancient settlement of a mound-building culture; located in present-day central Alabama. (33°N, 88°W) p. 79

Muncie The county seat of Delaware County, in east-central Indiana. (40°N, 85°W) p. 19

Nappanee A city in Elkhart County, in northern Indiana. (41°N, 86°W) p. 47

National Road An early road that connected Maryland and Illinois. p. 133

New Albany The county seat of Floyd County, in southern Indiana. (38°N, 86°W) p. 19

New France The possession of France in North America from 1534 to 1763. p. 99

New Harmony A town in Posey County, in southwestern Indiana. (38°N, 88°W) p. 142

New York City The largest city in New York; a major port city. (41°N, 74°W) p. 189

Noblesville A city in Hamilton County, in central Indiana. (40°N, 86°W) p. 41

Northern Moraine and Lake A broad plain covering the northern one-third of Indiana. p. 22

Northwest Territory Lands north of the Ohio River and west of the Appalachians. p. 110

Ocmulgee (ohk•MUHL•gee) An ancient settlement of a mound-building culture; located in present-day central Georgia. (33°N, 84°W) p. 79

Ohio River A large river that forms Indiana's southern border. p. 15

Oldenburg A town in Franklin County, in eastern Indiana. (39°N, 85°W) p. 47

Patoka Lake (puh•TOH•kuh) A lake on the Patoka River, in southern Indiana. p. 15

Patoka River (puh•TOH•kuh) A tributary of the Wabash River, in southwestern Indiana. p. 5

Pearl Harbor A harbor on Oahu, Hawaii, used as a United States Navy base. p. 177

Pennsylvania A state in the eastern United States. p. 189

Peru The county seat of Miami County, in north-central Indiana. (41°N, 86°W) p. 47

Portage A city in Porter County, in northern Indiana on Lake Michigan. (42°N, 87°W) p. 41

Port of Indiana-Burns Harbor/Portage A deep-water port on Lake Michigan; it is also known as the Burns Waterway Harbor. (42°N, 87°W) p. 233

Prophetstown An historic village; located near present-day West Lafayette. (41°N, 87°W) p. 111

Redstone Old Fort An American fort built in 1759, in present-day Pennsylvania. (40°N, 80°W) p. 103

Rensselaer (REN•suh•luhr) The county seat of Jasper County, in northwestern Indiana. (41°N, 87°W) p. 19

Richmond The county seat of Wayne County, in eastern Indiana. (40°N, 85°W) p. 19

GAZETTEER

Rochester The county seat of Fulton County, in northern Indiana. (41°N, 86°W) p. 47

Rockville The county seat of Parke County, in west-central Indiana. (40°N, 87°W) p. 47

 S

Salamonie River (SA•luh•moh•nee) A tributary of the Wabash River. p. 15

Salt Creek A tributary of the East Fork of the White River. p. 15

Serpent Mound An ancient site of a mound-building culture; located in present-day southern Ohio. (39°N, 83°W) p. 79

South Bend The county seat of St. Joseph County, in northern Indiana. (42°N, 86°W) p. 19

Southern Hills and Lowlands A region that covers the southern one-third of Indiana. p. 22

Soviet Union A country in Asia and eastern Europe during the twentieth century. p. 182

Spiro An ancient settlement of a mound-building culture; located in present-day Oklahoma. (35°N, 95°W) p. 79

St. Joseph River A river that flows across northern Indiana; one of two St. Joseph Rivers in Indiana. p. 5

St. Joseph River A river in eastern Indiana; a tributary of the Maumee River; one of two St. Joseph Rivers in Indiana. p. 15

St. Lawrence Seaway A canal system that connects the Great Lakes to the Atlantic Ocean. p. 233

St. Marys River A major tributary of the Maumee River. p. 15

 T

Terre Haute The county seat of Vigo County, in western Indiana. (39°N, 87°W) p. 19

Tippecanoe River (tih•pee•kuh•NOO) A tributary of the Wabash River. p. 19

Turtle Mound An ancient site of a mound-building culture; located on the present-day east-central coast of Florida. (29°N, 81°W) p. 79

 U

United States A country in North America. p. 12

 V

Valparaiso (val•puh•RAY•zoh) A city in Porter County, in northern Indiana. (41°N, 87°W) p. 41

Veedersburg A town in Fountain County, in west-central Indiana. (40°N, 87°W) p. 47

Versailles (vuhr•SAYLZ) The county seat of Ripley County, in southern Indiana. (39°N, 85°W) p. 22

Vincennes (vin•SENZ) The county seat of Knox County, in southern Indiana. (39°N, 88°W) p. 61

 W

Wabash (WAW•bash) The county seat of Wabash County, in northern Indiana. (41°N, 86°W) p. 22

Wabash River (WAW•bash) The longest river in Indiana; it flows west across the state from Ohio before turning south and forming part of the Indiana-Illinois border. pp. 14–15

Warsaw The county seat of Kosciusko County, in northern Indiana. (41°N, 86°W) p. 19

Washington The county seat of Daviess County, in southwestern Indiana. (39°N, 87°W) p. 19

Washington, D.C. Capital city of the United States. (38°N, 77°W) p. 189

Weed Patch Hill The highest knob in the Southern Hills and Lowlands region. (39°N, 86°W) p. 22

West Lafayette (lah•fee•ET) A city in west-central Indiana. (40°N, 87°W) p. 192

White River A large river that flows across south-central Indiana. pp. 14–15

Whitewater River A tributary of the Great Miami River; located in east-central Indiana. p. 5

Whiting A manufacturing center in northern Indiana. (42°N, 87°W) p. 216

Wickliffe Mounds An ancient settlement of a mound-building culture; located in present-day western Kentucky. (37°N, 90°W) p. 79

Wyandotte Cave A cave in southern Indiana. p. 19

Glossary

The glossary contains important history and social science words and their definitions, listed in alphabetical order. Each word is respelled as it would be in a dictionary. When you see the mark ´ after a syllable, pronounce that syllable with more force. The page number at the end of the definition tells where the word is first used in this book. Guide words at the top of each page help you quickly locate the word you need to find.

add, āce, câre, pälm; end, ēqual; it, īce; odd, ōpen, ôrder; tŏŏk, pōōl; up, bûrn; yōō as *u* in *fuse*; oil; pout; ə as *a* in *above*, *e* in *sicken*, *o* in *melon*, *u* in *circus*; check; ring; thin; this; zh as in *vision*

A

abolitionist (a•bə•li´shən•ist) A person who worked to end slavery. p. 151

absolute location (ab•sə•loot´ lō•kā´shən) The exact location of a place on Earth, using lines of latitude and longitude. p. 18

aerospace (âr´ō•spās) Having to do with the building and testing of equipment for air and space travel. p. 192

agriculture (a´grə•kul•chər) The growing of crops and the raising of farm animals. p. 35

allies (a´līz) Partners in war. p. 96

ancestor (an´ses•tər) An early family member. p. 77

appeal (ə•pəl´) To ask that a court case be judged again in a higher court. p. 243

appoint (ə•point´) To choose. p. 243

artifact (är´tə•fakt) An object made by people in the past. p. 88

automobile (ô´tə•mō•bēl) A vehicle that can move by itself, powered by its own engine; a car. p. 162

B

barter (bär´tər) To trade goods, usually without using money. p. 78

bill (bil) A plan for a new law. p. 242

biosphere (bī´ə•sfir) All living things and their environment. p. 32

bond (bänd) A document that allows the government to use a person's money for a certain amount of time and pay it back later. p. 167

border (bôr´dər) A line that divides one place from another. p. 13

budget (bu´jət) A written plan for how to spend money. p. 243

C

canal (kə•nal´) A human-made waterway that connects two bodies of water. p. 36

canyon (kan´yən) A deep, narrow valley with steep sides. p. 23

cardinal direction (kärd´nəl də•rek´shən) One of the main directions: north, south, east, west. p. I21

cause (kôz) An event or action that makes something else happen. p. 106

cease-fire (sēs´fīr) A temporary end to a conflict. p. 182

census (sen´səs) Official population count. p. 119

century (sen´chə•rē) A period of 100 years. p. 172

character traits (kâr´ik•tər trāts) A person's qualities and ways of acting. p. I5

choreographer (kōr•ē•ä´grə•fər) A person who creates dances. p. 57

chronology (krə•nä´lə•jē) Time order. p. I3

citizenship (si´tə•zən•ship) Full membership in a community or country. p. 254

civic virtue (si´vik vûr´chōō) An action that contributes to the smooth running of a democracy. p. 255

civility (sə•vi´lə•tē) Politeness. p. 255

civil rights (si´vəl rīts) The rights of citizens to equal treatment. p. 184

civil war (si´vəl wor) A war between people in the same country. p. 154

clan (klan) A group of closely related people. p. 87

climate (klī´mət) The kind of weather a place has over a long period of time. p. 29

cold war (kōld wôr) A war fought mostly with ideas and money instead of soldiers. p. 182

colony (kä´lə•nē) A settlement that is ruled by a faraway government. p. 94

communism (käm´ya•ni•zəm) A political and economic system in which all industries, land, and businesses are controlled by the government. p. 182

compass rose (kum´pəs rōz) A circular direction marker on a map. p. I21

competition (käm•pə•ti´shən) The effort among similar businesses to sell the most products. p. 215

constitution (kän•stə•tōō´shən) A written plan for government. p. 119

consumer goods (kən•sōō´mər gŏŏdz) Products made for personal use. p. 171

continent (kän´tə•nənt) One of Earth's seven largest landmasses. p. I16

county seat (koun´tē sēt) The city or town where the main offices of the county government are located. p. 247

culture (kul´chər) A way of life shared by a group of people. p. 44

debt (det) Something owed to someone else, often money. p. 109

decade (de´kād) A period of ten years. p. 172

delegate (de´li•gət) A representative. p. 119

demand (di•mand´) The amount of a product or service that people want and are willing to buy. p. 231

depression (di•pre´shən) A time when there are few jobs and people have little money. p. 175

dialect (dī´ə•lekt) A way of speaking. p. 54

discrimination (dis•kri•mə•nā´shən) The unfair treatment of people based on the color of their skin, their religion, or their ethnic group. p. 184

double-bar graph (də´bəl•bär graf) A graph that compares two sets of numbers. p. 236

drought (drout) A long period of little or no precipitation. p. 29

dune (dōōn) A hill of sand built up by wind. p. 22

economy (i•kä´nə•mē) The way people in a state, region, or country use resources to meet their needs. p. 213

effect (i•fekt´ or ē•fekt´) What happens as a result of something else happening. p. 106

efficient (i•fi´shənt) Productive with little waste of time or money. p. 191

elevation (e•lə•vā´shən) The height of land above or below sea level. p. 23

enabling act (i•nā´bə•ling akt) A special law that allowed a territory to become a state. p. 119

entrepreneur (än•trə•prə•nûr´) A person who takes a risk to start a new business. p. 223

equator (ē•kwā´tər) The imaginary line that divides Earth into Northern and Southern Hemispheres. p. I16

ethanol (e´thə•nōl) A liquid that can be used as a fuel in automobiles. p. 216

ethnic group (eth´nik grōōp) A group of people from the same country, of the same race, or with a shared culture. p. 46

evidence (e´və•dəns) Proof. p. I3

executive branch (ig•ze´kyə•tiv branch) The part of government that makes sure laws are carried out. p. 243

expedition (ek•spə•di´shən) A journey into an area to learn more about it. p. 94

explorer (ik•splōr´ər) Someone who travels to unfamiliar places. p. 93

export (ek´spôrt) A product sent from one country to be sold in another country. p. 234

extinct (ik•stingkt´) No longer in existence, which is what happens to a living thing when all of its kind die out. p. 78

fact (fakt) A statement that can be proved or supported by evidence. p. 158

fertile soil (fûr´təl soil) Soil good for growing crops. p. 14

fiction (fik´shən) A story that is made up. p. 158

flatboat (flat´bōt) A large, flat-bottomed boat that can only float downstream. p. 144

free state (frē stāt) A state where slavery was against the law before the Civil War. p. 151

glacier (glā´shər) A huge, slow-moving mass of ice. p. 21

grid system (grid sis´təm) An arrangement of lines that divides a map into squares. p. I22

gross state product (grōs stāt prä´dəkt) The total value of all goods and services produced by workers of a state in one year. p. 213

hatch lines (hach līnz) A pattern of stripes on a map that shows areas claimed by two or more countries. p. 98

hemisphere (he´mə•sfir) One half of Earth. p. I17

heritage (her´ə•tij) A way of life, including customs and traditions, that is passed down through a family or group. p. 46

high-tech (hī•tek´) Shortened form of the words *high technology*; having to do with inventing, building, or using computers and other kinds of electronic equipment. p. 192

historic (hi•stôr´ik) Existing after the beginning of written history. p. 83

historical map (hi•stôr´i•kəl map) A map that shows a place at a certain time in history. pp. I20, 98

human feature (hyōo´mən fē´chər) Something created by people that alters the landscape. p. 14

hydrosphere (hī´drə•sfir) The system of water below, on, and above Earth's surface. p. 31

illegal (il•lē´gəl) Against the law. p. 120

immigrant (i´mi•grənt) A person who comes from one country to live in another country. p. 46

import (im´pôrt) A product brought into one country from another country. p. 234

income (in´kəm) Money people earn for the work they do. p. 249

independence (in•də•pen´dəns) The freedom to govern on one's own. p. 101

industry (in´dəs•trē) All the businesses that make one kind of product or provide one kind of service. p. 16

inset map (in´set map) A smaller map within a larger one. p. I20

interdependence (in•tər•di•pen´dəns) The depending of people in each place on people in other places for resources, products, and services. p. 233

intermediate direction (in•tər•mē´dē•it də•rek´shən) One of the in-between directions: northeast, northwest, southeast, southwest. p. I21

interpret (in•tûr´prət) To explain. p. I3

interurban rail (in•tər•ûr´bən rāl) A network of rail lines connecting rural areas with nearby cities and towns. p. 170

investor (in•ves´tər) A person who puts his or her money at risk in hopes of making a profit. p. 225

judicial branch (jōo•di´shəl branch) The part of government that sees that the laws are carried out fairly. p. 243

labor union (lā´bər yōon´yən) A group of workers who join together to improve their working conditions. p. 164

legend (le´jənd) A story handed down over time. p. 89

legislative branch (le´jəs•lā•tiv branch) The part of the government that makes laws. p. 242

line graph (līn graf) A graph that uses one or more lines to show patterns in information over time. p. 186

lines of latitude (līnz əv la´tə•tōod) Lines on a map or globe that run east and west to help locate a position; also called parallels. p. 18

lines of longitude (līnz əv län´jə•tōod) Lines on a map or globe that run north and south to help locate a position; also called meridians. p. 18

lithosphere (li´thə•sfir) The soil and rock that form Earth's surface. p. 21

GLOSSARY

locator (lō´kā•tər) A small map or picture of a globe that shows where the place on the main map is located within a larger area. p. I21

longhouse (lông´hous) A large rectangular building, made from wooden poles and bark, in which several families could live. p. 86

manufacturing (man•yə•fak´chə•ring) The making of goods from raw materials by hand or with machinery. p. 163

map key (map kee) A part of a map that explains what the symbols on the map stand for. p. I20

map scale (map skāl) A part of a map that compares a distance on the map to a distance in the real world. p. I21

map title (map tī´təl) Words on a map that tell the subject of the map. p. I20

migration (mī•grā´shən) The movement of people from one place to live in another place. p. 141

mileage table (mī´lij tā´bəl) A table that tells how far apart two places on a map are. p. 250

militia (mə•li´shə) A volunteer army. p. 102

mineral (min´rəl) A natural nonliving substance. p. 35

missionary (mi´shə•ner•ē) A person who teaches his or her religious beliefs to others. p. 95

mound (mound) A large pile of hard-packed earth and other materials. p. 78

municipal (myoo•ni´sə•pəl) Having to do with a city or town. p. 247

natural resource (na´chə•rəl rē´sôrs) Something found in nature that people can use. p. 35

navigable (na´vi•gə•bəl) Wide and deep enough for ships to use. p. 144

nomad (nō´mad) A person who has no permanent home and moves from place to place. p. 77

opinion (ə•pin´yən) A statement that tells what a person thinks or believes. p. 158

opportunity cost (ä•pər•too´nə•tē kôst) The thing that is given up to get something else. p. 218

ordinance (ôr´dən•əns) A law or set of laws. p. 110

permanent (pər´mə•nənt) Long-lasting. p. 78

physical feature (fi´zi•kəl fē´chər) A feature formed by nature. p. 14

physical map (fi´zi•kəl map) A map that shows kinds of land and bodies of water. p. I20

plain (plān) An area of low, flat land. p. 14

plantation (plan•tā´shən) A huge farm that grows crops such as cotton, rice, and tobacco. p. 151

point of view (point uv vyoo) A person's perspective. p. I4

political map (pə•li´ti•kəl map) A map that shows cities, states, and countries. p. I20

pop art (päp art) An art style that uses common objects. p. 55

population density (pä•pyə•lā´shən den´sə•tē) The number of people who live in an area of a certain size. p. 45

population distribution (pä•pyə•lā´shən dis•trə•byoo´shən) The way in which a population is spread out over an area. p. 45

precipitation (pri•si•pə•tā´shən) Water that falls to Earth's surface as rain, sleet, hail, or snow. p. 29

primary source (prī´mer•ē sôrs) Any record made by people who took part in an event or saw it happen. p. 114

prime meridian (prīm mə•rid´ē•ən) The line that divides Earth into western and eastern parts as measured by lines of longitude. pp. I17, 18

proclamation (prä•klə•mā´shən) A public announcement. p. 97

productivity (prō•dək•ti´və•tē) The amount of goods and services produced in a period of time divided by the resources used to produce them. p. 213

profit (prä´fət) The money left over after all a business's expenses have been paid. p. 223

public service (pub´lik sər´vəs) The act of working for the good of a community. p. 254

GLOSSARY

rationing (ra´shə•ning) Limiting how much people can buy. p. 178

Reconstruction (rē•kən•struk´shən) A period of rebuilding the nation after the Civil War. p. 161

recycle (rē•sī´kəl) To use again. p. 178

refinery (ri•fī´nə•rē) A factory in which resources such as oil are made into products people can use. p. 163

region (rē´jən) An area with at least one feature that makes it different from other areas. p. 13

register (re´jə•stər) To sign up. p. 253

relative location (re´lə•tiv lō•kā´shən) Where a place is in relation to other places on Earth. p. 13

research (ri•sûrch´) To investigate. p. I2

revolution (rev•ə•loo´shən) A sudden, complete change of government. p. 101

right (rīt) A freedom that belongs to a person. p. 110

rural (roor´əl) Like, in, or of the country. p. 37

S

scale (skāl) A series of numbers or units that is used to measure something, such as distance. p. 250

scarce (skârs) Hard to find. p. 95

science fiction (sī´ənts fik´shən) Fiction about how real or imagined science affects people. p. 55

secede (si•sēd´) To withdraw from a group, often to form another group. p. 154

secondary source (se´kən•der•ē sôrs) A record made by people who did not take part in an event or did not see it take place. p. 114

segregation (se•gri•gā´shən) The practice of keeping people from one race or culture separate from other people. p. 184

service industry (sər´vəs in´dəs•trē) An industry in which workers are paid to do things for other people. p. 191

sharecropping (shâr´krap•ing) Farming a landowner's property for a share of the crop. p. 161

shortage (shor´tij) A low supply of something. p. 178

sinkhole (sink´hōl) A large, bowl-shaped hole that forms when a limestone layer above an underground hole collapses. p. 24

slavery (slā´və•rē) The practice of holding people against their will and forcing them to work. p. 120

slave state (slāv stāt) A state that allowed slavery before the Civil War. p. 151

specialize (spe´shə•līz) To work at one kind of job and learn to do it well. p. 84

stagecoach (stāj´kōch) An enclosed wagon that carried passengers and was pulled by horses. p. 145

steamboat (stēm´bōt) A boat powered by a steam engine that turns a large paddle wheel. p. 144

stock (stäk) A share of ownership in a company. p. 175

suburb (sub´ərb) A smaller community near a city. p. 38

suffrage (su´frij) The right to vote. p. 169

supply (sə•plī´) The amount of a product or service that is available. p. 231

surplus (sûr´pləs) An amount that is more than what is needed. p. 214

surrender (sə•ren´dər) To give up. p. 102

tax (taks) Money a government collects from citizens for the services it provides. p. 101

territory (ter´ə•tôr•ē) An area owned and governed by a country. p. 109

terrorism (ter´ər•i•zəm) The use of violence to promote a cause. p. 189

till (til) A mixture of clay, sand, and small stones that makes soil very fertile. p. 23

time line (tīm līn) A diagram that shows the order in which events took place during a certain period of time. p. 172

tornado (tôr•nā´dō) A funnel-shaped, spinning windstorm. p. 29

tourism (toor´iz•əm) The business of serving visitors. p. 217

township (toun´ship) One of the squares of land into which the Northwest Territory was divided by the Land Ordinance of 1785. p. 110

GLOSSARY

trade-off (trād´ôf) Giving up one thing to get something else. p. 218

treaty (trē´tē) An agreement among nations or groups. p. 96

tribe (trīb) A group that shares the same language and has the same leaders. p. 83

tributary (trib´yo͞o•ter•ē) A stream or river that flows into a larger stream or river. p. 14

Underground Railroad (un´dər•ground rāl´rōd) A system of secret escape routes that led enslaved people to free land. p. 152

unemployed (ən•im•ploid´) Without a job. p. 176

urban (ûr´bən) Like, in, or of a city. p. 37

veto (vē´tō) To reject. p. 243

voyageur (voi•ə•zhûr´) A French word meaning "traveler." p. 95

wetland (wet´land) Low-lying land where the water level is always near the surface of the land. p. 22

Index

The Index lets you know where information about important people, places, and events appear in the book. All entries are listed in alphabetical order. For each entry, the page reference indicates where information about that entry can be found in the text. Page references for illustrations are set in italic type. An italic *m* indicates a map. Page references set in boldface type indicate the pages on which vocabulary terms are defined. Guide words at the top of each page help you identify which words appear on which page.

INDEX

For permission to reprint copyrighted material, grateful acknowledgment is made to the following sources:

Alfred Publishing Company, on behalf of Chappell & Co.: Lyrics from "Can't Get Indiana off My Mind" by Robert De Leon, music by Hoagy Carmichael. Lyrics © 1940 by Chappell & Co. and PSO Ltd.; copyright renewed.

Jane Louise Curry: "Woodpecker and Sugar Maple" from *Turtle Island: Tales of the Algonquian Nations,* retold by Jane Louise Curry. Text copyright © 1999 by Jane Louise Curry.

New World Library: From *A Goose Named Gilligan* by Jerry M. Hay, illustrated by Phyllis Pollema-Cahill. Text copyright © 2004 by Jerry M. Hay; illustrations copyright © 2004 by Phyllis Pollema-Cahill.

Peer Music, on behalf of PSO Ltd.: Lyrics from "Can't Get Indiana off My Mind" by Robert De Leon, music by Hoagy Carmichael. Lyrics © 1940 by Songs of Peer, Ltd.; copyright renewed.

Simon & Schuster Books for Young Readers, an imprint of Simon & Schuster Children's Publishing Division: From *Abe Lincoln: The boy*

who loved books by Kay Winters, illustrated by Nancy Carpenter. Text copyright © 2003 by Kay Winters; illustrations copyright © 2003 by Nancy Carpenter.

INDIANA SOCIAL STUDIES GRADE 4 PHOTO CREDITS

Placement Key: (t) top, (b) bottom, (r) right, (l) left, (c) center, (bg) background, (i) inset.

Front Cover: Getty Images. Back Cover: Getty Images. Front End Sheets: Getty Images.

Title Page: Getty Images. Back End Sheets: Getty Images.

Frontmatter: [blind i] DigitalVision/ Superstock; [blind iii] (b) David Lawrence/ Panoramic Images ; I7 (cr) Andre Jenny/ Alamy.

UNIT 1

1A (bg) Jim Millay/Panoramic Images; 1A (br) Photri MicroStock; 1A (bl) Spectrum Photofile Inc./PhotographersDirect.com; 1B (cr) Tim Meyers/PhotographersDirect. com; 1 Layne Kennedy/Corbis; 4 (br) Indiana Department of Natural Resources; 5 (tl) Jeff Greenberg/Grant Heilman; 5 (cr) David Frazier/PhotoEdit; 5 (br) Cathy Melloan/PhotoEdit; 5 (tr) Cathy Melloan/

PhotoEdit; 7 (b) Gary Berdeaux/Cave Country Adventures; 14 (c) Mike Briner/ Alamy; 15 (bl) Harlan Taylor; 15 (tr) Indiana Department of Natural Resources; 15 (tl) Daniel Dempster/Alamy; 15 (br) David R. Frazier Photolibrary/Alamy; 16 (b) Ken Cave/ EyeGate Photography/PhotographersDirect. com; 17 (tr) Harlan Taylor; I7 (cr) Andre Jenny/Alamy; 21 (b) Photodisc/Superstock; 23 (tl) Dennis Flaherty/Photo Researchers Inc.; 23 (tr) age fotostock/Superstock; 25 (tr) Harlan Taylor; 26 (br) Lauren Victoria Burke/AP; 27 (bl) Marta Garcia; 27 (tl) AP; 27 (tr) Lloyd DeGrane; 28 (bc) Mike Briner Photography/PhotographersDirect.com; 28 (bl) Jeff Greenberg/PhotoEdit; 29 (br) Daniel Dempster/Bruce Coleman; 29 (br) Indiana Department of Natural Resources; 33 (tr) Frank Cezus/Getty; 34 (bl) Indiana Historical Society; 34 (b) Indiana Department of Natural Resources; 35 (tl) Rick Miller/Corbis; 35 (cl) Superstock; 35 (cr) J. Baumann/National Geographic Society/Image Collection; 35 (tr) STF/AP; 36 (br) Bass Photo Collection, Indiana Historical Society; 37 (br) Bass Photo Collection, Indiana Historical Society; 38 (tr) Workbook Stock/Jupiterimages; 40 (br) Superstock; 42 (b) Layne Kennedy/Corbis; 42 (cl) Calumet Regional Archives; 43 (br)

Dennis MacDonald/PhotoEdit; 43 (tr) United Way of Central Indiana; 43 (bl) United Way of Central Indiana; 44 (b) Tanya Constantine/Getty; 45 (t) Scott Boehm/Getty; 47 (tl) Mark Simons/Purdue University; 47 (cl) Mike Briner/Alamy; 47 (bl) Stuart Westmorland; 47 (cr) Elkhart Jazz Festival; 47 (cr) Indiana Black Expo; 47 (br) Larry Flinner Photography/Photographers Direct; 48 (br) M Stock/Alamy; 48 (bl) Abi Vanak/Photographers Direct; 48 (cr) Abi Vanak/PhotographersDirect.com; 49 (tl) Joe Raymond/AP; 49 (tr) Chuck Robinson/AP; 50 (br) Superstock; 52 (b) Indiana State Museum; 52 (cr) Indiana State Museum; 53 (tl) Kent Smith/Getty; 53 (tc) Ronald Martinez/Getty; 53 (tr) Donald Miralle/Getty; 54 (bcl) Jean-Christian Bourcart/Getty; 54 (bl) Seven Stories Press; 54 (bcr) William Pride/Permission Mari Evans; 54 (br) Just Us Books, Inc. 1999/Permission of author; 55 (bl) T.C. Steele State Historic Site; 55 (t) T. C. Steele State Historic Site/Indiana State Museum; 55 (br) Library of Congress; 55 (cr) Indiana Historical Society; 56 (tl) DiamondImages/Getty; 56 (cl) Michael Ochs Archives/Corbis; 56 (c) Hulton Archives/Getty; 56 (bl) Ben Sklar/Getty; 57 (bl) Steve Azzara/Corbis; 57 (br) Robbie Jack/Corbis; 58 (tl) John P. Filo/CBS/©2007 CBS Broadcasting Inc. All Rights Reserved.

UNIT 2

65A (br) Indiana Department of Natural Resources; 65A (bg) Indiana Department of Natural Resources; 65B (tr) Harlan Taylor; 65B (bl) Elena Rooraid/PhotoEdit; 67 Indiana Historical Bureau; 71 (br) Marilyn Angel Wynn/Nativestock; 80 (bg) Harlan Taylor; 80 (b) Marilyn Angel Wynn/Nativestock; 81 (cr) Glenn A. Black Laboratory of Archaeology; 81 (cl) Justin Rumbach/Evansville Courier & Press; 81 (tc) Harlan Taylor; 81 (tl) Marilyn Angel Wynn/Nativestock; 86 (t) Conner Prairie Living History Museum; 86 (tr) National Museum of the American Indian; 87 (b) National Museum of the American Indian, Smithsonian; 87 (bl) National Museum of the American Indian, Smithsonian; 88 (cl) Glenn A. Black Laboratory of Archaeology; 88 (bl) Indiana Department of Natural Resources; 88 (tl) Indiana Department of Natural Resources; 89 (tr) Indiana Department of Natural Resources; 90 (bl) Courtesy of the Eiteljorg Museum of American Indians and Western Art, Indianapolis; 90 (bl) Courtesy of the Eiteljorg Museum of American Indians and Western Art, Indianapolis; 90 Marilyn Angel Wynn/Nativestock; 91 Marilyn Angel Wynn/Nativestock; 91 Marilyn Angel Wynn/Nativestock; 92 (b) Don Smetzer/PhotoEdit; 93 (t) Bridgeman Art Library; 96 (tr) Library of Congress; 98 (bl) Bridgeman Art Library; 98 (br) Bridgeman Art Library, New York; 102 (c) Danita Delimont/Alamy; 103 (bc) U.S. Army Center of Military History; 104 (tl) Digitalvision/Superstock; 106 (r) Indiana State Museum; 107 (b) Indiana Historical Bureau, State of Indiana; 108 (b) Andre Jenny/Alamy; 111 (b) Ohio Historical Society; 111 (cr) Harlan Taylor; 112 (tl) Smithsonian American Art Museum, Washington, DC / Art Resource, NY; 114 (br) Indiana Historical Society; 114 (bl) Thomas B. Greenslade, Jr.; 115 (c) Indiana Historical Bureau; 116 (l) Archives of Ontario; 116 (r) North Wind Picture Archives; 117 (tl) Nativestock; 117 (tr) Detail of portrait:National Portrait

Gallery, Smithsonian Institution / Art Resource, NY; 119 (t) Daniel Dempster/Alamy; 119 (tr) Harlan Taylor/Indiana State Museum; 120 (bc) Bass Photo Co. Collection, Indiana Historical Society; 120 (br) Indiana Historical Bureau; 120 (bl) Daniel Dempster Photography/Alamy; 120 (bl) Museum of the City of New York/Corbis; 121 (bc) Indiana Historical Bureau; 122 (cl) Indiana State Archives, Commission on Public Records; 123 (tr) Michael Conroy/AP; 123 (br) David Snodgress/Bloomington Herald-Times/AP; 123 (b) Tom Strattman/Associated Press.

UNIT 3

128A (br) Andre Jenny/Alamy; 128A (bl) Tim Thompson; 128A (bg) Indiana Department of Natural Resources; 128B (tcr) Harlan Taylor; 128B (cr) Harlan Taylor; 129 Indianapolis Museum of Art, Gift of a Couple of Old Hoosiers; 135 (bl) J. C. Allen & Son; 142 (tl) Old Economy Village/State Museum of Pennsylvania; 142 (tc) H. Armstrong Roberts, Inc./Robertstock; 142 (tr) Indiana Historical Society; 142 (tc) Indiana Historical Society; 143 (tl) Bass Photo Collection/Indiana Historical Society; 143 (tr) North Wind Picture Archives; 146 (tl) Glenn A. Black Laboratory of Archaeology; 148 Richard Cummins/Lonely Planet; 148 (cr) Conner Prairie Living History Museum; 148 (bl) Conner Prairie Living History Museum; 149 (tl) Jeff Greenberg/PhotoEdit; 149 (tc) Derek Jensen; 149 (cl) Layne Kennedy/Corbis; 149 (tr) Gibson Stock; 150 (br) On to Liberty, 1867 (oil on canvas), Kaufmann, Theodor (1814-p.1887) / Private Collection, Photo © Christie's Images / The Bridgeman Art Library; 152 (cr) Levi Coffin House; 152 (bl) Levi Coffin House; 153 (cr) Levi Coffin House; 154 (tr) Indiana Historical Society; 154 (tl) Indiana Historical Society; 154 (cl) Indiana War Memorials Commission; 155 (b) Slavins Gallery; 156 (tl) Bettmann/Corbis; 158 (br) Bettmann/Corbis; 160 (b) Library of Congress; 161 (cr) Corbis; 161 (bc) Enrolled Acts and Resolutions of Congress, 1789-; General Records of the United States Government; Record Group 11; National Archives; 161 (tr) The Metropolitan Museum of Art, Morris K. Jessup Fund, 1940. (40.40) Photograph © 1985 The Metropolitan Museum of Art; 162 (bl) Northern Indiana Center for History; 162 (bc) The Henry Ford Museum; 162 (br) Ball State University Archives; 163 (br) Bass Photo Co. Collection, Indiana Historical Society; 163 (bl) Parma Conservation/United States Postal Service; 164 (c) Bass Photo Co. Collection, Indiana Historical Society; 164 (b) Madison-Jefferson County Public Library; 164 (bl) Library of Congress; 165 (tr) Indiana Historical Society; 166 (b) Library of Congress; 168 (t) Library of Congress; 169 (b) Indiana Historical Society; 170 (b) Harlan Taylor; 171 (tr) Bass Photo Co. Collection, Indiana Historical Society; 172 (bl) Harlan Taylor; 172 (br) Bass Photo Co. Collection, Indiana Historical Society; 173 (bl) Indiana Historical Society; 173 (bc) Scherl/SV-Bilderdienst/Image Works; 174 (b) Martin Collection, Indiana Historical Society; 176 (cr) Willard Library; 176 (tl) Bettmann/Corbis; 176 (tr) Parma Conservation/United States Postal Service; 177 (br) Evansville Museum; 177 (bl) Evansville Museum; 178 (tl) Martin Collection, Indiana Historical Society; 179 (br) AP; 180 (b) Studebaker National Museum, South Bend, Indiana; 181 (t) Willard

Library; 182 Harlan Taylor; 183 (t) Terry Fincher/Express/Getty; 184 (b) Indianapolis Recorder Collection, Indiana Historical Society; 185 (tr) Chuck Savage/Corbis; 186 (b) Bass Photo Co. Collection, Indiana Historical Society; 188 NASA Marshall Space Flight Center (NASA-MSFC); 189 (tl) Chris Collins/Corbis; 189 (t) Reuters/Corbis; 190 (t) Archie Carpenter/Getty; 190 Courtesy Farm Aid; 191 (b) Index Stock Imagery/Jupiterimages; 191 (br) Jeff Greenberg/The Image Works; 192 (b) Darron Cummings/AP; 193 (t) NASA; 194 (b) Bettmann/Corbis; 195 (t) Gerd Ludwig/Woodfin Camp.

UNIT 4

199A (bg) Dennis MacDonald/PhotoEdit; 199A (bc) Alamy; 199A (bl) Greg Mitchell Imaging/Indiana State House; 199B (cl) Alamy; 199B (tl) Dennis MacDonald/Alamy; 201 age fotostock/Superstock; 201 (br) AP Images; 204 (br) AJ Mast/Icon SMI/Corbis; 205 (cr) Dennis MacDonald/Alamy; 205 (br) AirPhotoNA.com; 205 (t) Greg Pease/Getty; 205 (tr) Mark Segal/Photolibrary; 207 (b) Peter Beck/Corbis; 212 (b) Alan Petersime/Indianapolis Star/AP; 213 (t) Inga Spence/Alamy; 214 (br) Indiana State Library; 215 (bl) J. C. Allen & Son; 215 (bc) Charles Fenno Jacobs/Time Life/Getty; 215 (br) V1/Alamy; 217 (tr) Mike Simons/Getty; 219 (t) Indiana State Museum; 220 (bg) Michael Kim/Corbis; 221 (tl) Schlegelmilch/Corbis; 221 (tr) Chad Buchanan/Getty; 221 (c) age fotostock/Superstock; 221 (tc) William Manning/Corbis; 222 (b) Mark Gibson Stock Photography; 224 (bl) Bass Photo Co. Collection, Indiana Historical Society; 224 (br) Studebaker National Museum, South Bend, IN; 225 (bc) Practical Patchwork; 225 (bl) Practical Patchwork; 225 (br) Courtesy Lilly Library, Indiana University, Bloomington, Indiana; 226 (tl) Harlan Taylor; 228 (cl) A'Lelia Bundles Walker Family Collection; 228 (bl) Thomas Dorsey/A'Lelia Bundles Walker Family Collection; 229 (tr) Harlan Taylor; 229 (cr) Dennis MacDonald/World of Stock; 230 (b) Harlan Taylor; 231 (t) Don Mason/Corbis; 232 (tl) Thinkstock/Superstock; 232 (tr) David R. Frazier Photolibrary/Alamy; 233 (tl) Ports of Indiana; 233 (tr) Alamy; 236 (b) Lisa F. Young/Shutterstock; 238 (cr) Visual Arts Library(London)/Alamy; 238 (bl) Marilyn Angel Wynn/Nativestock; 238 (br) Nancy Carter/North Wind Pictures/Alamy; 239 (tr) HIP/Art Resource; 239 (br) D. Hurst/Alamy; 242 (b) R. Krubner/Alamy; 243 (tl) Michael Conroy/AP; 243 (tc) Tom Strattman/AP; 243 (tr) Supreme Court of Indiana/AP; 244 (tl) Melanie Maxwell/The Star Press/AP; 244 (cl) State of Indiana; 244 (bl) Courtesy Indiana Secretary of State office; 245 (tr) Brooks Kraft/Corbis; 246 (b) Derek Jensen; 247 (t) Kelly Wilkinson/The Star RM; 248 (b) Jim West/PhotoEdit; 248 (tc) Kitt Cooper-Smith/Alamy; 249 (tr) Alamy; 253 (b) Supreme Court of Indiana; 254 (b) Joseph C. Garza/Tribune-Star/AP; 254 (l) Alamy; 255 (tr) Kim Komenich/Time Life Pictures/Getty; 256 (tl) Indianapolis School on Wheels; 258 (cr) Coinery/Alamy; 258 (bl) Library of Congress; 259 (bl) Phil Martin/PhotoEdit; 259 (cr) Harlan Taylor.

BACKMATTER

R19 Andre Jenny/Alamy.